Maryland's Eastern Shore:
A Journey in Time and Place

by John R. Wennersten

Tidewater Publishers
Centreville, Maryland

Library of Congress Cataloging-in-Publication Data

Wennersten, John R.
    Maryland's Eastern Shore : a journey in time and place / by John
R. Wennersten. — 1st ed.
      p.   cm.
    Includes bibliographical references and index.
    ISBN 0-87033-428-X :
    1. Eastern Shore (Md. and Va.)—History.   I. Title.
F187.E2W46   1991
975.2′ 1—dc20   91-50584
                                            CIP

Manufactured in the United States of America

First edition

For Ruth Ellen, Stewart, and Matthew
Come here, raised here, born here on the Eastern Shore

Contents

Preface

Long before there was a United States, there was an Eastern Shore. A long diamond-shaped peninsula that extended between the Chesapeake Bay and the Atlantic, the Eastern Shore was a feisty, provincial, self-absorbed part of the Maryland colony. Its early society was erected on a tobacco base and slavery, but its agricultural economy grew exceptionally more diverse in the late eighteenth century.

Until just recently, the Eastern Shore was one of the most geographically isolated regions on the Atlantic coast: It was difficult to get to and difficult to leave. The Eastern Shore never got caught up in the surge of westward expansionism in the late eighteenth and nineteenth centuries; its people were simply left behind. Over the years it grew slowly and matured as a separate society in which agriculture, race, and seafaring have been the important factors that have given it a significant degree of uniqueness. Put simply, in its historical evolution the Eastern Shore has been a blend of soil, soul, and sea.

The Eastern Shore of Maryland is to the historian what the oil-rich Permian Basin is to the geologist—a vast and rich resource. After World War II, Charles B. Clark, a historian at Washington College, edited a three-volume work called *The Eastern Shore of Maryland and Virginia.* To this day it remains a classic and illustrates how exceptionally fruitful is the history of the region. This study does not attempt to duplicate or update Clark's splendid work. I am fully aware that each of a score of topics or ideas that I have accorded a paragraph or merely a sentence deserves extended study.

Rather, what I have chosen to do is present the reader with a journey through time and place to understand a region that has been a distinct society for over three centuries. On the Eastern Shore people are history-conscious, and issues that may be long forgotten or enmeshed in the cobwebs of obscurity are treated here as current events. "A hundred years ain't a very long time on the Eastern Shore," local farmers and watermen used to say, and it is a telling refrain. Past and present mix so easily together here, each informing and anchoring the other, that it is difficult for a writer to differentiate the two. In this respect, as well as with regard to certain local customs and habits of language, the Eastern Shore is very much still an old-fashioned English society.

Although I am not a native Eastern Shoreman, I have spent many delightful and instructive years in the region. I have traveled widely in the Chesapeake region, sailed and canoed its waters, trod its farms and fields, and spent time in its many small towns and villages. When occasionally I wax lyrical about the Eastern Shore, I receive a skeptical poke from my wife. Regions to be understood, she cautions, have to be seen at their worst as well as their best.

Much that was distinctive about the Eastern Shore, especially in the maritime industry, disappeared before my arrival, and is now the stuff of history. Unfortunately, in the last decade the forces of economic change and metropolitan development seem to have dramatically accelerated and the Eastern Shore is being transformed. The Eastern Shore has a fatal beauty to it. This lovely land of beaches, farms, and seaside towns is too popular and too close to major urban centers to remain unchanged.

Above all, this book is a modest call to readers to think of America as a land of distinct regions. Regions like the Eastern Shore are cultural rather than governmental units. The Eastern Shore has been formed out of the history, geography, economics, literature, and folkways of the Chesapeake. Also, the regional life-style of the Shore extends beyond food and dialect to include the more imprecise habits and sentiments of local people. Despite the homogenizing influence of television and mass culture, Americans remain a people as different as we are similar. On the Eastern Shore these differences have been nurtured over the centuries and the region marches to the beat of its own sociocultural drum.

This book would not have been possible without the regional insights of colleagues, acquaintances, and friends. I am especially indebted to Bonnie Joe Ayers, Earl Brannock, Donald

Cathcart, Charles Clark, Mary Corddry, John Dennis, Cathy Fisher, Patrick Hornberger, John Jeffries, Varley Lang, Sidney Miller, Dick Moore, Jim Nelson, L.Q. Powell, Tom Stanley, Orlando Wootten, and William Wroten. Also, over the years I have benefited enormously from the insights of George H. Callcott. He is the scholar of Maryland par excellence. Any errors or mistakes that I have made, however, are my own responsibility.

A writer's life has its own unique stresses, and this book would not have been possible without the support and good humor of my wife, Ruth Ellen, and my sons, Stewart and Matthew.

Part One

SOIL: Country Life in the Chesapeake

1

On the Eastern Shore

*We don't give a damn 'bout the whole state of Maryland.
We're from the Eastern Shore!*

—Popular Song

STRIDING the waves like a giant steel behemoth, the Chesapeake Bay Bridge connects Annapolis and the west with Maryland's Eastern Shore. Each year over 12 million motorists cross these spans, mostly in a pell-mell rush to get to the Atlantic resorts of Ocean City and Rehoboth Beach. The bridge crosses the Bay in a gentle arc, the curve being necessary to comply with federal regulations that a bridge must cross the Chesapeake's main ship channel at a right angle. As you drive, the bridge ascends gradually until you can see the vast expanse of Kent Island in the distance. An engineering triumph, the bridge provides one of the most scenic vistas along the Atlantic seaboard.

Yet despite its multilane comfort and steel-girder security, the bridge terrifies many motorists. Even veterans who drive it regularly are occasionally haunted by the feeling that they will lose control and plunge into the watery depths far below. For acrophobes the bridge is an unmitigated nightmare that produces a rapid pulse, sweating palms, and nausea.

"The bridge immobilizes lots of people," says Terry Hunter, a trooper with the Maryland Toll Facilities Police. "Sometimes they just stop dead on the bridge and refuse to drive because they're so scared," he says. "Sometimes they try to back up to get off the span." The Toll Facilities Police annually chauffeur

3

over a thousand phobics across the bridge, thus providing a service that is perhaps unique in the country. Some whimper or cry as they are being driven over. Others ask to be blindfolded. One man required that he be locked in his car trunk by police during the crossing. Once a year the bridge is open for pedestrians to walk across, but it is not a walk for the fainthearted.

The first span of the William Preston Lane, Jr., Memorial Bridge was built in 1952. It was a monumental engineering task that required 118,000 cubic yards of concrete, 2.5 million cubic yards of earth, 151,000 tons of stone, and 42,500 tons of structural steel. The state of Maryland added a second parallel span in 1973. The spans cross over four miles of water and their cable towers reach 354 feet above the water. The original span of the bridge cost $41 million to build. The second structure escalated to $120 million—a monument to inflation and political ineptitude.

As toll facilities go, the bridge is inexpensive. Eastbound cars are charged $2.50 per trip. The toll collectors on the western side of the bridge have the thankless task of taking nearly four hundred payments per hour, and some drivers with a nasty streak pay the fare in pennies. Some stick coins and a dollar bill together with gum; others throw their money at the collector. One bridge regular known as the "tin man" wraps his fare in foil.

Regardless of how one feels about toll bridges, the Bay spans are important arteries of commerce for the Eastern Shore that carry billions of dollars in goods and services annually. The two spans also link the largely rural and small-town society of the Eastern Shore with fast-paced metropolitan life.

The first proposal to span the Bay came in 1907 when Baltimore merchant Peter J. Campbell envisioned a bridge that would extend the city's trolley lines to the Eastern Shore. With the rise of the automobile industry, however, developers lost interest in Campbell's trolley bridge. In 1926 the Chesapeake Bay Bridge Company received a charter from the state to construct a bridge from Miller Island near Baltimore to Tolchester Beach in Kent County. Maryland shelved this plan during the Depression of the 1930s.

After World War II, economic considerations made the construction of a bridge across the Bay to the Eastern Shore appear a necessity. Without a bridge, argued planners and highway experts, the Eastern Shore of Maryland would remain economically depressed. The more the bridge idea was discussed in Annapolis, the more it became a hot political issue. Merchants and realtors clamored for it, saying that it would be good for tourism and economic development. Conservative Eastern Shoremen, however, feared that a bridge would open their pristine, tradition-bound region to strange ideas and foreign life-styles. Many politicians bemoaned the construction costs. One Republican, John H. McFaul, Jr., even went so far as to warn that a Bay bridge would be a natural target for a Russian nuclear bomb.

Until the bridge opened in 1952, passage to the Eastern Shore was either by Chesapeake Bay ferry or by a tiresome auto route through Cecil County via Elkton. Three ferries regularly crossed the Bay. The steamer *Governor Harrington* offered services between Claiborne in Talbot County and Annapolis. The *Philadelphia*, operated by the Pennsylvania Railroad, cruised from Love Point on Kent Island to Light Street at the harbor of downtown Baltimore. This two-hour-and-twenty-minute ferry ride was a favorite of men who relished a good whiskey and a leisurely card game while their wives enjoyed the Bay air. The ferry that most old-time Marylanders remember, however, was the *Harry W. Nice*, a car ferry that ran between Matapeake on Kent Island to Sandy Point in Anne Arundel County. The Matapeake run took forty minutes, about an hour shorter than the Annapolis-Claiborne trip. The ferry cost passengers a dollar each way.

The fifty-car Matapeake ferry was not as romantic, however, as old Marylanders make it out to be. In the peak summer season in the 1940s, a Sunday observer could easily spot the three-mile-long line of cars waiting to take the ferry back to Annapolis. Tempers flared easily in the congestion, and occasionally arguments over one's place in the ferry line turned into fist fights. In winter, ferries sometimes got trapped in Bay ice and passengers spent a chilly night on board before they were rescued by the Coast Guard.

Before World War II, the ferries offered easy connections with Eastern Shore trains. From Love Point a traveler could take the Maryland, Delaware, and Virginia line to Lewes, Delaware. From the Claiborne wharf in Talbot County beachgoers could take the Baltimore, Chesapeake, and Atlantic

Railway to Ocean City. For holiday merrymakers, the train trip across the flat Eastern Shore peninsula was as much fun as the ocean itself.

July 30, 1952 was a day to remember in Maryland—William Preston Lane, Jr., Memorial Bridge Dedication Day. It was the first and last time that Marylanders would be able to drive across the span without paying a toll. Named after the former governor William Preston Lane, Jr., the Chesapeake Bay Bridge ended three centuries of geographic isolation of the Eastern Shore from the rest of the state. During the ceremony, a band blared the state song, "Maryland, My Maryland," with the words that might unsettle reflective Eastern Shoremen—"the despot's heel is on thy shore." The ferry boats from Matapeake gave free rides on that historic day. Historian Dickson J. Preston wrote of the passing of an era: "At 5:30 P.M. ferries pulled out from the two terminals at the same time. As they passed in mid-Bay, they sounded their horns in mournful salute. As soon as they touched the other side they went out of service for good."[1]

In the first ten years after the bridge opened, traffic doubled. During the month of July 1963, traffic so choked the span that it had to be operated in one direction eighty-one times. Shortly thereafter, the state appropriated funds for a second span. By 1988, however, the twin spans seemed hardly able to handle the immense flow of commuter and tourist traffic.

A favorite fantasy of many Eastern Shoremen is that of blowing up the Bay Bridge in order to preserve and protect what is left of the region. "It is the latecomers who are most intrigued by the fantasy," says Shore sociologist Howard Rebach. "Now that they are here, they don't want anyone else to come." After a few years on the Eastern Shore these affluent newcomers behave as if their residence carried with it the same serenity and pride of place as that of a family whose roots can be traced back seven generations to when the region was England's colonial frontier. While the bridge, according to some, may be the devil's work, few people wish to turn the clock back to the steamboat era. According to architect Gilbert Sandler, "The bridges have brought the Eastern Shore into the twentieth century, showering on it the largess of a boom in real estate, tourism, and land development that has forever changed the Shore's physical and psychic landscape."[2]

The bridge connects metropolitan Maryland with a vast history-soaked agricultural region of over 3,500 square miles. The Eastern Shore is a flat coastal plain, and nowhere on the Shore does elevation reach a hundred feet. If you fly over the Atlantic seaboard between Boston and Richmond, you will be struck by the simple fact that the Eastern Shore is the last major green space left in this megalopolitan strip. It is a land of pine and honeysuckle, a land of fields loaded with corn, grain, and truck produce. The marine climate of Chesapeake Bay makes winters mild, and temperatures rarely stay long below the freezing mark. Summers are ferociously hot and humid, almost subtropical in nature. It is a rainy climate: the region averages about two inches of rain a month. Thunderstorms in summer are frequent and fierce. It is the kind of climate that encourages loafing, hunting, fishing, and general revelry. For Eastern Shoremen, happiness is to run into a school of "blues" while fishing on a lazy summer day or to savor the deep dark red skies of a summer sunset. The region does little to encourage moral or philosophical speculation.

*　　*　　*

The Chesapeake Bay country of Maryland's Eastern Shore was known to explorers as early as the sixteenth century. Giovanni da Verrazano, a Florentine navigator in the hire of the king of France, touched land along the Bay of Chincoteague in 1524 and explored part of what is now Worcester County. This "Arcadia," as Verrazano called it, was a deeply forested region inhabited by shy Indians who probably thought that the white men who came ashore were torch-bearing demigods. Verrazano also may have been the Shore's first anthropologist for he commented at length in his log about the habitat and dress of the Indians he observed. Most, he noted, were either naked or scantily clad and subsisted on a diet of fish, game, and wild peas. Later, Spaniards sailed into the mouth of Chesapeake Bay in search of booty and empire in 1573 but it is doubtful they explored this new dominion of soil and sea that they had discovered.

The first English account of the Eastern Shore of the Chesapeake Bay country is probably that of Sir Ralph Lane in the late sixteenth century. Lane was an experienced soldier of England's Irish wars who accompanied Sir Richard Grenville on a military expedition to Sir Walter Raleigh's ill-fated Virginia colony in 1585. During a scouting expedition in the Chesapeake, he reported that the natives were amiable and curious and that the land seemed good. The region was pleasant "for fertility of the soil and for the commodity of the sea, besides multitudes of bears (being an excellent good victual) with great woods of sassafras and walnut, not to be exceeded by any other whatsoever."[3] While his account is interesting, its veracity is open to question. Lane, however, did report elaborate networks of Indian fishing weirs, which reflects in a small way both the complexity and sophistication of aboriginal society on the Chesapeake shore at that time.

The Indians of the Eastern Shore were fishing Indians of Algonquin stock. They planted permanent settlements near the waterside and raised maize, beans, and tobacco. They ranged the Bay widely in dugout canoes that took them from the mouth of the Sassafras River in the north to the mouth of Chesapeake Bay. On the Eastern Shore even today shell banks and kitchen middens of a people who may have resided here as early as the time of Christ can be found. One tribe of this stock, the Nanticokes, lived in bark huts and fortified villages. For the Indians tobacco was a sacred herb to be used in important ceremonies and religious ritual. Little did they know that the white man would come to the Eastern Shore and found a slave empire on tobacco. While a few people calling themselves descendants of the Nanticoke reside today in the Indian River area of Delaware and in Dorchester County, only the Indian names remain on the land of Maryland's Eastern Shore. They are names like the following:

> Manokin—the earth is dug out
> Pocomoke—dark water or broken ground
> Tony Tank—where there is a stream at the little rock
> Assateague—the place across the water
> Nanticoke—those who play the tidewater stream
> Quantico—dancing place[4]

The Eastern Shore of Maryland has had its share of swashbuckling braggarts, opportunists, and liars, but none more illustrious than Captain John Smith. When Smith sailed up Chesapeake Bay in a tiny barque with a frightened and befuddled crew of six gentlemen, seven soldiers, and a "Doctor of Physicke" in June 1608, he had already lived several lives as a soldier of fortune. While a Hapsburg mercenary in the defense of Vienna, for example, he was captured by the Turks. He escaped from prison and narrowly missed a eunuch's fate. Later he fastened his colors with England's Virginia Company and sailed for the Jamestown colony.

Captain John Smith left the fledgling settlement of Jamestown in the summer of 1608 to explore the Chesapeake region. Sailing in an open barque of "three tunnes burthen," he headed northward. For a man of Smith's military background and good sense, he was ill-prepared and ill-equipped, by his own account, for the voyage. Wrote Smith: "We discovered the winde and waters so much increased with thunder, lightning, and raine, that our mast and sayle blew overbord and such mighty waves overracked us in that small barge that with great labour we kept her from sinking by freeing out the water." The crew members ultimately were forced to repair the sail with their shirts. Apparently the "gentlemen" on board got more than they bargained for from a Chesapeake squall. They subsisted on oatmeal, water, roots, and fish. After years of scholarly controversy, it has been determined that Smith sailed up the Pocomoke River in search of fresh water. The islands off Pocomoke Sound still bear Smith's name. After storms, thirst, and several misadventures with hostile Indians in the area of the Nanticoke River, Captain Smith sailed his barque into the Sassafras River.

Fish were so plentiful in the rivers and the Bay that he and his men attempted to catch them with frying pans. Ever the gallant soldier, Captain Smith even speared a stingray with his sword and received a poisonous wound from the ray's tail which caused him considerable torment. The expedition found, however, neither gold nor lasting peace with the Indians.[5] In sum, Captain Smith's voyage northward was a bungled affair. Yet in 1608 Smith called the region "the Eastern Shore" and the name took hold. Today the term Eastern Shore refers to all that is now the Delmarva Peninsula—the land east of the Chesapeake Bay and south of the Elk River.

*   *   *

The Eastern Shore of Maryland has often been referred to as the land that time forgot. Stretching from Cecil County in the north, the region follows the Chesapeake Bay southward to form a diamond of tidewater counties shaped over the millennia by the sand deposits of the Susquehanna River. Until

The William Preston Lane Memorial Bridge links the rural Eastern Shore with metropolitan Maryland. Photograph by Pat Vojtech.

Kent Narrows. Photograph by Pat Vojtech.

recently, the Eastern Shore was so isolated from the commercial and social mainstream of Maryland that residents usually thought of themselves as living in a land apart from the state. Three states, Delaware, Maryland, and Virginia, have sovereignty over the Eastern Shore; and the name Delmarva (as the region is popularly referred to) testifies to the political allegiance of its inhabitants. Most residents identify more with the region as a social entity than with its hyphenated political structure.

The Eastern Shore of Maryland has always had an uneasy relationship with Annapolis. Over the centuries the Eastern Shore has tried to secede from the state and form an independent commonwealth. As early as the Maryland Convention of 1776, delegates from the Eastern Shore attempted to proclaim its legal right to secede. Even at the time of the Revolution, politicians from the Eastern Shore were aware that they were a special group within the state of Maryland. In 1833 there was an uproar on the Eastern Shore over the way that state money was poured out for the construction of the Chesapeake and Ohio Canal and the Baltimore and Ohio Railroad. The Eastern Shore was easily outvoted during the appropriations fight. According to local historian James C. Mullikin, "a resentful Cinderella, watched gloomily as the parent Legislature pawned the family jewels, so to speak, to deck in splendor Cinderella's sisters, Baltimore and the Western Shore."[6] The last such secession effort blossomed in the 1950s under the leadership of Senator Harry Phoebus of Somerset County. While the legislature dismissed Phoebus as something of a tidewater tomfool, the senator delighted in reading angry letters from his constituents and others on the floor of the legislature. One secessionist went so far as to argue that the Eastern Shore should declare its independence from America and threaten to go Communist if it did not receive foreign aid. Examples of this sentiment are still seen on the Eastern Shore. Motorists proudly display bumper stickers on their cars that read "Secede Now" or "There Is No Life West of the Chesapeake Bay."

Settled in the seventeenth century, the Eastern Shore has the oldest or "most American" of populations. Most of the people on the Eastern Shore can trace their roots to the colonial migrations from England and Ireland in the seventeenth and eighteenth centuries or to the African slave trade.

The population of the Eastern Shore has "set" for three centuries and local residents still do not take easily to outsiders. Anyone not a native of the Eastern Shore is immediately dubbed a foreigner, and candidates for public office at election time go to great lengths to assure voters that they were "born and raised on the Eastern Shore." That phrase has almost totemic value and often Shore residents will vote for a local dullard over a talented outsider. The passionate concern for "us versus them foreigners" is reflected in a famous anecdote of Queen Anne's County. In the late nineteenth century a Baltimore couple came to live on Kent Island with their baby girl. The baby grew up on the island, married, had children, and became a prominent local matron. When she finally passed away at the age of ninety, her obituary in the local paper read: "Baltimore woman dies."

Outsiders have difficulty understanding the contrariness and the stubborn independence of Eastern Shoremen. Pete Switzer, a Tilghman Island waterman, explains it this way: "Once there was an old waterman, about eighty years he was. He got so that he was too feeble to work. Everybody on the island knew him and was willing to help the old guy. He was proud, though, and chose to starve rather than take handouts."

In a way the Eastern Shore is a cultural gestalt—a unity of the Chesapeake Bay, the land, and the people conditioned through time. The issues of two centuries past are still debated on the Eastern Shore and its intensely conservative citizenry stand fast against the forces of social change. Eastern Shoremen have always been reluctant to embark on radical social and economic reforms and are resentful of government interference. Labor unions have withered on the vine as locals have a grudge against anything that places a restraint on economic individualism. People place great emphasis on kinship and heritage; personal accomplishment is secondary to one's family name.

Given the lushness of nature and the rivers and creeks that run into the Chesapeake Bay, the great bounty of the region is easily at hand. Between local agriculture and hunting and fishing, the Eastern Shore is still a place where a man can live a life of ease and independence on a modest income. One Eastern Shoreman summed it up this way: "So what if I only make minimum wage. The freezer is full of goose and deer and sea trout and I take off when I want. If the boss gets rough, I'll find me another job. Don't bother me no way at all."

Eastern Shore life also has its dark side. Slavery existed here for over two centuries and the institution died hard. During the age of tobacco empires on the shore in the eighteenth century, rich planters set the mold of racial feudalism. After the Civil War and emancipation, Jim Crow laws separated the races and intensified personal antagonisms. The public schools of the region were some of the last in the South to integrate, and at times the National Guard has been called out to keep racial peace. In matters of racial accommodation white Eastern Shoremen can be singularly tough-minded, especially if they feel that they are being bullied by outsiders. Recently, however, economic and social conditions for black people have improved on the Shore and the region now has a small but increasingly powerful black middle class.

Maryland's Eastern Shore has always loomed large in the popular imagination of the Atlantic seaboard. In the 1870s big city writers like John Williamson of *Century Magazine* and others wrote romantic tributes to the Eastern Shore. It was for them an enchanted region of colorful manor houses, genteel traditions, and pleasant living. Writing in a promotional pamphlet to attract farmers to the region in 1879, writer W. Halstean exclaimed that people should "consider our healthful and agreeable climate, mild winters, pleasant summers, highly fertile soil, only a few hours ride to our largest cities, excellent society . . . and is it a wonder that northern, western, and even southern people are locating here as fast as it is made known to them?"[7] Such themes continue to be echoed today in publications such as *The National Geographic* and *The Washington Post* that herald the Eastern Shore as a majestic region of independent farmers and watermen. For the media the emblem of the region is the proud sailing skipjack oyster boat. Mary Corddry, who covered the Eastern Shore for many years for *The* [Baltimore] *Sun*, often sent dispatches to Baltimore that contradicted this Edenic myth. They were rarely published, though her stories of proud watermen and oyster boats made the front pages. Even those unfamiliar with the region are still able to make an association with Chesapeake crabs and oysters. Also, James Michener's novel, *Chesapeake*, so romanticized the region that the book added fuel to an already explosive boom in Eastern Shore real estate development.

*   *   *

A trip to the Eastern Shore via Kent Island is an adventure in time-travel. As the oldest continuous settlement in Maryland (1631), Kent Island's well-recorded heritage opens a centuries-old window on the Eastern Shore experience. In the early seventeenth century, the island was a frontier outpost manned by fur traders who swapped trinkets, guns, and hatchets for the rich beaver pelts of the Matapeake and Susquehanna Indians. The founder of the outpost, William Claiborne of Virginia, was an affluent and politically well-connected Englishman who feuded for decades with Lord Baltimore and the Calvert family over the destiny of the island. Claiborne, an ambitious second son of an aristocratic family, held the position of royal surveyor of the Virginia colony. Eager to make his fortune in the Chesapeake through court influence, Claiborne obtained a royal license from King Charles I to trade and make discoveries "in any and all parts of North America not already pre-empted by monopolies." This license was granted a year before the Calverts received their proprietorship of Maryland and from it and the lucrative Indian trade in fur arose much of Lord Baltimore's trouble with Claiborne and his London allies.

Beginning in 1629 when George Calvert made an unwelcome visit to Jamestown and expressed interest in Virginia, the Chesapeake country became a bauble of English court rivalry. At times Claiborne and his faction in London had the upper hand. At other times the quiet diplomacy of the Catholic proprietorship won the island for Maryland. At stake was a rich fur trading business and the military and political control of the upper Chesapeake. After George Calvert's death, Claiborne continued to press his claim and stirred up the Indians of the Kent Island area with visions of Catholic settlers seizing Indian domains and driving away the wild game.

Finally, in exasperation, Cecil Calvert instructed his brother, Leonard, then sitting as governor of Maryland, to seize Claiborne and take possession of the island. Maryland naval forces captured one of Claiborne's boats, the *Long Tayle*. In angry retaliation Claiborne outfitted an armed pinnace, the *Cockatrice*, and vowed war against Calvert. He soon met his match. Governor Calvert sent two armed vessels, the *St. Margaret* and the *St. Helen* down the Bay and the rival boats clashed in Pocomoke Sound in April 1635. This was the first naval battle on the Chesapeake Bay and Calvert's forces prevailed, killing three Virginians in the fire. Shortly thereafter the Calverts proclaimed Claiborne a pirate and sought to extradite him from Virginia. Further, the proprietor issued a bill of attainder, confiscating his Kent Island property.

Unfortunately the overthrow of the Stuart king of England and the ascendancy of Oliver Cromwell and his Puritan faction brought the royalist Calvert fortunes to a low ebb. The ever-resourceful Claiborne plotted anew; and counting on the anti-Calvert Puritans in Maryland, the wily Virginian led a rebellion against the proprietorship. With short dispatch, Claiborne and his followers seized the Maryland colony and forced Governor Leonard Calvert into exile in Virginia. Although the Calverts eventually retook the island with an armed force, Kent Island's fate, like that of Maryland, swung in the balance for several years. After 1666 with the restoration of the English monarchy and the Calverts' assumption of the proprietorship of Maryland did the struggle with Claiborne and his Virginia faction end.[8]

Kent Island was a rich Chesapeake prize. Its control determined the fate of Maryland. Small wonder that all the weapons of deceit, fraud, diplomacy, and violence were used in this high stakes scramble for empire during the colonial period.

The picaresque quality of Kent Island and the Chesapeake generally in the late seventeenth century is well documented in the writings of George Alsop and Ebenezer Cooke. Between 1660 and 1700 George Alsop and Ebenezer Cooke visited Maryland and the Eastern Shore and each wrote an intriguing and largely truthful account of his experiences. When George Alsop published his *Character of the Province of Maryland* in 1666, he wrote that he was so excited about Maryland "that I am almost out of breath." Alsop had served as an indentured servant at Patuxent on the western shore in exchange for his six-pound passage to the New World. During his service he had ample opportunity to observe daily life in the colony and his account of the richness of the Chesapeake region excited London readers. "Deer are as common as London cuckolds," he wrote, and the wild life was so ample that no man starved in Maryland. The Chesapeake Bay was loaded with fish and oysters and a life of ease was available to those venturing westward to Maryland. Religious toleration, Alsop noted, was a well-established practice in the colony. Even Presbyterianism, that "profuse profaneness that issues from the prodigality of none but cract-brained sots," thrived in the colony. "Dwell here and be rich," Alsop advised. "For here every man lives quietly and follows his labor . . . . Here's no Newgates for pilfering felons, nor any Bridewell to lash the soul of Concupiscence into chaste repentance."[9]

It is also from Alsop that we obtain our first glimpse of tobacco planting in Maryland. The custom of smoking tobacco was universal among the Indians of the Chesapeake when the first white settlers arrived. While tobacco for the Indians was a sacred herb used only in solemn ceremony, this addictive drug quickly became a cash crop for white farmers. Despite King James I's pronouncement that it "fowled the lungs," tobacco became fashionable with the British elite and thousands of other Englishmen as well. Thus was an agricultural empire founded in the Chesapeake upon smoke.

Tobacco season, Alsop reported, began in March and April with the sowing of thousands of tiny tobacco seeds in special soil beds protected from the elements. In June the small tobacco plants were transplanted and set in little hillocks. During the summer planters pruned off excessive leaves from the tobacco stalk and by mid-September the crop was cut down and hung in sheds to dry. Once dried, the tobacco was tied into bundles and packed into hogsheads—large wooden barrels holding a thousand pounds of tobacco that men could roll along farm paths to a nearby wharf.[10] The tobacco shipping fleet arrived between November and January to transport the crop to London and Bristol.

Given the shortage of hard currency in the colony, tobacco itself became a kind of money. "Tobacco is the current Coyn of Maryland," Alsop observed, "and will sooner purchase commodities from merchants than money."[11] On the Eastern Shore planters purchased dry goods with tobacco, bought slaves with tobacco, and left estates to heirs valued in tobacco. For much of the colonial period the rule of thumb was that a pound of tobacco was equal to one English penny. To those unfamiliar with the system, the tobacco economy fosters visions of colonists groaning under immense loads of tobacco as they trudged about the region purchasing items. In reality, most tobacco didn't leave the hogshead. Colonists trafficked in tobacco certificates from various warehouses that were seldom redeemed in small cash matters.

The Maryland observed by Ebenezer Cooke in his delightful poem, "The Sot Weed Factor or a Voyage to Maryland" (1708), was rougher and more vulgar than that reported by Alsop. If Maryland was a haven of tolerance, employment, and plenty for Alsop, for Cooke it was a land of rogues and drunks who would steal your last farthing.

Little is actually known of Ebenezer Cooke. His father was a man of some means, owning two houses in London and one at Cook Point on the mouth of the Choptank River in Dorchester County. Scholars speculate that Cooke was born in London in the late 1660s and was a resident of the Maryland colony as early as 1694. In that year Ebenezer Cooke signed a petition against removing Maryland's capital from St.Mary's to Annapolis. During this time, Cooke, though a bit of a colonial greenhorn, tried to make his fortune as a tobacco trader, with disastrous results. Back in London in 1708, Cooke penned a biting satirical poem of his experiences, which he sold in London for five pence. Historians speculate that Cooke was probably a London gentleman decayed by fast living.

Ebenezer Cooke in addition to calling himself the "poet laureate of Maryland," also practiced law, but not successfully. He spent his last years in poverty on the Virginia side of the Potomac River. Cooke is also known for his poem "Sot Weed Redivivus or the Planters Looking Glass," which he published in 1730. It celebrates the Maryland tobacco planters and claims that tobacco is "Industry and not a nauseous Weed/Must cloath the naked and the Hungry feed." He also denounced ship captains for usuriously profiting from the colonial planters and urged agricultural diversification into grain, hemp, flax, cotton, and rice. The exact date of Cooke's death is unknown, but he was approximately sixty when he wrote his last poem, quite an advanced age when most men in Maryland rarely lived past forty. He probably died in Maryland. Despite his economic failures, Cooke has left us with a distinctly American satire and a memorable, sharp-eyed glimpse of the Maryland colony in 1700.[12]

The curse of unkind friends and an empty purse made Cooke take leave of "Albion's Rocks." Cooke's voyage took three months, time enough to test the strength of any man. Landing in the Bay of Piscataway on the western shore, the usual place where ships anchored in Maryland, he beheld a society such as he had not imagined—a raw primitive frontier society "where no good sense is found, But conversation's lost and manners drowned." It was a society of shoeless and sockless sunburned tobacco planters—"In hue as tawny as a Moor." Colonists subsisted on a diet of Indian corn pudding, hominy, and apples amply washed down with large gulps of rum from the cask kept in the family chest. Although the food was poor, the rum was excellent and occasionally Cooke overindulged.

Court day was a drunken festival. Most of the judges and lawyers were illiterate, Cooke reported, and court sessions were nothing more than a drunken brawl: "And straight the lawyers broke the peace, wrangling plaintiff and defendant . . . with nonsense stuff, and false quotations, with brazen lies, and allegations." After viewing and no doubt frolicking in this spectacle, Cooke went to bed in a nearby inn. He awoke to find his hat, wig, shoes, and stockings had been thrown into the fire by the celebrating, half-savage planters. Such was life in a rude newly settled country, peopled with adventurous men hell-bent on acquiring land and wealth as tobacco planters. While hospitable to strangers, they liked to play tricks on them, too. Cooke saw little of the refined colonial cavalier upon which so many myths of old Maryland and the Eastern Shore have been built.

Determined to make his way, Cooke sailed across the Chesapeake Bay to the Eastern Shore with a load of British trade goods, probably to Kent Island. Unfortunately Cooke is silent on how he got either the money or the credit to acquire the goods. He negotiated a deal with a planter for ten thousand pounds of tobacco, only to find after trading his wares that the tobacco was not forthcoming. The "rogue Quaker" ran away from his creditor and Cooke was forced to pursue his case in Annapolis. The justice ruled that the debtor could pay Cooke for the merchandise over time in the fare of the country—corn, lumber, and cider.

In any event, the English goods had vanished, the tobacco never materialized, and Cooke cursed Maryland as a place "where no man's fruitful or a woman chaste." Back in England he had time to reflect upon his unfortunate experience with the rogues of the "Eastern Shoar." Cooke, however, would not be the last sheep to be fleeced by shrewd Eastern Shoremen.[13]

Of the majority of English inhabitants of the Eastern Shore at this time, Alsop and Cooke say little. These were the indentured servants and convicts who gave the region its special flavor of license and mayhem during the early colonial period. Indentured men and women agreed to serve from four to seven years hard labor in exchange for the price of their transport to the colony. Convicts were usually of the cutpurse and convict quality popularized by Daniel Defoe in *Moll Flanders*. Their deportation to Maryland relieved England of much of its prison population.

Until after 1700 when Maryland became flooded with Negro slaves from Barbados and Africa, white servile labor was in high demand in the Chesapeake. In order to understand the significance of indentured servitude on the Eastern Shore at this time, it is necessary to explain labor's value in the colony. For the most part, land was cheap. Free white labor, however, was quite expensive as few freemen wished to work for a planter when they had visions of becoming planters themselves. Therefore, what came to solve this labor shortage was an interesting breed of slovenly men and sluttish women who were to transform the region from wilderness to farmland. Usually one servant could till six thousand hillocks of tobacco and hoe five acres of corn, and many hard-driving planters got double this amount from their servants. Using two indentured servants, a planter in a good year could produce a hogshead of tobacco, notes historian Thomas Scharf. This was sufficient to purchase all the staples that a colonial family would need in the course of a year.[14] In Somerset County, for example, Randall Revell ruthlessly drove a dozen servants to carve out of the wilderness a thousand-acre plantation called Double Purchase.

Often servants were grossly mistreated. A revolting case of cruelty came to light in Kent County Court on September 28, 1674, when William Drake, a servant of John Welles, testified that "your petitioner's master has several times abused me by giving me unlawful correction . . . hanging me up to ye gunne racks and whipped me without mercy giving me at least one hundred blows upon my bare skin."[15] Few instances of cruel treatment resulted in court action, however.

As late as the 1770s William Eddis, an Englishman resident in Maryland, remarked that indentured servants were harshly dealt with and "only the Negroes were kindly treated."[16]

After 1700 the condition of servants was regulated solely by the price of Negroes, and, like blacks, white servants could be bought and sold at auction. It seems hardly worth noting that few indentured servants went on to become great planters when they received their freedom. Most joined the ranks of a frequently impoverished lumpen proletariat that was a cause of much concern to colonial authorities, especially when significant numbers of former white servant girls took black slave husbands.[17]

It was also the scarcity of labor that made the sale of convicts easy in Maryland in spite of local sentiment against the practice. Until well into the eighteenth century convicts in Maryland outnumbered indentured servants. While Maryland was not a penal colony in the strict sense that Australia was in the early nineteenth century, it did receive very large numbers of convicts. The historian Abbot E. Smith estimates that convicts came to Maryland and the Eastern Shore in two waves. In the 1633-1680 period, he writes, 21,000 convicts were sent to Maryland plantations. In the 1746-1775 period, another 9,360 convicts were transported to Maryland. It is useful to note that many convicts were happy to arrive in Maryland. Barbados in the Caribbean, the alternative destination for convicts, was much worse. In the Caribbean, convicts were worked to death on sugar plantations.[18]

Despite continuous waves of immigrants, the population of the Eastern Shore grew slowly in the seventeenth century. Seasoning, the adjustment to the New World disease climate, took its toll. Although there was a significant number of women, the society could not reproduce itself. Malaria and cholera carried off large numbers of adults and infant mortality was high.[19]

In times past Eastern Shore wags joked that Kent Island was shaped like a woman's leg—tempting and exposed. While the anthropomorphic outline of old Kent Island is open to debate, in the seventeenth century it was a land of roguish sexual mores. When Maryland publicist George Alsop happily discoursed in 1666 on how four years in the colony could result in good fortune and "copulative matrimony," he failed to mention that adultery and bastardy flourished with abandon on the Eastern Shore and Kent Island.

Illicit sex was most prevalent among the servant class. And planters who had a significant financial investment in their indentured female servants did not look kindly on the bastards who drained their purses and their labor supply. In Talbot County a woman servant who had an illegitimate child, like Elizabeth Wharton, received thirty lashes "well laid on her Bare Backe for having a bastard child."[20] If the father of the illegitimate child could be identified, he was usually fined and whipped as well. After Elizabeth Johnson was publically whipped in Somerset for producing a bastard, the justices ordered her lover, Peter Calloway, to pay her "one hundred pounds of tobacco for her abuse."[21]

Occasionally a pregnant maiden proved more formidable than either the courts or her lover had suspected. Mary Hartwell, a pregnant free woman from Virginia, followed Joseph Wickes, her lover, to Kent Island and sued in the court for marriage and the legitimization of the child. She lost the battle in court "for lack of evidence," but won the war. Wickes married her, though he refused to claim the child. As she and her husband refrained from making the child a public charge of Kent Island, the new Mrs. Wickes was spared the sheriff's whip.[22]

The sexual transgressions of seventeenth-century servant girls pale in comparison to that infamous Kent Island couple, the Bradnoxes. The wild behavior of Thomas and Mary Bradnox, who owned a plantation at Love Point—significantly—fill the pages of early Kent Island history. They are characters worthy of Hogarth's brush or a Defoe novel and probably a source of embarrassment to Kent Island's staid genealogists. In the 1650s and 1660s the Bradnoxes were known on Kent Island and beyond as wild drunkards, thieves, liars, adulterers, and traitors. In the last regard, the Bradnoxes participated in the Ingle uprising against Lord Baltimore when civil war raged in the colony in 1646.

Yet Tom Bradnox's reputation scarcely held him back in Kent Island society. From 1658 until his death in 1661 Bradnox served as a Kent Island justice and supervised the disposition of wills and estates. He also served as a witness to the court in important legal matters. After his death it was found that Bradnox had stolen the county's militia funds.[23]

The sexual escapades of the Bradnoxes spilled over into Kent County Court in April 1653 when Mrs. Mary Bradnox sued John Salter, a Kent Island planter, for slander. While Salter had blamed the Bradnoxes for stealing hogs on the island, it subsequently came out in court that Mrs. Bradnox and her drunken friends had gone off whoring in Virginia. Salter's position in court became complicated when his wife, Janne, and a servant girl, Ann Stanley, caught John Salter with his britches down and Mrs. Bradnox "upon her bed with her coats up as high as her brest."

The slandered and cuckolded Tom Bradnox threatened a fist fight and a civil suit. Salter swore an oath that this was "no more than you have done to my wife," and he could prove it.[24] While the personal and legal battles of the fighting cuckolds raged, Salter discovered what he thought was incontrovertible proof of his wife's infidelity with Bradnox. Armed and not a little drunk, Salter rode out to the six-hundred-acre Love Point plantation and broke down the front door of the Bradnox house. Although Mary and Tom Bradnox were able to calm Salter's temper, it would not be the last time he would break down their door in search of his whorish wife. Eventually peace must have come to this "ménage à quatre" for Salter and Bradnox worked together on land and tobacco sales.

We leave Tom Bradnox in his favorite recreation—drinking and partying with Colonel Robert Vaughan, commander of Kent Island, and his friends. In the wee hours of the morning, after chasing servant girls, Bradnox fell drunk and smashed his nose on the floor. No doubt in this case as in others involving his riotous behavior, he would be defended by Mary Bradnox who practiced as his attorney before the court.[25]

The Bradnox battles must be seen as part of a larger historical tapestry in which fights over cattle grazing, livestock stealing, and slander were everyday matters. Even Colonel Robert Vaughan, the respected and extremely able military commander of Kent Island, was a rough and insolent man used to having his own way. He mistreated his servants and several times was fined by Kent justices three hundred pounds of tobacco for "insolent language to the court."[26]

In addition to unruly neighbors, Kent Islanders also had to worry about hostile Indians. In the seventeenth century the Chesapeake Bay was a war path for the Susquehanna Indians. The Susquehannas were so strong and daring that they once captured an armed Dutch sloop on the Chesapeake and looted it of its cargo, gunpowder, and arms. The local Matapeake Indians of Kent Island stole cattle and kidnapped white children to hold for ransom. Occasionally the Indians massacred whites and burned their homes. In 1650 the Kent County Court passed legislation that prohibited Indians from coming onto Kent Island without giving notice. The court also authorized the militia to shoot, kill, beat, or take prisoner any Indian violating this law. Indian depredations continued until Colonel Nathaniel Utie blocked the route of the Susquehanna Indians in Cecil County with a fort on Spesutie Island in the mouth of the Susquehanna River.

By the time that Kent Island was absorbed by the newly created Queen Anne's County in 1706, the Indian menace had diminished to a minor nuisance. By then the major concern of Kent Island planters was the destruction of local agriculture by herds of wild hogs, and the Matapeakes enjoyed a nice living by killing the hogs for the government.

As late as 1743, Henry Callister, a tobacco factor for a London firm in Oxford, Maryland, could refer to the Eastern Shore as a "Purgatory of Rogues and Fools." Although there were rogues and fools aplenty in this tough and increasingly region-conscious land, there were also sober and industrious planters and craftsmen. These men were quite different from the Cavalier imagery of ancestor-worshiping moderns. The inventory of Robert Short, for example, who died in the fall of 1651, listed five head of cattle, one gun, a small bed with blankets, one pair of shoes, some old lumber, a frying pan and an iron pot, and 3,523 pounds of tobacco. In the eighteenth century these men and their families would tame the land and make it one of the most charming locales in British North America. As Stephen Bordley, the elder brother of John Beale Bordley and himself an Eastern Shore planter, saw it in 1740, the farmers of the Eastern Shore live "amidst a great plenty of everything, [and] we enjoy as fine and serene an air as any in the world."[27]

Although Maryland settlers began to make a distinction between eastern and western shore as early as 1631, Eastern Shore regional consciousness did not fully develop until the beginning of the eighteenth century. The Chesapeake Bay set Eastern Shoremen as a breed apart from the rest of Maryland, and the Bay was their own wondrous highway. They traded and traveled on it, fought on it and frolicked on it. Its inlets, rivers, and creeks were so numerous and accommodating that nearly every planter could live near navigable salt water. In an age when it took the royal English court five days to travel the short distance from London to Bath, Eastern Shore planters could easily cover the same distance in a day's sail.

Although Eastern Shore planters eventually raised fine Georgian homes on the Eastern Shore, settlements were not as diffused in the region as in the counties of England. Given the Bay and the geography of countless nooks and creeks, rivers, and necks, the planters tended to adopt wholly different settlement patterns on the land. Settlement on the Eastern Shore was more a scattering of isolated habitations connected to England by a tobacco-merchant fleet of several hundred ships. The great majority of settlers lived within a few miles of shipping in a water-laced countryside. Life and commerce in the Chesapeake tended to be simple. A small elite quickly capitalized in the early eighteenth century on the tobacco revolution to obtain through political and social means the best land. The remainder of small yeoman farmers lived simple lives with a very modest dwelling, a rifle, a few spoons, and a cooking pot.[28]

Eastern Shoremen personalized their land grants with names that betrayed bold ambition and lust for life: Bennet's Adventure, The Hazard, and David's Destiny. Others like Makepeace in Somerset County and End of Controversy in Dorchester reveal the more pacific dreams of the early Eastern Shoremen. Some grants like Crooked Intention in Talbot County may have been patented by less honorable men.

*   *   *

In addition to rogues and Indian raids, Kent Island has also had to endure pirates and hurricanes. It was invaded by the British during the War of 1812 and its history shows the people of Kent Island to be a very resilient breed. During World War I, the federal government attempted to uproot the island community and turn Kent Island into an army munitions testing site. The islanders fought back in the legislature and in the press and federal authorities backed off. The army chose another site up the Bay, which is now the Aberdeen Proving Ground.

Kent Island has always been a good place to make money. The land is fertile and the oyster packinghouses of Kent Narrows have produced their share of affluent watermen. The bars and taverns of the area draw a good crowd. The Angler's Restaurant at the Narrows is a favorite haunt of those who want country music, soft-crab sandwiches, and little inter-ference from the Lacoste crowd that seems determined to turn every Eastern Shore honkytonk into a fern bar. While only a short time ago oyster shuckers and restaurant workers lived in poverty reminiscent of Mississippi, the island now hums with prosperity. In recent times the island has succumbed to tourism and metropolitan sprawl with its attendant motels, fast-food restaurants, and singles' bars.

In times past, tobacco and oysters were the gods that Kent Islanders worshipped. Today real estate speculation has be-come Kent Island's driving force. The island's few remaining farmers sit on land passed down through the centuries. Soon it will all be subdivisions, marinas, and boatels. Anne Arundel County's tightly packed middle class is spilling across the Bay Bridge in quest of cheaper housing on the Eastern Shore. Only recent state legislation barring intensive waterfront develop-ment has spared what is left of Kent Island's coastline. Also, the rapid growth of Kent Island has been unsettling to Queen Anne's up-county farmers who have run the county for genera-tions from their sleepy courthouse citadel in Centreville.

Many natives have come to lament "the passing of Kent Island." As Dr. Reginald Truitt, a long-standing resident of the island put it, "Kent Island is now a suburb of Annapolis. It's not part of the Eastern Shore anymore."

2

The Wye Country

I can shine where I please, in a church, a drawing room, a grog shop or a brothel.

—Jacob Gibson, 1813

Queen Anne's County is the gateway in the west to the heart of the Eastern Shore. Named after England's feisty and politically astute Queen Anne, who lived from 1665 to 1714, the county was organized in 1706 out of slices of Talbot County that included Kent Island. Today in the county little is known of Queen Anne save that she desperately wanted an heir. Tragically she conceived fourteen children, all of whom were lost by miscarriage or at childbirth. A fifteenth child, a boy, died at an early age.

As a county, Queen Anne's is a beautiful Stuart jewel caressed by three gentle rivers, the Chester, the Corsica, and the Wye. It is a peaceful, quiet land defined by necks—small peninsulas that stretch out into tidal rivers on which many of the great estates of the Eastern Shore are located. It was here in Queen Anne's that the region's tobacco empire came of age in the eighteenth century, producing a tidewater aristocracy that easily rivaled that of England.

Tobacco is a luxury crop. It is hard to store and hard to ship and for much of the colonial period Navigation Laws, which limited the colonies to trading with the Mother Country, prevented it from being marketed locally. Between 1680 and 1720 tobacco prices fluctuated wildly on the British and European markets. During this period, notes historian Gregory Stiverson, many small planters sank into tenancy and debt.[1] Only those who had the capital and ability to diversify their farming operations were able to prosper.

Slavery made the difference in the making of the tidewater gentry. In counties on the Eastern Shore only slaveowners and their children could exploit opportunities in farming and the tobacco trade and prosper. Those who could afford it were possessed by "the Negro fever" in the eighteenth century. Slaves were far more profitable than indentured servants, and their labor and offspring could be exploited across the generations. In 1707 there were scarcely 2,000 Negro slaves on the Eastern Shore. By 1755, however, planters would own over 17,000 black slaves in the region. Ultimately the slave population on the Eastern Shore would peak at around 37,000 with about 100,000 statewide in 1790. Tobacco and slaves reinforced one another on the Eastern Shore, and planters using human capital reaped a fortune when tobacco prices improved.

Slaves, however, were a most troublesome property, especially those who had not been seasoned in the Caribbean but came directly from Africa's western coast. Today, at the Hall of Records in Annapolis, visitors can easily find scores of levy lists for Eastern Shore counties during the colonial period where local governments annually appropriated funds for "the suppression of tumults of Negroes." Further, although the region easily adapted to changes in the labor system from white indentured servitude to black slavery, interracial sex was a troublesome political problem. Were the offspring of black-white unions slave or free? This was an important question that struck at the legal definition of slavery. The Act of 1681 in Maryland declared that children born of white servant women and Negroes were free. By 1715, however, ministers were prohibited from marrying any white to "any Negro whatsoever, or Mulatto slave." Finally in 1728 the Maryland legislature went so far as to prohibit the marriage of free mulatto women with Negro servants. Given the large mixed race population that emerged in the region in the next hundred years, one can only conclude that these race laws were observed more in the breach than in practice.[2]

One highly individualized problem came to the Eastern Shore in 1730 in the form of an African slave known as Job. Purchased by the Tolsey family of Kent Island, Job was a Moslem priest from the Gambia region of west Africa. Job spoke his tribal language and was fluent in Arabic. He had been captured in the Futa (modern Fouta) region and sold into slavery by an enemy tribe. Politically adroit and well schooled in the Koran, Job was useless as a servant and a social threat to the plantation regime. Ultimately the devout Moslem was purchased by a group of Queen Anne's planters and sent back to Africa via London.[3]

For certain members of the tidewater gentry the plantation system paid fabulously well. Today you can still see on the Eastern Shore many of the grand eighteenth-century plantation structures like Wye House in Talbot, Teackle Mansion in Somerset, and the riverfront mansions of Kent along the Chester River. These attractive buildings with their long hallways, colonnades, and formal gardens are still much sought after by the region's wealthy even though the way of life that brought them into being has long since disappeared.

From the southern tip of Kent Island it is an easy sail across Eastern Bay to the Wye River. Named by Welsh settlers, the Wye has always been the cradle of wealth in the Chesapeake. In the early eighteenth century the Wye country was the home of Richard Bennett III, one of the richest men in America at that time. Bennett owned 1,300 slaves and 25,000 acres of farmland in Kent, Queen Anne's, Talbot, Dorchester, and Somerset counties.

Richard Bennett of Wye was the grandson of Richard Bennett, the shrewd Puritan governor of Virginia who was appointed by Oliver Cromwell to make peace with the Susquehanna Indians and extinguish Catholicism on the Eastern Shore. Ironically this Puritan's son would marry the Catholic daughter of the lady-in-waiting of Queen Henrietta Maria of England. Named after the queen, Henrietta Maria Bennett was a headstrong determined woman who raised her two children as devout Catholics. She defied Protestant bigotry, established a small Catholic chapel, and defended Catholic priests from persecution. After her husband's death, she married Philemon Lloyd, a wealthy Protestant planter in the region. After much contention, she agreed to raise any children by Lloyd as Protestants. The Bennett children, however, were the main focus of her religious attention.

Either because of his being persecuted as a Catholic or because of his family and business connections with the Lloyds, Richard Bennett plunged into land speculation as a young man and became a farmer and shipper of tobacco. His additional activities as a money lender were pursued with the same ferocious energy that characterized all his interests. Even in an age of intensely ambitious tobacco planters he was a phenomenon; and by 1700 his name was on hundreds of deeds for land in Queen Anne's and Dorchester counties. He also acquired Wye Mills, a flour milling operation that today is a historic landmark. By 1715 he was one of the most important shipbuilders of the region as well. No recluse, Richard Bennett loved public argument, tavern brawls, and lawsuits. Once in Talbot County during court day Bennett and several of his rowdy friends rode their horses into the justices' chambers and turned the courthouse into a drunken carnival.

When he died at the age of eighty-two in 1749, secure in his Catholic faith, Bennett left a sixteen-page will with 275 beneficiaries. Ultimately his estate totalled over 200,000 pounds sterling—a vast fortune for either side of the Atlantic at that time. The cycle of religious irony begun by his Puritan fore-bearers was completed in Bennett's will. The overwhelming bulk of his estate went to the resolutely anti-Papist son of his half-brother, Edward Lloyd III.[4] Today Bennett Point, where this tidewater aristocrat held sway in the Wye country, is the secluded preserve of expensive waterfront estates.

By 1770 there were distinct social classes on the Eastern Shore based on land and slaves. In that year Maryland's tobacco crop fetched 300,000 pounds sterling in the ports of Bristol and London, and planters had enough money to satisfy nearly every material want. Many tobacco nabobs lived only for the moment as fluctuations in the world tobacco market could make today's aristocrat tomorrow's pauper. Such high-consumption living produced a class of Eastern Shoremen who spent much of their time in foppish pursuits in Annapolis. Dressing in the effeminate Italian fashion of that day, these "macaroni," as they were called, were a source of vexation to sober-minded farmers like John Beale Bordley. Many planters, Bordley complained, left their estates to the care of overseers to indulge in "Foppery, idleness, and dissipation," gambling their heritage and slaves on the throw of the dice.

In the eighteenth century John Beale Bordley of Wye Island exemplified the finest qualities of the Eastern Shore gentry. A man of excellent education and social connection, Bordley was one of the first farmers in the region to switch from tobacco to wheat farming. Grain, he quite correctly believed, freed Eastern Shore planters from the tyranny of the London-controlled tobacco market and could be sold more easily on the European continent than the royal weed. Bordley was especially irked by the British Navigation Laws and on the eve of the American Revolution he preached colonial self-sufficiency. Practicing what he preached on Wye Island, Bordley turned his plantation into a self-sufficient agricultural and industrial estate. He established a carpentry shop and smithy and built a small textile mill for wool and hemp spinning. His brickyard, kiln, and ropewalk turned a handsome profit and his milk house and granary kept the Bordleys and their servants well fed. Bordley was also an excellent brewmaster and his beer was highly popular with the local squires.

John Beale Bordley was also something of a snob and was appalled by the low-class behavior of tenant farmers in Queen Anne's County. They were poor and worthless, Bordley reasoned, because they were creatures of the moment who "hurry to the tavern, the race, nine pins, billiards, excess upon excess of toddy, and the worst nonsensical and idle chat with exclamations and roarings and foreign to common sense and manners . . . ." In sum, they behaved just like the "macaroni" of Annapolis but without slaves or great reserves of cash. Such behavior in his countrymen made Bordley gloomy about the future of the Eastern Shore.[5]

Just off the island at Wye Narrows lived Bordley's brother-in-law, William Paca. Bordley and Paca married the Chew sisters, heirs of the Richard Bennett fortune with family connections to the Lloyds. While they made exceptionally shrewd marriages, neither man lacked talent and political connections in his own right. The Pacas, for example, were part of the Baltimore County squirearchy on the western shore. After receiving a good education in Philadelphia, Paca studied law under Stephen Bordley, the well-known barrister of Annapolis and brother of John Beale Bordley.

As squire of Wye Narrows and part owner of Wye Island with his brother-in-law, John Beale Bordley, Paca drifted easily into land speculation and colonial politics. During the revolutionary era, Paca was one of the Eastern Shoremen who signed the Declaration of Independence. Three times member of the Continental Congress, Paca was also elected twice to the governorship of Maryland.

While Paca's responsibilities during the Revolution often kept him in Annapolis and Philadelphia, he was well informed about Eastern Shore politics. When he received word that the Tories on the Eastern Shore were doing everything possible to hamper the patriot cause, he used his influence and his money to quell their insurrectionary plots in Queen Anne's and Caroline counties. The Tories, he suspected, were being led by "scoundrel Methodist preachers." While Paca's plantation somehow escaped the depredations of British raiding parties in the Wye country during the Revolution, marauders did row their barges to Wye Island and sacked the estate of John Beale Bordley who had done so much to furnish Washington's troops with grain and fresh beef. Both Paca and Bordley subsequently had their own armed boat on the Wye to protect their estates until the war ended.

The Pacas emerged from the Revolution as rich as feudal lords and they were the absolute rulers of Centreville society. Always at the center of political power, the Pacas maintained a thirty-seven-room mansion with extensive gardens in Annapolis. Unfortunately, the sons who followed in the Paca line were arrogant men who were out of tune with the democratic sensibilities of a new postrevolutionary age on the Eastern Shore. Paca's grandson, William Paca II, fathered a generation of men who came to no good. During the Civil War, William Paca II was a staunch belligerant Unionist who despised his nephews for their Confederate sympathies. Paca secretly maneuvered to have their estate confiscated and sold at auction. When his relatives challenged him, Paca shot and killed Jack Paca and his uncle, Alfred Jones.

William Paca had his trial moved from Centreville to a pro-Unionist court in Talbot County and a judge found him innocent. Eastern Shore society, however, shunned Paca and his family for his foul crime and the family spent its last years in seclusion. One son committed suicide and a daughter died mysteriously from poison that she had mistaken for medicine. Both the Bordley and Paca plantations have long since disappeared and the accomplishments of these proud colonial families are largely forgotten in the region. [William Paca is buried near the Wye Institute, and his grave looks out on his beloved Wye River.][6]

The Lloyds carried on the family name and exercised considerable power in the region until the waning years of the nineteenth century. The Lloyds traced their power and wealth back to the end of the seventeenth century when Edward Lloyd II of Talbot County was appointed councillor to the proprietor. The Lloyds were part of a native-born aristocracy on the Eastern Shore that enjoyed good health, made advantageous marriages, and consolidated its wealth in each locality. As early as 1700, for example, over fifty percent of the large landowners on the Eastern Shore were linked to each other through kinship or marriage. Together with his brothers, Philemon and James, Edward Lloyd was a major economic and social power in the eighteenth-century Chesapeake country. From portraits and historical record the Lloyds appear to be a singular breed of "stout men, hardheaded, prudent, eminently respectable, never given to excess, and singularly unimaginative." After 1760 the Lloyds joined the aristocratic anti-British faction and lent their talent and money to the Revolution of 1776.

They, too, are now gone from the land of Wye and a new aristocracy of wealthy outsiders—sportsmen, real estate developers, corporate executives, government officials, and celebrities—has replaced the old landed gentry of the land of Wye.

Yet none of these newcomers will ever have the magnificent character of Jacob Gibson. In the early nineteenth century, Gibson was one of the most warm-hearted, fun-loving, and mischievous planters on the Eastern Shore. A passionate admirer of Napoleon, he named his Miles River plantation Marengo and named all his other farms after Napoleon's victories. When the British invaded his plantation at Sharps Island during the War of 1812, Gibson talked his way out of imprisonment and argued successfully for reimbursement for the cattle the British soldiers took. After his release he sailed up the Miles River in his barge with his slave beating a tune on an empty barrel and Gibson flying his old red bandanna as a flag. From a distance the good citizens of St. Michaels thought this was the vanguard of the British invasion and the panic-stricken town prepared for the worst. Thus they were less than amused when they learned that the old prankster Gibson had played a joke on them again. Gibson liked to call himself "sunburnt and mad," and he feuded constantly with his neighbors in the local press and in the county court. Sometimes he won, sometimes he got a severe beating for his outspoken remarks. He also wagered heavily

The bridge to Wye Island connects the visitor to the Eastern Shore's plantation past. Photograph by Pat Vojtech.

The county courthouse plays a large role in Eastern Shore political and social life. Queen Anne's County's namesake is prominently displayed on the county courthouse grounds. Photograph courtesy of the Chesapeake College Library.

on congressional elections, at times winning $3,000. Yet, if Gibson had anything, it was a strong ego, and at Marengo plantation he boasted: "I can shine where I please, in a church, a drawing room, a grog shop, or a brothel." The gentry detested him and the women loved him dearly.

*   *   *

When the late Arthur A. Houghton, Jr., a wealthy glass manufacturer, first moved into the Wye River country in the 1930s, he found a region ravaged by decades of agricultural neglect. In fact, the Depression of those years merely brought to a sad end the already déclassé life-style of the aristocratic tidewater. The land, however, was beautiful and Houghton picked a farm overlooking the Wye River and took to building an estate that would be known throughout the region for its elegant parties and scientific husbandry. A strong-willed man whose business acumen would serve him well in the amassing of a large fortune, Houghton nonetheless did not try to play the role of the imperious landlord. He blended in well with the locals.

After World War II Houghton took a serious philanthropic interest in trying to bring about the economic and social improvement of a region he had come to love. An outgrowth of these philanthropic efforts was the architectural rescue of historic buildings and churches and the creation in 1963 of the Wye Institute. More than just an organization to dispense philanthropy, the Wye Institute was an activist organization that pursued a vision of the great society for the Chesapeake Bay country. From its base on a three centuries' old estate at Cheston-on-Wye near Queenstown, the Wye Institute was charged by Arthur Houghton to work with the people of the nine counties of the Eastern Shore of Maryland in their efforts to strengthen and expand educational, cultural, and economic opportunities. Houghton recruited an affluent and like-minded Baltimore attorney, Clarence Miles, to serve as president of the institute and the two men immediately set to work. In the first year of its existence, the institute published a highly regarded economic survey of the Eastern Shore region that pinpointed many of the problems affecting the region. How could the Eastern Shore, asked Miles and the consultants recruited for the institute, be improved by comprehensive zoning and vocational education programs? How could they help to stem the flow of young local talent away from the region toward Baltimore and Delaware and other metropolitan regions of the country? Men like Donald Shank, Clarence Miles, and John Ward were accustomed, like Houghton, to socializing with the rich and powerful and used their network of corporate and political contacts to make the Eastern Shore a focus for the study of regional problems in the state. While they at times found stubborn Eastern Shoremen and provincial governments more than a match for their well-intended altruism, the leaders of Wye Institute did score some notable successes within a short time. In numerous publications the Wye Institute advertised the region's economic potential and its labor force. It publicized the need for improved hospitals and better access to higher education in the region. The Wye Institute sent Eastern Shore school teachers to Europe during the summer to expand their horizons. In the 1960s when there was little talk on the Eastern Shore of regional economic development, the Wye Institute established the Eastern Shore Community Council to provide a setting for business planning and to serve as a forum for the discussion of the region's problems.[7]

Wye Institute reports were occasionally controversial. In 1964 the Maryland Chesapeake Bay Affairs Commission took sharp exception to a Wye study that argued that the resources of the Bay were being mismanaged. And seafood processors in Somerset Country criticized the institute for attempting to meddle in Eastern Shore politics. Donald Shank, the director of the institute, down-played the affair, however. The report, he said, was merely a "starting point for future study." The institute also encouraged the agricultural research component of the University of Maryland to use Wye acreage for important test plots of corn, soybeans, and other crops. Ultimately the Angus beef herd that had been owned by Arthur Houghton was donated to the University of Maryland to further research in animal husbandry on the Shore.

In the 1960s most people still thought of the Eastern Shore as a depressed backwater and the Wye Institute was one of the few forces for change and uplift in the region. Today many adult men and women on the Shore remember the summer camps they attended at Wye Institute, and scientists reflect upon the fact that the Wye Institute was interested in protecting both the landed heritage of the region and the environment of the Chesapeake Bay when few others were.

At the end of the 1960s Arthur Houghton devoted most of his energy to running his firms, Steuben Glass and the Corning Glass Works, and recruited James G. Nelson, an energetic and talented Crisfield businessman, to direct the affairs of Wye Institute. Within a short time Nelson emerged as a resourceful leader and consultant on Eastern Shore affairs. The secret of the Wye Institute was that it seldom gave large gifts of money to any organization or charity. Rather, the Wye Institute preferred to look for those small activities that would ultimately influence economic and social life on the Eastern Shore and provided these activities with grants of "seed money." Whether it has been publishing books about the Eastern Shore, conducting economic studies, or hosting the world-famous Aspen Institute for university dons and corporate and political leaders at the institute's plush headquarters, the Wye Institute has never wavered from its original mission of assisting the educational, economic, and cultural advancement of the Shore. In 1984, the Wye Institute scaled down its efforts because other state, community, and business organizations are now in place to carry on the work of the institute. According to James Nelson, the Wye Institute exists now only as a small grant-making organization.

While the late Arthur Houghton and the Wye Institute scored some notable accomplishments in aiding the region's economic development, others were not as successful. In 1974 James Rouse, the famous Baltimore developer, obtained a real estate option on Wye Island, an exquisite parcel of 2,800 acres of farmland, and unfolded for Queen Anne's County a plan to build a secluded retreat of fancy homes on the island. Rouse, a native of Talbot County, believed that the development of Wye Island would stimulate the region's commercial life and provide hundreds of jobs for the local labor force. To Rouse's surprise and chagrin, his plan was soundly defeated by an unlikely coalition of farmers, stubborn politicians, and environmentalists who were profoundly suspicious of big-time developers, even if they were born and raised on the Eastern Shore. Rouse never got the zoning approval for the island that he needed and he abandoned the project. The fight over Wye Island, admirably chronicled by Boyd Gibbons, an environmental affairs writer, brought forward the old struggle over who was right—those who sought to preserve their community or those who wanted to improve a community by changing it.[8]

The Wye Country

Today Wye Island is a nature conservancy owned by the state of Maryland. Crossing the old wooden trestle bridge to the island, one encounters an overpowering stillness on a late summer afternoon. Only the occasional cyclist or birdwatcher intrudes upon the quiet landscape. At twilight, the mists of Wye River caress the island and the gentle winds carry the distant lowing of cattle and, sometimes, refrains of chamber music from a poolside quartet at the Wye Institute.

3

From the Sassafras to the Susquehanna

Some of the halcyon days remain as memories.
—William E. Burkhardt

F rom Queen Anne's County northward the countryside on the Shore becomes more rolling, and the landscape is dotted with numerous dairy farms. Names on country byways like Clabber Road and Creamery Lane attest to the importance of the dairy industry on this part of the Eastern Shore. During the week Route 213 is almost a deserted highway. Only occasional grain and milk trucks with their grinding gears disturb the stillness of the countryside.

Kent and Cecil counties are old well-settled communities. Kent's name is rooted in English local history and grew out of the contest between Lord Baltimore and William Claiborne for Kent Island. Kent County is often referred to as the "Mother County of the Eastern Shore" and traces its birth to 1642. Cecil is the namesake of two individuals: Sir Robert Cecil, a staunch ally of the Calvert family in the seventeenth century and Cecil Calvert, the son of the first Lord Baltimore. The landscape of these counties is dotted with colonial structures and federal period homes which remind the visitor that this once was the economic heartland of the Chesapeake Bay country.

Route 213 leads directly to the Sassafras River country and to Cecil County beyond. Named for the tree with its famous medicinal bark, the Sassafras is considered by many to be one of the most beautiful rivers on the Eastern Shore. Unlike the marshy tidal rivers of the southern Eastern Shore, the Sassafras is high banked and well defined. Atop gentle slopes that lead to the water's edge stand some of the proudest old estates and plantations in Maryland. The Sassafras offers safe and delightful anchorage to hundreds of Chesapeake yachts in summer; and the torrents of fresh water that pour into the Sassafras make its river mouth one of the few swimming areas in the Bay that are relatively safe from sea nettles in summer.

Captain John Smith sailed up the Sassafras in 1608 and named it Tockwogh after the Algonquin Indians who lived here. Because of the difficulties of commuting to metropolitan areas, the Sassafras Country retains an unspoiled beauty. Along the river the country looks much like it was in Captain Smith's day, though Smith's jerry-rigged sailing barge today would have to navigate its way precariously through the highly congested traffic of summer pleasure boats on the Sassafras.

The region abounds in historical markers and famous old houses that attest to its heritage. Just outside of Kennedyville, a historical marker indicates the birthplace of General John Cadwalader who was a close friend of General George Washington and a revolutionary war patriot. When he learned of the "Conway Cabal" to depose Washington from his office, Cadwalader challenged General Thomas Conway to a duel and wounded him in the mouth. Cadwalader subsequently boasted that "I have stopped that damned rascal's lying tongue at any rate."

Continue on Route 213 and you will come to the Kitty Knight House. Now a famous inn that straddles a bluff overlooking the Sassafras River, the Kitty Knight House is named for an intrepid woman who stood up to Admiral Cockburn's invading English armada in May 1813. According to local history, Kitty Knight extinguished fires in two houses with her broom as fast as the British soldiers lit them until a sympathetic officer ordered that these two houses be spared.

Unlike other regions of the Chesapeake, the Sassafras country did not get swept up in the Methodist revivals of the late eighteenth and early nineteenth century. Although George Whitfield preached in the region in 1740 and the Jesuits proselytized here, neither evangelical enthusiasm nor religious radicalism took hold here as it did in Somerset and other counties of the south Chesapeake. (The only spate of religious intolerance was the Labadist commune which was short-lived.) In the colonial period and after, the only religion in the Sassafras country was farming and trade. Also, inasmuch as the region enjoyed flourishing maritime and overland commerce it was constantly being exposed to new ideas and values from urban regions like Philadelphia, New York, Baltimore, and Wilmington. Others have argued that the land was simply too pleasant and the living too easy to give much thought to the salvation of one's soul and life in the next kingdom.

Within easy proximity by boat were the mighty Susquehanna and the Bohemia River, a waterland rich in wildlife and fertile fields. In their journal of a trip to Maryland in 1679-1680, Jasper Danckaerts and Peter Sluyter, two Dutch immigrants, wrote of ducks and geese: "The water was so black with them that it seemed when you looked from the land below upon the water as it were a mass of filth or turf, and when they flew up there was a rushing and vibration of the air like a great storm coming through the trees, even like the rumbling of distant thunder." Danckaerts and Sluyter reported that it was easy to get six ducks with one shot by firing into the mass.[1]

It is here in this land of rolling hills and stunning river vistas that the coastal plain of the Eastern Shore meets the Piedmont. Although part of the Eastern Shore, Cecil County is different, more connected to urban regions, more dominated by the state of Delaware than other parts of Maryland's Eastern Shore. The life-style is more working class than agrarian or maritime and indeed there are parts of Cecil County that are more reminiscent of West Virginia than the Delmarva Peninsula.

When the famous American writer, Bayard Taylor, visited Cecil County in 1871, he found a land that was "rich and cheerful" and saw vast orchards as lovely as those he had seen on the island of Majorca in the Mediterranean. Taylor was one of the first writers visiting the Eastern Shore after the Civil War to observe that the death of slavery in the region was a good thing. The region's market garden economy had great potential, despite the fact that rail service in the area was dismal. Only one cloud troubled Taylor's sunny estimate of the region. Everywhere he went in Cecil County and beyond he saw "the old imposing mansions of former feudal lords." Deploring what he called the power of "transmitted ideas," Taylor feared that the region's past would so haunt the countryside as to make it incapable of coping with social and economic change. Said Taylor: "I heartily sympathize with an affectionate regard for the past, both of families and communities; but nothing can be more fatal than to set the standard of life behind instead of before us."[2] Taylor may have been right, for the land between the Sassafras and the Susquehanna remains haunted by the past. It was in this region, for example, that feudalism came closest to taking root on Maryland's Eastern Shore.

In an age when men were carving empires for themselves out of the rich forests of the Eastern Shore, none was more illustrious than George Talbot. In 1680 this frontier explorer and Indian fighter obtained patent to Susquehanna Manor, a 32,000-acre estate that enabled him to hold court like the nobility of England, a right never extended to others in Maryland. A feisty Irishman from Castle Rooney in Roscommon County, Ireland, Talbot was a cousin of Cecil Calvert and received this vast domain in consideration of his having brought to the Eastern Shore at his own expense 580 English and Irish immigrants. His domain extended from the Northeast River westward and ten miles up the Susquehanna.

Talbot was not intimidated by the fierce Susquehanna Indians and maintained a small private army of rangers. When danger threatened, Talbot had fires lit on hillsides at night to summon his men. In daytime, the firing of three musket shots in rapid succession warned of the approach of the Indians. On his manor Colonel Talbot made his own law. In 1684 when his family was out of favor in England, Talbot ran afoul of a British tax collector named Christopher Rousby. When Rousby and other officials attempted to assert the authority of Oliver Cromwell and diminish the claims of the Calvert family, Talbot became incensed. During a shipboard argument, Talbot took out a knife and stabbed Rousby to death.

Talbot was quickly arrested and taken by ship back to Virginia. When all attempts by the Maryland government to rescue him failed, Talbot's wife, a feisty person in her own right, and a few friends went to Virginia and rescued him. Although Talbot was ultimately pardoned for his crime because of his connections with the lord proprietor of Maryland, he had to remain in hiding for a long time. A popular local legend has it that while Talbot hid in a cave above the Susquehanna River, he was fed by two falcons who shared the cave with him. Each day the falcons swept over the Bay and river in search of waterfowl which they shared with Talbot and prevented him from starving.[3]

In the late seventeenth century, Augustine Herrman, a native of Prague and former resident of New Amsterdam, came to the Eastern Shore and carved out a medieval barony of over 20,000 acres that encompassed some thirty-one and a half square miles. How he traveled to the Eastern Shore and acquired this land is part of the dynastic story of the Lords Baltimore and their struggle to hold on to their land and resist the encroachments of Virginia and Pennsylvania. It is also the story of a famous map and the fortunes of Maryland.

When Augustine Herrman published his map of Maryland in 1674, he included a carefully executed miniature portrait of himself on the margin of the work. The miniature shows a man with long flowing locks, prosperous chin, directed nose, and imperious wide-set eyes. It is a portrait of a shrewd opportunist. Born in 1608, Augustine Herrman emigrated to the New World as a young man, serving as an agent of Dutch commercial interests in New Amsterdam and Philadelphia. In the seventeenth century, Dutch military and commercial interests in the Chesapeake held considerable sway and England feared for the security of her fledgling Atlantic colonies. The Dutch were well known as pirates and the Chesapeake tobacco fleet, which annually sailed out of Virginia, was frequently plundered by these marauders. The Dutch had established settlements at Lewes and other points along the Delaware coast and were economically and militarily strong enough to contemplate snatching portions of Pennsylvania and Maryland for their own commercial interests. Thus Augustine Herrman would be forced to thread his way through the uncertainties of the Dutch-English rivalry.

As a resident of Manhattan in New Amsterdam, Herrman became a member of the colony's important inner council called "The Nine Men." Herrman was associated with Laurents Cornelissen as an agent in New Amsterdam for Peter Gabry and Sons, the prominent merchant traders of Amsterdam. Owing to business problems with the parent Dutch firm, Herrman struck out on his own and soon became involved in the salt and lumber trade between New Amsterdam and Curacao, the Dutch colony in the Caribbean.

Such was his knowledge of Dutch shipping that he derived an income sufficient to build a substantial house on Pearl Street with a large orchard. Peter Stuyvesant, the governor of New Amsterdam, disliked Augustine Herrman's outspoken ways, however, and on one occasion had him jailed for insubordination. Yet when Dutch interests were threatened in the

New World, Stuyvesant sent Herrman down into the Chesapeake to serve as the Dutch ambassador to the Maryland colony.

On more than one occasion the Dutch and Marylanders had met in skirmishes in the region of the Susquehanna. The Susquehanna Indians had firearms supplied by Swedish and Dutch traders who had a vested interest in keeping the frontier in turmoil and the fortunes of Maryland in jeopardy. Finally a small army of grizzled Indian fighters led by Colonel Nathaniel Utie overwhelmed the Dutch force and ordered it out of the region. Utie, a soldier experienced in fighting off the fierce raids of the Susquehanna Indians on settlements in the upper Chesapeake, had taken over an island in the Susquehanna and heavily fortified it.

When Herrman arrived on the Delmarva Peninsula in 1659, he quickly sized up the situation. The Dutch, he realized, would never force the English out of the Susquehanna. And in an age of loose allegiances and constant change, Herrman decided to join the English and cast his fortunes with the Maryland colony. By then middle-aged, he was sensible enough to recognize that his fortunes might fare better under English rule rather than Dutch. Herrman knew enough Latin to detect a serious flaw in the land grant of Lord Baltimore that would jeopardize the future of the Calvert land holdings. In their land grant, the Calverts enjoyed the right of *hactentus inculta*, which meant that they had the right to own all the land "hitherto unoccupied by civilized man." Thus, any other European settlement in Maryland would seriously diminish their land grant.

On January 4, 1660, Herrman and his family received a decree of denization, a right to live in Maryland. Lord Baltimore needed a reliable map of his province and Herrman dreamed of becoming a feudal overlord in the New World. The Bohemian was a skilled surveyor in addition to his other talents as a businessman, and Herrman agreed to make a map that would make *hactentus inculta* a descriptive term and not a restrictive injunction. In return for his map and his labor, Lord Baltimore promised to award him a land grant of 20,000 acres. Today the Bohemia River (named after Herrman's native land) flows serenely through the land upon which Herrman built Bohemia Manor. It was here on the upper Chesapeake that Herrman relocated his wife and five children.

The mapping of Maryland took nearly ten years and in 1670 Herrman dispatched it to William Faithorne, a London engraver. When Herrman saw the work he was not pleased. The map, Herrman complained bitterly, was "slobbered over by the engraver Faithorne, defiling the print with many errors."[4] After corrections were made, Augustine Herrman forwarded the map to Lord Baltimore in London. Officially published in 1674, the map carried the official escutcheons of the Calvert family as well as the previously mentioned miniature of Augustine Herrman. Herrman himself spent 220 pounds sterling on the project, a considerable sum for those days. Apart from its geographic significance, the map had true artistic merit, and Faithorne, the unknown English engraver, more than atoned in his final draft for his earlier "slobberings."

Herrman's map only intensified Lord Baltimore's troubles with the proprietors of Pennsylvania, though. The new map established Maryland's claim to its northern boundary at the 40th degree, thus giving Lord Baltimore a strong claim to most of the navigable part of the Delaware River. Shortly thereafter William Penn asserted his claim to the Sassafras country and told the startled Herrman that he should cease paying his taxes to Lord Baltimore as he was living in Pennsylvania. A long, drawn-out controversy ensued which was not settled amicably between the two colonies until 1767 when the famous Mason and Dixon line running between 39 degrees, 43 minutes and 26.3 seconds and 39 degrees, 43 minutes and 17.6 seconds was established. Thus most of Herrman's survey was maintained, and Maryland only lost a small fraction of the land originally surveyed by the Bohemian geographer.[5]

True to his word, Lord Baltimore made Herrman a generous gift of thirty-one and a half square miles of land for which the new lord of Bohemia Manor was required to send annually to Lord Baltimore three arrowheads in token of fealty. The new Lord of Bohemia Manor carved a tobacco plantation out of the wilderness and experimented with the production of indigo, a valuable commercial dye. In order to have access to the Delaware River and the port of New Castle, Delaware, Herrman had a twenty-two-mile ox-cart road carved through the forests of the Delmarva Peninsula. Lord Baltimore wanted to reward Herrman in a manner befitting his talent and ambition and conferred upon him the special title "Lord," one of the few instances of a special title of nobility being conferred on a

British subject in the New World. At the height of his prosperity, Herrman owned about 25,000 acres of some of the best land in North America and was without doubt one of the largest landholders in seventeeth-century America. His estate, Bohemia Manor, included the land between the headwaters of Chesapeake Bay and between the Elk and Bohemia Rivers eastward to the current Delaware line.

As the upper peninsula of the Eastern Shore is in reality an isthmus between the Chesapeake and Atlantic, Augustine Herrman drew up plans for the construction of a canal that would connect the two great bodies of water and develop waterborne commerce in the region. He died, however, before his dream could be implemented. Today the Chesapeake and Delaware Canal traverses the route that Herrman envisioned, and oceangoing vessels navigating from Philadelphia to Baltimore do not have to undergo the expense and delay of sailing down the coast to the mouth of the Chesapeake and then up the Bay.

Herrman quickly became known throughout Maryland as an excellent farmer and the generous lord of Bohemia Manor. He constructed a large manor house reminiscent of the great estates of his native Bohemia and had a private deer park established for his private hunts. During the halcyon days of Bohemia Manor, friends and visitors reported that at the Herrman estate "it snowed of meat and drink." Later in life Herrman drew considerable income from tolls charged for using his highway across the peninsula.

Unfortunately Bohemia Manor fell upon evil days shortly after the arrival in 1677 of Dutch Labadist mystics who chose Bohemia Manor as a site for their little theocracy. The Labadists were disciples of the teaching of Jean de Labadie, a French Jesuit turned radical Protestant. The Labadists were communal farmers and industrialists and sought to found communities based upon principles of joint effort and shareholding much in the manner of today's rural communes. Initially the Labadists founded a successful sanctuary in Holland and attracted rich women of high social rank like Princess Elizabeth, the granddaughter of King James I of England.

The Labadists were ascetics with radical notions about marriage. They considered marriage a "Popish superstition" and declared that "hell was full of ordinary marriages." They wore only dark garments and admitted no class distinctions in their commune. They also preached that mankind should revert to a primitive basis of civilization. Whether the Labadists believed in plural marriage is difficult to ascertain. What is certain, however, is that their righteousness and asceticism offended Dutch authorities in Holland and the normally tolerant Dutch encouraged the sect to search for land in the New World. After rejecting Surinam as a possible site for a Labadist colony, the communal leaders led by Peter Sluyter and Jasper Danckaerts sailed for Maryland. The two Labadists arrived on the Eastern Shore in October 1679. When the Labadists came to Cecil County seeking new land for a small industrial and farming community, they were welcomed by Augustine Herrman and the tolerant Protestant agreed to sell the Labadists a tract of land.

Sluyter was a powerful preacher and quickly made a profound impression on Herrman's son, Ephraim, and his wife. Fearing that the Labadists might get too influential a hold on his children, Herrman refused to sell the land he had promised. When Sluyter and the 100 colonists returned to the region in 1684, they sued Herrman for the land that he had promised to sell them and they won a tract of 3,700 acres.

Although the teachings of the Labadists forbade slavery, tobacco, and indentured servitude, Peter Sluyter soon had the community growing tobacco for export. And within a short time the Labadists began to use slave labor in their tobacco fields. In the meantime, the commune of a hundred men, women, and children functioned as a kind of moral dictatorship. No dissent was tolerated in the community and most of the efforts of the communalists were controlled by Peter Sluyter and his wife.

Peter Sluyter died a rich man in 1722 at the age of seventy-seven; and shortly thereafter the community disbanded. Today only a few historical markers near the old Bohemia Manor survive to chronicle this brief interlude of radical Protestantism in the upper Chesapeake.[6]

*   *   *

Cecil County in the colonial period was a freewheeling community of farmers, land speculators, and river traders. Using tiny sailing craft, merchants from Annapolis, Baltimore, and other western shore communities crossed the Bay and traveled upstream on the Bohemia and Sassafras to sell bolts of cloth, salt, and the hardware necessary for daily farming. Cecil County benefited from the fact that Philadelphia Quakers refused to spend money on roads developing the interior of Pennsylvania. Thus, as a result, an enormous amount of commerce came down the Susquehanna River and the mountain roads southward into Cecil.

The Elk River divides Cecil County into two complementary regions. The connecting link in colonial times was the Elk River ferry between Oldfields and Courthouse Point. In a time when a trip from Onancock, Virginia, to Philadelphia took five days on horseback, Cecil was an important way station and hostelry. The residents of Cecil were known to be highly disputatious and the county court was so unruly that the local government had to issue a specific set of rules regarding smoking, vulgarity, and noisy behavior. The worst offenders were the lawyers. According to historian George Johnston, Cecil's lawyers of that period "were probably as ignorant of the law and as unskillful in the practice of it as the courts were in the dispensation of justice."[7]

Until well after the American Revolution, Cecil was dominated by an elite of well-connected families who made their money in farming, lumber milling, and shipping. At the pinnacle of Cecil society were families bearing the name Hall, Gilpin, Mitchell, Ramsay, and Mauldin. These families owned most of the good farmland and tightly controlled the social and economic life of Elkton and the surrounding countryside.

Charlestown, which was founded in 1742 on the Northeast River, was the seat of Cecil County until the courthouse was moved to Elkton in 1786. Until its river became unnavigable for Chesapeake Bay commerce, Charlestown rivaled Baltimore as a port and shipbuilding center. There was a racetrack at Charlestown and cockfighting and gambling were a regular part of life in this rough-hewn county seat. During the American Revolution Charlestown was a major supply depot of grain and salt for Washington's Continental Army. In 1777 General Howe sailed up the Chesapeake and a British force ascended the Elk River. The British intended to use Elkton as a base for the invasion of Pennsylvania and the capture of Philadelphia. At that time the town of Elkton was called Head of Elk after the nearby river, and both Elkton and Charlestown experienced the depredations of the British. The region lay astride the major transportation routes of the mid-

Atlantic and it is not suprising that General Washington worried constantly about the fate of his storehouses in Cecil during the war.[8] During the conflict, Cecil's farmers lost wagons, cattle, grain, and horses to the British and received only paper currency of dubious worth from the hapless revolutionary government. Also, Elkton was an important medical center for Washington's army, and the Mitchell House on East Main Street, which still stands, was used as a hospital for the wounded. In 1781 General Lafayette passed through Head of Elk with a military force en route to Annapolis to put an end to the raids by British troops in the lower Chesapeake led by General Benedict Arnold. Washington and his army also passed through Head of Elk on the way to the seige of Yorktown. As the town was such an important crossroads, it was often filled with rowdy soldiers from Washington's patriot army. Grogshop fights were common, and in one brawl a Negro patriot soldier named Forteen Stodder shot a sailor and killed him. Stodder was indicted for murder and convicted of manslaughter. For his punishment he was branded on the left thumb with a hot iron. The records do not indicate whether this was a harsh punishment or a lenient one for a revolutionary soldier in Cecil County. The record does show, however, that the region was quite patriotic. Cecil sent three battalions of seventy-five men each to Washington's Army, and Tories in the county kept their mouths shut and their persons out of harm's way.

After the American Revolution Cecil's economy stagnated. The inflation of American currency after the Revolution coupled with the loss of British agricultural markets fostered hard times in the region. During the War of 1812 and afterwards the local economy declined; and by 1830 Cecil's most important crop was the people emigrating from the county to Baltimore and the West.

It was the rivers that first brought the English settlers to Cecil County during the colonial period, and in the 1820s and 1830s the Susquehanna and Northeast Rivers attracted large crowds of visitors each year for the first spring run of herring. In those days the region processed thousands of barrels of salted and pickled fish and German families from Lancaster County, Pennsylvania, traveled through the backwoods on treacherous country roads in Conestoga wagons to fish in the river. The annual herring run was a time for socializing and drinking strong spirits and Cecil was most obliging in its hospitality. Fish were caught in such large quantities in the region that they were used for manuring farms in Cecil County. On the Northeast River, for example, farmers caught 2,700 barrels of herring during a twenty-six-day period in 1819 at one place on the river and with only one haul of the seine each day.

On the north bank of the Susquehanna the town of Port Deposit became an important milling and lumbering center. In 1833 a wildcatting Pennsylvania entrepreneur named Jacob Tome came down the Susquehanna on a huge lumber raft and proved that it was possible to move large amounts of timber down the shallow and dangerous river. In 1840 alone, Tome's lumber operations sent 250 million board feet of timber down the Susquehanna and the town of Port Deposit prospered mightily. Jacob Tome settled in Port Deposit and established a milling and lumbering operation that quickly made him a millionaire. In the land of the fast buck, Cecil County had in Jacob Tome a hero of its own. Tome's lumber ships regularly plied the waters between Port Deposit and Baltimore, and the flamboyant lumber king became a leader in the Republican Party and close friend of President Ulysses S. Grant after the Civil War.[9]

When the railroads became an important transportation force in Maryland, Port Deposit languished. The construction of the Conowingo Dam across the Susquehanna in the 1920s cut the port off from the river commerce of Pennsylvania and nearly destroyed the town's fragile economy. High on the hillside overlooking the Susquehanna stand exquisite stone Victorian houses that testify to the town's former greatness. For years Port Deposit was known as a town that was slowly dying on its feet, but it is now feeling the first stirring of gentrification and state-sponsored economic development.

Elkton is the home of one of the most venerable news-papers in America, *The Cecil Whig*. The paper has been an important force in Cecil County life since 1841 and has itself been the focus of great controversy in the region. Residents continue to recount the story of the famous showdown at the Elkton post office in 1843 when Palmer Ricketts, the editor of the *Whig*, killed Amor Forwood, editor of the *Cecil Democrat*. Ricketts got away with the crime even though the whole town saw him do it.

The argument originated in a political quarrel between the two men over the desirability of paying off the state debt.

The financially conservative *Whig* argued against state debt and inflation and criticized the Democratic Party as a party whose deeds were "evil." It also stated that Forwood showed a great deal of greenness in editorial capacity. The crowning blow came on August 26 when Ricketts wrote on the editorial page of the *Whig* that his opponent's paper was full of "philological errors," and that the editorial content of the *Cecil Democrat* was "insipid and puerile." Forwood exploded in anger and vowed to cowhide Ricketts and cut off his ears with a pair of scissors. He also made threatening assertions that both men could not live in the same world together. Ricketts armed himself with a revolver and prepared for a confrontation. When they encountered each other on August 29 at noon at the post office a fist fight ensued. During the struggle, Palmer Ricketts took out his revolver and shot his editorial opponent. This was the only time a man has died on the Eastern Shore over issues of philology and English grammar. Ricketts claimed self-defense and subsequently lamented in the pages of the *Whig* that "No man, God knows, can regret the occurrence more than we do, yet no man we venture to assert would have done otherwise than we did." Tempers flared easily in Cecil in those days, and Ricketts was as anxious to protect the good name of *The Cecil Whig* as he was his own personal reputation. In the highly emotional jury trial that followed, Ricketts was acquitted. He resumed his editorship of the *Whig* and lived an illustrious life as a respected Eastern Shore newspaperman until his death in 1860.[10]

*   *   *

In its heyday in the late nineteenth century, Cecil County was the hunting capital of the Eastern Shore, and the region attracted celebrity hunters like Theodore Roosevelt and President Benjamin Harrison. The Susquehanna Flats, a vast area of Chesapeake shallows created by the river deposits, was the breeding and roosting area of millions of ducks and geese, and individual hunters and market gunners shot thousands of birds annually for fun and profit. Also, the Susquehanna Flats encouraged a very profitable decoy industry, and duck hunters branded their decoys to prevent theft just as cattlemen branded their steers. The popularity of waterfowl hunting on the Susquehanna Flats indirectly contributed to the prosperity of Abercrombie and Fitch, an extraordinary outfitting firm in New York City. Duck and goose hunters demanded sturdy clothes that would both last and protect them from the elements; and Abercrombie and Fitch boasted that its hunting clothes could easily be worn for twenty years.

While Cecil never attracted large numbers of vacationers and wealthy businessmen looking for second summer homes, it did attract a sizeable number of visitors each year because of the Chesapeake and Delaware Canal. First envisioned by Augustine Herrman in the seventeenth century, the canal that connected the Chesapeake with the Atlantic Ocean formally opened for business in 1829 after two decades of construction. The 13.6-mile-long canal cost $2,250,000. As the Chesapeake was seven feet higher in elevation than the waters of the Delaware River and the Atlantic, the canal had three elaborate locks. The noted Baltimore business publicist, Hezekiah Niles, called the canal "a stupendous public work." One of the major locks was located at Chesapeake City. Starting as nothing more than a lock house and a tavern, the town grew quickly and flourished as a canal port.

From its inception the Chesapeake and Delaware Canal was a tourist attraction. Canal passenger barges were well appointed and comfortable. Historian Ralph Gray comments on the barges: "Pulled by five or six horses hooked in tandem and moving at a rapid trot, they could traverse the canal in approximately two hours, thereby completing the all-water communication between Philadelphia and Baltimore. The time required for the three-stage journey (overland) was eight to ten hours." Chesapeake tourists of that era were good customers, and the passenger barges earned the canal $20 for a one-way trip. Today you can still see the old steam engine and giant waterwheel that pumped water into the lock at the local Canal Museum at Chesapeake City.

Within a short time canal authorities could boast that nearly 170 vessels a month passed through the canal creating toll revenues of $2,289 for January 1830. Unfortunately, the canal became an economic prize that investors and politicians fought over and it never lived up to its promise as a major transportation artery on the Atlantic coast. Also, after the Civil War the big money-maker for the canal was coal tonnage, and regional railroads like the Baltimore and Ohio offered competitive rates that cut heavily into canal revenues. By the 1880s

the Chesapeake and Delaware Canal was a struggling operation that was plagued by "dissensions and defalcations."

The canal was purchased by the federal government and
enlarged in 1919. Unfortunately, on the Delaware end of the
canal, the Army Corps of Engineers dredged a new route that
bypassed the canal port of Delaware City and the town's
prosperity evaporated.

Yet the canal maintained its romantic image. Until 1919
on the Chesapeake and Delaware Canal, narrow steamers
on the Baltimore and Philadelphia route traversed the waterway and were quite popular with excursionists. A voyage on
the Chesapeake and Delaware Canal, wrote Edward Vallandigham, "seemed like an adventure in toyland." On the upper
deck of the tiny canal steamer there was just room enough
for an officer and six passengers. The stateroom and galley
were equally cramped, but the canal journey was exciting,
especially the journey from the Delaware River to the final
lock at Chesapeake City. Although conditions on board were
far from luxurious, the hospitality of the crew was legendary.
As was the case with most Chesapeake steamers, travelers
remembered the insinuating courtesy of Negro waiters who
would whisper in their ears at breakfast: "De's ham, an' lam,
an' chicken, an' fried oyste's, and clam fritte's, an' sof crabs;
and Ah rekon ya'll have yo' aigs sof bil't, and surrup with
yo' griddle cakes?"[11]

The Chesapeake and Delaware Canal today remains an
important highway of commerce for large vessels and Chesapeake City has become a flourishing tourist center. Four
hundred and fifty feet wide and thirty-seven feet deep, the
canal cuts off 340 miles for ships traveling between Baltimore
and Philadelphia. Its importance to the mid-Atlantic economy
was demonstrated during World War II when it provided an
alternative route to the upper Chesapeake for ships that
normally would have been the prey of Nazi submarines prowl-
ing the Atlantic.

Complementing the Chesapeake and Delaware Canal's
history is the Bainbridge Naval Training Center. Unlike the
canal the Bainbridge Center is defunct, but during World War
II this 1,200-acre facility trained nearly a half-million sailors.
Closed in 1948, it was reactivated in 1952 to train men for the
Korean War. It was an important source of prosperity for Cecil
County. When it finally closed in July 1976 after serving briefly

Chesapeake City on the Chesapeake and Delaware canal. Photograph by Pat Vojtech.

Chesapeake telescope house circa 1800. Photograph by the author.

as a nuclear power school for sailors, its passing was much lamented in the community.

* * *

In keeping with its flamboyant past, Cecil County is best known for its matrimonial industry. During the 1930s the town of Elkton was the marriage capital of the mid-Atlantic. Some people called it "Reno in reverse." Until well into the 1960s, couples traveled from all over the mid-Atlantic region to get married at the Cecil County Courthouse, and E. Day Moore, the deputy clerk of the court, married as many as a thousand couples a month. Visitors to Elkton often quipped that Moore had "the happiest job in Maryland." Elkton's fame as a marriage center is easily explained. Couples had to wait only forty-eight hours after filing their license to get married and the county required no blood test. In both Delaware and Pennsylvania the marriage laws were far stricter. Before the 1930s the county didn't even require a waiting period; many couples from Philadelphia and Wilmington chartered a taxi for the day to go to Cecil County to get married, and hotels and restaurants advertised "newlywed specials."

* * *

Today Cecil County is being brought into the suburban orbits of Baltimore and Wilmington. While the downtown core of Elkton slowly languishes, low-income real estate developments and recreational communities are spreading rapidly. Many people in the county fear that this spread of the metropolitan life-style into their community will bring in its wake a higher crime rate, drugs, and social disorganization. Despite its proximity to Bay recreation areas and urban centers, Cecil County remains a blue-collar minimum-wage economy. In part Cecil's lack of economic growth can be explained by its traditional Eastern Shore reluctance to accept outside assistance from state and private agencies for fear of losing its independence. "People of the Eastern Shore . . . don't live all that badly," argues Senator Walter Baker of Cecil County. "What we should have an opportunity to do is to govern ourselves." The problem of poverty in Cecil County is "a very real problem," says Jerilyn Ayers, a local citizen activist. There has been an escalation of welfare rolls and an escalation of the working poor, Ayers notes. At a community roundtable hosted by *The Cecil Whig* in the spring of 1986, community leaders and educators called the county's negative image its biggest problem. Some county residents believe that banks, out of snobbery or fear of a poor return on their investment, discourage middle-class professionals from buying homes in Cecil County. For example, Richard Davis, the former manager of Morton Thiokol, a chemical firm, reports that he was encouraged by his bank to buy a house in New Castle, Delaware, rather than settle in Cecil County.[12]

Despite Cecil's problems most residents argue that this is probably one of the most pleasant regions in which to live. The fishing and hunting are good, and the taverns and stores of the village of North East hum with activity and good-natured banter on the weekends. Men still wear T-shirts and Levis for practically every social activity save churchgoing, and the local restaurants serve good food at reasonable prices. Tourism has made only a minimal impact on the areas's social economy.

Thus, in retrospect, it seems that Cecil County has not strayed very far from its historic origins. It remains a working-class community with a small elite at the apex of power. Over three centuries Cecil has experienced enormous change. The heavily trafficked Route 40 now covers the route that Nathaniel Utie, the old Indian fighter, explored in 1652. Farms and plantations have given way to trailer parks and jerry-built shopping centers. With the spread of suburbia into Cecil, social tensions are inevitable. Commuters want peace and quiet and protest against the noise of harvesting and the smells of agricultural life. Meanwhile farmers are demanding the passage of laws to protect them from being declared a "public nuisance" by the Volvo set. And as local writer William E. Burkhardt has observed of Cecil, "Some of the halcyon days remain as memories."

4

From Kent To Caroline

*The people now call it Delmarva. Still to me it's just my home
sweet home.*
—Dale Wimbrow, "The Good Old Eastern Shore"

K ent County is one of the most beautiful and historically
intriguing regions of Maryland's Eastern Shore. It is a
peninsula bounded by water—the Chester River to the south,
the Sassafras to the north, and the Chesapeake Bay to the
west. Its historic roots stretch deep into the seventeenth
century when Lord Baltimore and William Claiborne fought
over Kent Island and the land was a rough frontier environment. [Ironically, Kent Island is now part of Queen Anne's
County, a matter which confuses visitors.] Kent County is the
home of Washington College, one of the oldest schools of higher
education in the nation, and Chestertown, a delightful small
town that still exudes colonial charm. Kent is also one of the
smallest counties on the Eastern Shore and one of the wealthiest in terms of its agriculture.

For nearly two centuries tobacco and corn were the
principal crops of Kent, and the general trend of settlement
was up the Chester River. Slavery came to dominate the local
economy at an early date and Kent never had much of a small
farmer class during the antebellum period. Although a settlement existed on the Chester River earlier, Chestertown was
not laid out as the county seat until 1706. The town grew over
time as it was a port of entry for Cecil, Kent, and Queen Anne's
counties. When the world market for tobacco turned sour after

1715, the farmers and merchants of Kent focused on grain and livestock, and Chestertown became a flourishing port with a trade that was almost exclusively with the sugar islands of the Caribbean. By 1750 Chestertown was one of the leading ports in the Maryland colony, second only to Annapolis. Chestertown also had the distinction of being a ship auction center, and many vessels like *Pocomoke Industry* fell under the auctioneer's gavel in 1732. Maritime creditors also sold parts of salvaged ships and the trade in spars and rigging was brisk. So busy was the port that the town had three large warehouses on the river wharf and employed two full-time customs inspectors. Chestertown was part of the Patuxent River Customs District for several years before becoming a separate district in 1742.

Among the prominent merchant families of Hanson, Smyth, and Hand, none was more illustrious than that of Thomas Ringgold. Born in 1721, Thomas Ringgold earned enough money in shipping to be classed as one of the wealthiest men in the colonial period. His mansion in Chestertown bore elaborate wainscoting and all the other trappings of an aristocratic manor house in England. The Ringgold house was nicknamed "the Abbey" to give it an old English flair, and, with its parties and sumptuous feasts, it was known as one of the gayest homes on the Eastern Shore. Today this proud mansion with its secluded walled gardens is the home of the president of Washington College. Also during this time Chestertown developed a wealthy society that far exceeded what one might expect from the neighboring countryside.[1]

Kent's history as the "home of the Cavaliers" can be traced back to 1658 when Lord Baltimore gave a gift of land to Colonel Henry Coursey for his role in negotiating peace with the Indians. Lord Baltimore granted Colonel Coursey as much land on the south side of the Chester River as he could cover on a map with his thumb. Thus in this unique fashion did the Coursey family lay claim to most of the land that currently surrounds the village of Queenstown in Queen Anne's County. In any event Colonel Coursey's peace treaty with the warlike Iroquois nation kept the region tranquil.[2] The Coursey's set Kent County's aristocratic tone and the Chester River merchants made it a local way of life.

In the colonial period Chestertown (which in its early stage was referred to as Chester Town) was known as a fashion center and its reputation for frivolity, gaiety, and extravagance spread far and wide. Ladies imported hair dressers from Philadelphia and paraded around Chestertown in expensive coaches and sedan chairs. The male dandies of Chestertown society were often wealthy, though dissolute, sons of local merchants who strutted about the courthouse and the taverns like roosters in embroidered waistcoats. Wine, rum, and other liquor was cheap and the taverns were lively and crowded. Given the amount of molasses beer, brandy, sherry, port, claret, Madeira, and cider that was consumed in the ordinaries and taverns of colonial Chestertown, it is surprising that any work at all was accomplished in this tidewater port.

Merchants, flush with the wealth from the Caribbean trade, constructed substantial homes along the Chester River. Many of these homes still remain and give the town a Georgian ambience. Mansions, like Widehall, which was owned by Colonel Thomas Smyth, the well-known shipbuilder, stand in gardens of boxwood and shrubs on lawns that stretch to the banks of the Chester. Dancing, theater, horse racing, fox hunting—all the trappings of colonial society—developed here as they did in Annapolis. Chestertown's merchants aped the English aristocracy and helped to turn their county seat into one of the most fashionable places on the Eastern Shore. In a rough and unschooled region like the Eastern Shore, Chestertown boasted the civility of a full-time book merchant. Although booksellers on Maryland's colonial Eastern Shore were hard pressed to earn a living, they seem to have done quite well in Chestertown. Ironically, despite Chestertown's wealth, artists and school teachers had difficulty making a living in the town. The father of the great portrait painter of the American Revolution, Charles Willson Peale, had trouble earning a living as headmaster of the Kent Free School. Charles Willson Peale and his son, Rembrandt Peale, spent little time at Kent, preferring the more lucrative portrait market of Baltimore's affluent mercantile society.

Each spring modern Chestertown decks itself out in colonial finery to reenact its own revolutionary tea party of 1774. Although Chestertown's tea party is less famous than the one that occurred at Boston, it was more daring, for the men showed themselves without disguise. In broad daylight the outraged patriotic citizens of Chestertown forced their way aboard the ship *Geddes*, off the foot of High Street, to dump tax-burdened tea into the Chester River. Every May the taverns and hostelries of Chestertown are filled to the brim as the sounds of fife and drum lead citizens down to the river edge to witness the great blow struck for economic and personal liberty in old Kent on the eve of the American Revolution. The town also remembers that it once sent food supplies to Boston when the British closed the New England port to punish it for its tea party.

Chestertown society probably reached its zenith during the American Revolution and directly after when Tench Tilghman, General Washington's aide de camp, made his famous ride from Yorktown to Philadelphia announcing the surrender of Cornwallis. Tilghman landed at Rock Hall and passed through Chestertown on horseback, becoming something of a local hero as the news bearer of American victory. Although the Tilghmans were part of the gentry of Queen Anne's and Talbot counties, they could often be found on social occasions among Chestertown's well-dressed glitterati. The letters of Tilghman's sisters, Henrietta and Mary, offer ample insight into the life of upper-class families in Chestertown at this time.

Then, as now, wealthy families stalked the sons of affluent merchants, and marriages with wealthy "macaroni" like Edward De Courcey were celebrated with the same triumph as that which accompanied Washington's victory. The Tilghman sisters described the "superb" wedding of Betsy Worrell to Captain John Hyland sometime in 1785:

> "A number of elegant Cloaths, 6 Brides Men and Maids . . . Between fifty and sixty people were present at the Ceremony, who danced till 4 o'clock (A.M.). Some of the Company retired at twelve being afraid (I suppose) of injuring their healths by keeping such riotous hours. They kept up the Ball till Monday (the wedding was on the previous Thursday), then went to middle Neck, accompanied by 6 Carriages well filled. The Bride and Brides groom led the Van in a new Phaeton . . . ."[3]

The balls of Chestertown were gay affairs and the women drank as much claret as the men. The Tilghmans reported that during the Christmas celebration of 1786 some of the "Bucks of true spirit" drank too much and broke windows. Though the play that the Tilghman sisters saw was boring, the dress and costumes of both the cast and the audience were elegant; and it was such a high fashion affair that "the Ball gave such a spring to the Spirit of our Beaux that they have made up a Subscription for Assemblies, and the first is to be tomorrow night." High fashion, drama, and flirtation with the opposite sex, fueled with copious amounts of claret, spelled an exciting Christmas social season.[4]

One of the greatest annoyances to Eastern Shoremen during this era was the interruption of the winter social season by the British during the War of 1812. Eastern Shoremen who accepted invitations from friends and kinsmen in Baltimore never knew whether they would get there or end up as prisoners on a British man-of-war. To outsmart the British, Eastern Shore swains and their lady friends used small but swift packet boats that could outrun the more cumbersome warships. Besides, the element of danger on the Chesapeake added zest to local social life and few of Chestertown's smart set remained at home because of the British.

During the War of 1812 Kent was the locale of the only land battle fought between the Americans and the British soldiers on the Eastern Shore. In their attempt to capture Baltimore, the British feinted an invasion of the Eastern Shore to dilute the American defense of that port. The British sent Captain Peter Parker in his sloop *Menelaus* to capture small bodies of American troops along the Eastern Shore and to destroy farms and crops. The *Menelaus* was a powerful ship of 38 guns and had a squad of 120 soldiers on board. The warship was also accompanied by two other vessels. The American defenses near the present site of Tolchester beach were led by Colonel Philip Reed of Chestertown. Although Reed's 174 men were fairly well equipped with muskets, they had little ammunition. On the night of August 30, 1814, Captain Parker decided to have it out at last with the Americans and landed his troops at Caulk's Field. The British suffered a crushing defeat with fifteen troops killed, including the thirty-eight-year-old Captain Parker. With little ammunition and great determination the Eastern Shoremen had repulsed an invasion of Kent County. Church bells rang in Chestertown, and Colonel Philip Reed was proclaimed a hero. No doubt this heroic feat made him very popular with the well-dressed ladies of Chestertown society.[5]

*   *   *

Neither the War of 1812 nor the Civil War disturbed Chester-town that much. The rise of the American West and the shift of commerce from maritime routes to railroads prompted Chestertown's gradual decline. As H. Hurtt Deringer, editor of the *Kent County News* said in 1990, "Like most of the Eastern Shore, we have gone our own way—hard-headed, stubborn and insulated from the rest of the world until the Bay Bridge." Yet Chestertown retains its easygoing cosmopolitan flavor, and, if the Eastern Shore has a cultural capital, it is certainly to be found here, for a brisk walk north from the old colonial houses on Water Street sits Washington College.

The eighteenth-century founder of Washington College, Dr. William Smith, was a well-educated clergyman associated with founding the University of Pennsylvania in Philadelphia. Smith became master of Kent County Free School in 1782 with 142 students, and the energetic parson worked to have the school chartered as a college on May 24, 1782, as a school "in honorable and perpetual memory of His Excellency General Washington, the illustrious and virtuous commander in chief of the armies of the United States." In November 1782, the Maryland state assembly, prodded by the Eastern Shore squire-archy, appropriated 5,992 pounds, fourteen shillings, and sixpence for the college. The school was to have a three-year curriculum with emphasis on mathematics, navigation, meta-physics, Latin, Greek, and French. However, French was to be studied only in spare time, not taught. When the college held its first commencement on May 14, 1783, Governor William Paca attended and was honored with thirteen charges of cannon. George Washington visited the college in 1784 to the delight of the Eastern Shore. Several years later on July 11, 1789, the school awarded General Washington an honorary doctorate. Unfortunately, falling enrollments in the 1790s resulted in termination of state funding in 1798. A foreign visitor, Duc de la Rouchefoucault, found the college in 1796 in a deplorable state of repair—windows without glass, en-trances to the buildings without steps.

After the War of 1812 the college settled into its role as a small-town school. Then, as now, students complained of the monotonous college food. The daily student menu in the 1820s consisted of salt meat every day and fresh meat and salt meat for three days, with plain dessert and two vegetables. The college served only breakfast and supper.

A fire in 1826 destroyed the school's only building, and it was not until after the Civil War that the fortunes of Washington College improved considerably. In addition to raising money for the school, the main task of the administration was to impose discipline on the loutish students from the farms and plantations of the Eastern Shore. The college entered a new era during 1873-1887 when Principal William J. Rivers, former professor of ancient languages and literature at the University of South Carolina, raised standards during his tenure. Despite an inadequate library and a small and underpaid teaching staff, Rivers did produce a number of lawyers, ministers of the gospel, and physicians. Washington College went co-ed in 1891; the college needed the ladies' tuition money. Although the school was convulsed in the late 1960s with students protesting the administration's in loco parentis approach to education, the school survived. By the 1970s the college had acquired the reputation as a genteel liberal arts college and enrollment grew to over six hundred. The blossoming of Washington College during the period from 1950 to 1970 was largely the work of President Daniel Z. Gibson, and the school's growing reputation helped attract sophisticated well-to-do people to Chestertown.[6]

The graduates of Washington College defend their alma mater with an almost messianic zeal, and few students really want to leave this bucolic environment once they have finished their studies. On the Chester, the rowing shells of the college crew club move delicately on the water with the precision of water bugs and in the old crew house you can still see the autographed oars of rowers who gave their all for Washington College. The faculty is gentle and caring. Seminars are often held in faculty members' homes at tea time; and in the homes of faculty members good sherry and classical music are the sine qua non of existence. Students get an education worthy of a lady or gentleman of the Republic, for the college will not tolerate an ignoramus. There is also time for fun and sport on the playing fields of Washington College, and it is casually mixed in with the discipline of the liberal arts. Occasionally the students get a little high-strung, but both the college and the town are watchful, protective, and tolerant. The good students go on to well-paying jobs in major corporations; the exceptional ones go off to the heady world of scholarship at Cambridge and Oxford.

Washington College is also known for the Sophie Kerr Literary Prize, an excellence in writing award given each year to an outstanding senior. Sophie Kerr was a famous novelist from Denton who gave the school a generous endowment. As a writer and investor, Kerr made a lot of money in her day, and the annual prize, depending on the fluctuations of Wall Street, is worth between $25,000 and $35,000. Good writing is highly prized at Washington College and the college administration encourages students to read the novels of their fellow students if they are incapable of writing their own. Every year about a half dozen students hole up in the O'Neill Literary House to put the finishing touches on manuscripts that they hope will enable them to win the coveted prize. The endowment also helps students to meet the giants of the American literary scene. John Barth, Edward Albee, William Styron, and poet Allen Ginsberg have all passed through and talked of the joys and torments of writing. Practically no one who has ever won the prize, though, has gone on to amount to much as a writer. When a newspaper reporter asked why this was so, an English professor replied that he thought that God was on their side. Yet the Sophie Kerr prize is tax free and it gains the school an enormous amount of publicity each spring when the young writers of Washington College spill out of O'Neill Literary House clutching their manuscripts and hoping that fate will be generous.

But on the whole, Sophie Kerr is more interesting than the literary prize she left behind. In her lifetime Sophie Kerr learned that it was one thing to live on the Eastern Shore and another to write about it. The Denton native spent most of her time as a literary exile in New York as her creative muse could not root in the local culture of the Eastern Shore. Much like Sinclair Lewis, Sophie Kerr had an intense love-hate relationship with the Eastern Shore that was often reflected in her novels. In her lifetime Kerr wrote twenty novels, several plays, and a large number of light essays. While she is largely unread today, her prose has a vitality to it that forever captures the spirit of the Eastern Shore. Two novels especially are revealing of Eastern Shore life in the 1920s, her most creative period. In *One Thing Is Certain* (1922), a young Denton girl is forced to marry a despotic and cold church deacon. The story is a reflection of the small-town excessive puritanism that existed on the Eastern Shore at that time. Like Hester in Hawthorne's *Scarlet Letter*, the heroine commits the unpardonable sin of adultery with her lover after her marriage to the deacon. In *Mareea-Maria* (1929), Kerr again focuses on the puritanical intolerance of the Eastern Shore by having a young female cannery worker who is Italian and Catholic marry one of the most eligible Methodist men in the town. The public stir that this "unholy union" creates in the Eastern Shore locality illustrates how hard it was for anyone to deviate from small-town social norms. Thus it is not surprising that Sophie Kerr only came back to the Eastern Shore to visit. Ironically, when her novels went out of fashion, Kerr earned a living writing in women's magazines, extolling Eastern Shore country fried chicken and other regional recipes of her homeland. When she died she was more known as the Eastern Shore's beloved food writer than as a critical novelist of Chesapeake society.

Today 280-year-old Chestertown survives not as a quaint suburb, wrote the *Washington Post*, "but as a living specimen of a seminal American entity—the small town." Unless you really want to go to Chestertown, you will miss it as it is on no main highway. Among the things that Chestertown has to recommend it are the quiet beauty of its colonial homes and peaceful streets, the majestic Chester River, and the carefully tended lawns that roll to the water's edge as they did in colonial times. The town is sedate, self-possessed, and Episcopalian. Chestertown has no shortage of both new and old wealthy residents, and many people who fled the town in their youth are returning. It is a friendly town; race relations are good and tourists are welcome as long as they speak well and mind their manners. As a newspaper reporter once wrote of Chestertown, "Norman Rockwell would find plenty to paint and Sinclair Lewis would be busy taking notes." And if you listen hard on a spring evening you may be able to hear the refrains of harpsichord music and the gentle tapping of a colonial dancing master's cane.

*　　*　　*

During the golden age of steamboats on the Chesapeake before World War II, Kent County was the playground of Baltimore. In summer, crowded steamers would dock at the resorts of Betterton and Tolchester beach, as Baltimoreans sought to escape the heat and congestion of the city. Tolchester was a wonderful resort for the weary vacationer. It had a large bathing beach and a twin-towered pavilion, and there was a large hotel on the hill overlooking the Bay where many Baltimore families spent a week or two on vacation. When the steamboat *Emma Giles* arrived at Tolchester, its horde of summer passengers always cheered. By the standards of the late Victorian era, Tolchester Beach was a summer wonder. The brightly painted resort sprawled over 150 acres and the architecture suggested not a Chesapeake resort but a fancy Renaissance villa. The park had a merry-go-round with brightly colored elephants, lions, bear, and giraffe to delight the children. The resort also had a small roller coaster, picnic groves, and a miniature train that delighted adults and children alike. There were movie boxes you could look into for a penny. You turned a little crank and a succession of pictures flicked by. Those seeking escape from the summer heat could stroll around a miniature lake or visit the bathhouse and take a plunge in the Bay. At night you could get a meal of succulent seafood in the hotel restaurant, sit in a rocking chair on the two-hundred-foot veranda, or go dancing at the pavilion. The summers at Tolchester Beach were golden and even today the memories of happy times linger though the resort has long been torn down. Today's vacations are more like frenzied diversions than they are a release from the work and heat of summer. The innocent fun and relaxation of a Tolchester vacation is gone.[7] Yet people remember the pavilion orchestra that played late into the night and Dale Wimbrow, a young graduate of Washington College, who crooned a happy song:

> On the Good Old Eastern Shore. On The Good Old Eastern Shore. They've got so much they couldn't ask for more. Where good folks stick together like the good folks ought to do. On the Good Old Eastern Shore!

*   *   *

Caroline County is the only land-bound county of the Eastern Shore. A practical hardworking blue-collar county, it has few rich newcomers and none of Talbot's feverish social life. In the nineteenth century Caroline was an important milling center, and the flour mills along Hunting Creek made excellent stone-ground flour. Caroline was named for Lady Caroline Calvert, the sister of Frederick, the last Lord Baltimore. It was created in 1763 to offset the creation of Harford County on the western shore and to maintain a regional balance of delegates in the colonial legislature. Denton, the county seat, remains today what it was in the last century, a peaceful Choptank river town. Although the town boasts that Andrew Jackson once stopped there, Denton has little romance to brag about. The town, however, is not without its own fierce pride. In 1865 when the town received word of the end of the Civil War, the patriotic Unionists of the town got so excited that they nearly burned down the town with fireworks. Today the old cannery festivals of ginger cake and persimmon beer have given way to oyster roasts and volunteer firemen's parades. Harry Hughes, who was born in Easton but grew up in Denton, served as governor of Maryland; however, the locals hardly mention it.

Denton was originally named Edenton in honor of Sir Robert Eden, the proprietary governor of Maryland from 1769 to 1774. After the Revolution local patriotic sensibilities called for the dropping of the E from the town's name. As the county seat of Caroline, Denton flourished as a warehouse town and storage depot for ships coming up the Choptank River from Cambridge. As early as 1827 Denton's fresh produce, butter, and eggs were much prized by steamboat pursers who in turn shipped them to a receptive market in Baltimore. Slaves, as well, were regularly auctioned off in Denton on the public square facing Market Street. This practice was roundly condemned by the Nicholites, a Quaker-like religious group founded in the county by Joseph Nichols in the late eighteenth century. In the 1790s the Nicholites bore testimony to their strong anti-slavery beliefs by refusing to wear dyed or cotton clothing produced by forced Negro labor.[8]

Denton also served as a major financial center and the town, on the eve of the Civil War, boasted three commercial banks, a fact of considerable importance in a capital-poor region like the Eastern Shore. After the war Colonel Philip W. Downes, the president of Denton National Bank, guided the town's business life, and he and other bankers in the town were instrumental in attracting canneries and basket-making companies to the river town.

In the nineteenth century steamboats came up the Choptank River to Denton and landed south of town at Pig Point.

The river was Caroline's main contact with the outside world and was a very easy travel route. The steamboats *Joppa* and *Avalon* regularly plied the waters of the Choptank and were fascinating emissaries of Baltimore and the outside world. In the 1890s the *Avalon* left Denton at one o'clock and stopped at all the county wharves along the way. For the inhabitants of isolated Denton the coming of the steamboat was a great occasion, and town boys would race down to the wharf to greet the chugging sidewheeler when it hove into view on the Choptank. The trip to Baltimore from Denton on the *Avalon* was an overnight voyage, but the dinners on board were excellent. You could stuff yourself on platters of Maryland chicken and deviled crab for less than a dollar and later you could relax on a deck chair and watch the river bank slide lazily by as the boat sailed down river for Cambridge and the Chesapeake Bay. By midnight everyone had trailed off to their berths or staterooms for a good night's sleep. The steamer's whistle would wake them in the morning when the *Avalon* entered the Patapsco River and the outskirts of Baltimore.

In the days before World War I, Denton was an important center for horse racing and the half-mile dirt track in town was popular with sportsmen who liked to bet on the sulky racers. Men came from as far away as Philadelphia to attend the races. The Brick Hotel in Denton was a thriving inn filled with drummers and merchants who did business every month with the local canneries and shirt factories in the county. Occasionally men would amble over to the local plum pudding factory and buy several cans of plum pudding to take back to their girl friends and wives in Baltimore. Just outside Denton was a large camp of gypsies who used the village as a way station during their wanderings on the Eastern Shore. The gypsies traveled in Dearborn-style wagons and wore brightly colored clothes. To the somber citizens of Denton the gypsies must have been a more than curious sight.

Few people today visit Denton; most speed through the slumbering town on Route 404 en route to the beach resorts of Delaware. This is all to the good as the town retains its Eastern Shore provinciality, and long after other places in the region have succumbed to tourism and metropolitan sprawl, Denton will still be the heart in the heart of the country—a small town of Fourth of July parades with fire engines dressed up in bunting, crab feasts and quiet afternoons with a fishing

Among the things Chestertown has to recommend it are the quiet beauty of its colonial homes, the majestic Chester River, and the well-tended lawns that roll to the water's edge as they did in colonial times. Photograph by Pat Vojtech.

Denton, an enduring and close-knit Chesapeake country town. Photograph by Pat Vojtech.

pole on the banks of the Choptank, chats with the old folks on the benches in front of the courthouse, and eating sugary watermelons on the screened-in porch on a summer night.[9]

*   *   *

Denton's commercial sister, Federalsburg, grew much more rapidly in the late nineteenth century than the county seat; and even though the town was based on the banks of the shallow Marshyhope Creek, it became an important farm and market center. In the early days of the Republic, Caroline County was the stronghold of the Maryland Federalist Party and its citizens were stalwart defenders of General George Washington and Alexander Hamilton. This is how Federalsburg got its name, and on the Eastern Shore the town is well known for its patriotism and red-white-and-blue bunting on holiday occasions.

Before the Civil War, Federalsburg boatyards were famed for their shallow-draft river vessels. There were large oak forests nearby and the creeks were dammed to provide water power for local saw mills. The town also boasted a popular old-fashioned tavern that was more like an English pub than an American saloon. The Federalsburg Tavern was located on the creek bank on the northwest fork of the Marshyhope and was popular with rivermen who shipped bark, lumber, cordwood, and produce downstream on small craft that resembled Missouri River keel boats. In 1900 Federalsburg was the home of Messengers Mills, one of the largest flour milling operations on the Eastern Shore. The mill handled about 150,000 bushels of grain a year. At harvest time the streets of Federalsburg were choked with grain-heavy farm wagons and the town seemed to have an ambience that was more midwestern than Chesapeake provincial.

Even today Caroline County retains this kind of midwestern outlook. The people are calm, reliable, and straightforward. Being in Federalsburg, remarks one resident, is sort of like being in Kansas. It is pleasant, but not very exciting.

In the 1970s Federalsburg seemed destined to become a ghost town until the community rallied. Led by hardworking citizens like Frank Adams, Paul Wise, John Hargreaves, and Lee McMahan, the Federalsburg Economic Development Commission attracted several new industries for the ailing town. Local businessmen gave $100 each toward securing a new industrial park on fifty acres on Route 313 at the Preston-Federalsburg Road intersection. Today, boasts Mayor Torbert Williamson, Federalsburg is a success story that any small town its size would envy. With the growth of the DuPont plant in nearby Seaford, Delaware, and the proliferation of ancillary food, trucking, and light manufacturing industries, Federalsburg's future seems secure. While the town is not immune to social problems like drugs and crime, there is still an easygoing friendliness here on the Marshyhope Creek that transcends racial differences.

*　　*　　*

When railroad building was at its peak on the Eastern Shore in the late nineteenth century, a group of Philadelphia businessmen conceived an idea for a fully planned town in the forests and fields of Caroline County. This dream town of Ridgely was to be an entrepôt of the Maryland and Delaware Railroad. Founded in 1867 as a real estate development by the Maryland and Baltimore Land Association and named after a local parson, Reverend Greenbury Ridgely, the contemplated city never got off the ground and the beautiful streets and avenues planned by Philadelphia architects remained blueprint schemes. After decades of neglect, Ridgley did emerge as a town and became an important railroad center with a cannery and a shirt factory. Unlike most villages on the Eastern Shore, the broad main street and false-front architecture make Ridgley resemble a stage set of a western town. Ridgely almost became a city and it almost became an important commercial center; it nearly achieved what the land promoters of Philadelphia had planned. But then the railroads and steamship companies went out of business and Ridgeley now is but a forgotten dream of yesteryear.

5

Main Street Methodists

The country town is one of the great American institutions
. . . giving character to American culture.
—Thorstein Veblen

here is something distinctive about small-town life on Maryland's Eastern Shore that is both sentimentally attractive and disturbing. Shore towns like Salisbury in Wicomico County are safe, secure, rooted places where people feel that they have somehow escaped the dominant contagions of modern metropolitan life. While this perception of small-town folks may not exactly be true, they nevertheless act upon it, and it becomes the daily canon of their lives. Its life seems secure enough and rich enough to contain their imagination. Race and class sometimes play an ugly role in town life, however. And outsiders find that it takes time to adjust to small-town life on the Shore, for until the 1960s few people from beyond the immediate countryside emigrated to these towns and outsiders were greeted with the sobriquet, "foreigner." In the past who your parents were was even more important than who you are; and family names like Adkins, Laws, Jackson, Truitt, Bailey, Grier, Long, and Todd to a great extent determined one's status and opportunity in these towns.

It is easy to mock small-town life on the Eastern Shore. The towns are provincial worlds within themselves. People cling to old ideas and antiquated ways; and business community boosterism seems lifted right out of the pages of Sinclair Lewis's novel *Main Street*. From a political standpoint town life reflects an ideological world view that to a great extent was shaped on the Eastern Shore during the 1950s when Dwight D. Eisenhower was president of the United States. Town life on the Shore is busy, confident, suspicious of left-wing nostrums, enterprising, conservative. Local conservatism, however, is defined more in terms of property and "hands-off" entrepreneurship than in resistance to all social change.

Small-town society is also deeply rooted in the churches of the region which exercise enormous power. Church is not a casual weekend affair. It is a social institution, a religious center, a school, a recreation facility, a welfare organization, and an oral newspaper bound into one. An Eastern Shore small town may reflect the virtues and defects of main street provinciality, but in its heart it is practical do-good Methodist.

Methodism came to the Eastern Shore in the eighteenth century and took root in fertile ground. Methodist preachers on horseback spread a spiritual message that challenged the sterile gentry-dominated Presbyterian and Anglican faiths. Methodism appealed to the heart and not to the intellect and presented a view of religion that was both practical and democratic. The spread of Methodism on the Eastern Shore was, however, to a great extent the work of one man, Francis Asbury. Arriving on the Delmarva Peninsula from England in 1772, Asbury transformed religious life on the Eastern Shore and soon became the leader of American Methodism. Asbury was a man of small stature, but his piercing blue eyes, broad forehead, and flowing blond hair gave him a presence in the pulpit. Prior to the American Revolution, Asbury and his Methodist colleagues had to tread warily in Eastern Shore society. Anglicanism was the established faith of the crown and to challenge its doctrines was tantamount to treason.

Asbury's sermons were especially well received among the poor and middling planters of the lower Eastern Shore. Riding his horse over fields, around marshes, and through forests, Asbury made himself available to most of the rural population. Asbury maintained that to serve God and his ways required a rejection of the ways of men. Loosely translated this meant a rejection of gambling, drunkenness, horse racing, and general reveling that marked the leisure moments of the gentry. Asbury also called into question the need for people to defer to

higher rank. Thus did the Methodist message stress serious-
ness for frivolity, cooperation for competition, compassion for
brutality, and egalitarianism for deference.[1]

Belonging to a Methodist Church was also an exercise in
self-criticism, and many of the soul-revealing testimonies in
the little Methodist societies offered instruction in righteousness, economic self-help, and upward social mobility. Methodism also provided women with opportunities to serve in the
church and find self-fulfillment. Stressing the importance as
well of a conversion experience over religious instruction, the
new Methodist faith appealed to illiterates and blacks. Methodist distaste for slavery and interest in the salvation of Negroes
in order to prevent them from becoming "vassals of Satan" won
many blacks to the new church. Thousands of Eastern Shore
blacks have remained in the Methodist fold ever since.

On the Eastern Shore Methodism began as a countryside
faith. It was slow to enter the towns, which were largely
Anglican strongholds. But in the nineteenth century, however,
the "hope" and "certainty" of the Methodist faith began to filter
into town life and, by the Civil War, every community had its
small flourishing Methodist church with its emphasis on
saving souls and doing good in the community. In 1876 there
were over thirty Methodist churches in Wicomico County
compared to only five Baptist, three Presbyterian, seven Episcopalian, and one Catholic.[2] Methodism, with its emphasis on
self-help and community solidarity, attracted town civic leaders;
and often the two most important leaders in Salisbury were
the preacher and the mayor.

The Asbury Methodist Church sits triumphantly on the
south side of Salisbury. It is one of the most affluent churches
in the region. Asbury has over 1,600 members and distributes
a photo directory of the membership so that people can
connect names with the sea of faces. Its complex of administrative offices, school rooms, and recreation facilities requires the
direction of three ministers and an administrative assistant,
and the political clout of its parishioners is reflected in their
positions on bank, hospital, company, and philanthropic boards
of directors. Asbury Methodists are "socially concerned." The
church has played an important local role in AIDS education
programs and the congregants help build homes for the poor
on the Eastern Shore and in Appalachia. Adult Sunday-school
classes focus more often on community issues and individual

psychological well-being than on religious salvation. Also, church members support an amazing amount of private and public philanthropy, which, in turn, gives them a secure grip on the levers of social change in their town.

*   *   *

Most outsiders don't know Salisbury very well because it is a town easily bypassed on Route 50. Like most tidewater towns, Salisbury is centuries old, a commercial center whose fortunes have fluctuated with the large agricultural region that surrounded it. Located on the upper reaches of the Wicomico River, Salisbury began as a tobacco wharf known as Handy's Landing. Throughout the colonial period the town grew slowly despite its being officially created as Salisbury Town by the Maryland Assembly in 1732. Until the Civil War era, Salisbury was part of Somerset County and the planters and merchants of Princess Anne showed little interest in the economic development of this river town to the north. Salisbury was known for its mills, and farmers from the surrounding area brought their grain to be milled at the Humphrey grist mill.[3]

The Civil War and railroad building changed the fortunes of Salisbury and by the late nineteenth century Salisbury was an important business hub of Maryland's Eastern Shore. Union soldiers occupied Salisbury during the Civl War and used it as a base to quell secessionist and pro-Confederate movements in the region. From their base at Camp Upton in Salisbury two regiments of well-armed soldiers carried out General Henry H. Lockwood's orders to confiscate contraband, disarm Confederate volunteers, and arrest seditious persons. Perhaps the most vociferous defender of Dixie in Salisbury was a strong-willed woman named Clara Gunby who refused to walk under the Stars and Stripes. When a Union flag was draped over the door of her house, she climbed through a window. Worried that Miss Gunby would become something of a local heroine, the army arrested her and then exiled her to the Confederacy for the remainder of the war.

By the end of the Civil War, the Eastern Shore Railroad had reached Salisbury, and the town flourished because it was able to ship food and lumber simultaneously by rail and water. With prosperity came Salisbury's resentment over the control of the town's business and civic life by county politicians. Many merchants yearned for the creation of a new county and feared that unless this were done, Salisbury would slowly strangle. Salisbury stood to benefit greatly from the creation of a new county for it would be the seat of government. Also, reformist elements in Annapolis in 1867 were looking for allies on Maryland's Eastern Shore who would help break the control of the old planter elite in the legislature.

The move to create Wicomico County prompted passionate debate in the region. Many feared that this would open Pandora's box for the creation of a host of smaller counties in the state. Furthermore, delegates to the state constitutional convention in Annapolis from Worcester and Somerset argued that the state had no right to dismember their counties just so Salisbury could be a county seat. Salisbury, however, lobbied vigorously and in the end won out. The secessionists named their new county Wicomico; it would be the only political subdivision on the Eastern Shore of Maryland to bear an Indian tribal name.[4] Inasmuch as one of the strongest arguments against creating a county was the cost of erecting a new courthouse, a group of local businessmen pledged to build it from private subscription. When the courthouse was finally completed in 1878, it was a large Victorian monument to civic pride and a reflection of the can-do spirit that has characterized Wicomico County life ever since. Significantly, the courthouse was the only building in Salisbury to survive the disastrous fire of 1886 which leveled the town.[5]

Phoenix-like, Salisbury rebuilt itself from the ashes, and, by 1904, Main Street was a crowded jumble of stores and warehouses that had grown up without plan or concern for design. Yet it was a happy market town. Railroad cars loaded with fruit, potatoes, and tomatoes left the railroad yards of Salisbury for Philadelphia daily; and there were plenty of jobs to be had in the icehouses and fertilizer plants along the river.[6]

It was the lumber business that built Salisbury, and the Adkins and Jackson families owned profitable saw mills in the county which supplied rough lumber used to construct the burgeoning cities of New York and Baltimore in the Gilded Age. By 1900, for example, the timber holdings of William Jackson's family included large acreage on the Eastern Shore plus over 140,000 acres in Alabama. Timber fortunes like these paved the way for local political careers and Elihu and William Jackson became pillars of the Democratic party. Elihu rose like a comet through the state legislature to be elected governor of Maryland in 1887; and his brother served in the state senate. While most people thought of Governor Jackson as a stolid lumberman, he was also a politician of some intellect. He sought to prevent the railroads of Maryland from consolidating and becoming too powerful in state affairs and attempted to have large corporations bear their fair share of taxation in the state. When Governor Jackson left office in 1892, he was one of the few politicians in the Democratic party who had survived the tidal wave of Republican party victories in Maryland. In a callous and corrupt age, he kept his business prosperous and his personal reputation intact.

These were prosperous years for Salisbury; money flowed into the region and Salisbury emerged as a growing commercial metropolis. Salisbury has never stopped growing. Neither a terrible Negro lynching in town during the 1930s nor the Great Depression dampened its optimistic spirit, and Wicomico County between 1920 and 1960 had a population growth of almost 75 percent when other counties on the Eastern Shore were declining. Salisbury was a Rotarian town, a community that never stopped promoting itself. The business of Salisbury was business and that ethic carried over into all walks of life—from the courtroom to the classroom and Sunday school. It was a town of outdoor band concerts at the city park on lazy Sunday afternoons; of oyster feasts and muskrat suppers at local churches; of entrepreneurs like Avery Hall and I.L. Benjamin who were eager to do some good for the town and good business for themselves.

Salisbury, however, was far from being a tidewater Utopia. It grappled with the problem of being a low-wage economy and worried that a haughty commercial and legal aristocracy with imposing houses on Camden Avenue might polarize caste and class in town. Yet when towns in the Midwest were losing their agricultural hinterland, Salisbury continued to flourish as an important market town for farmers. Many who did leave farms in Hebron and Powellville settled in Salisbury and strengthened the economic bonds between farm and city in the tidewater. Also, by the 1960s Salisbury's professional population had grown, spurred in part by Salisbury's growing legal importance as a county seat and the town's enhanced reputation as a medical center. Yet it was chicken and not law or medicine that made Salisbury a flourishing country town in the modern era.

*　　*　　*

Nighttime is chicken time on the New Jersey Turnpike and fifty bright yellow tractor trailers carrying iced fresh-killed chicken to urban centers in the Northeast are as much representatives of Salisbury's thriving economy as they are vassals of Frank Perdue, the poultry king. The poultry industry saved rural Delmarva in the 1960s and early 1970s when truck crops failed because of soaring labor and transportation costs. Farmers who once staked their fortunes in watermelons and tomatoes turned to raising chickens, corn, and soybeans for large growers like Frank Perdue.

Taking over his father's small hatchery and poultry operation in Parsonsburg, Perdue applied the techniques of Madison Avenue and mass marketing to capture a major share of the fresh urban poultry market. At a time when the price of beef was rising 20 percent yearly, Perdue and other processors kept poultry prices competitive. Labor costs in the Salisbury area were low. A minimum-wage environment assured plenty of unskilled workers in Perdue's processing plants, and farmers and their wives were delighted to have a means to stay on the land and turn a tidy profit as poultry growers and grain farmers. Salisbury tax revenues grew as well, and Perdue became something of a local folk hero to town boosters. Perdue's accomplishment as a mass marketer of fresh chicken was indeed considerable for he virtually created the market for name chicken with a wing tag and a slogan: "It takes a tough man to make a tender chicken." And Frank Perdue was certainly tough. He ruthlessly used and fired top-wage talent and was not averse to calling key executives about business in the middle of the night. Perdue snarled at union organizers and fought against collective bargaining in his plants.[7]

Meanwhile Perdue scrapped with his competitors and fought over the New York market with the zeal of an enraged prize fighter. All the while on national television Perdue appeared as the gentle and homely bird man from Salisbury who proclaimed that "My chickens eat better than you do." Dashing about Delmarva, Perdue appeared to be everywhere at once, a seemingly inexhaustible chicken crusader who fought other poultry processors like Paramount, Holly Farms, and Cookin' Good as if they were the infidel.[8]

By 1979 Frank Perdue was selling between 1.2 and 1.3 million birds a week in metropolitan food markets. Nationwide the price of broilers in supermarkets dropped in that year from 55 cents a pound to 38 cents, thanks in no small part to the aggressive marketing of Frank Perdue. In New York City the battle for market control between Perdue, Holly Farms, and Cookin' Good was so intense that news columnists referred to it as the "Great New York City Chicken War." Frank Perdue worked hard, but he played hard too; and there was always time for fast cars and fashionable society.

Meanwhile Perdue's plants and grow-out operations extended southward to the Eastern Shore of Virginia, into the Shenandoah Valley, and North Carolina. By 1986 Perdue Farms was listed as a Fortune 500 industry with 14,000 employees on the Shore and in the South. The company processed six million broilers a week and Perdue boasted sales of $964 million in fiscal year 1986-87. The huge chicken processing plant in Salisbury hummed with activity and poured millions of dollars into the local economy. Chicken gave employment to agronomists, food technicians, unskilled workers, salesmen, truck drivers, dispatchers, clerks, computer operators, public relations men, accountants, and lumber workers. Frank Perdue gave millions to Salisbury State College to endow a school of business bearing his name. He spun off agribusinesses, escorted school children through his chicken houses, and served as a driving economic force of a vertically and horizontally integrated poultry empire. It was an empire that began with corn and fertilized eggs and ended with precooked ready-to-eat chicken in grocery stores.

Commercial poultry is a scientifically controlled industry that processes nearly half a billion birds each year on Maryland's Eastern Shore. "Integrators" like Perdue and Conagra hatch the chicks from fertilized eggs in incubators, vaccinate them, and then transport them to chicken houses on Maryland farms in old school buses. The birds have been debeaked, meaning the upper part of their bills have been trimmed back to prevent the birds from pecking each other to death in the stress of crowded conditions and to make them more efficient eaters. Thousands of birds cluster in a climate-controlled chicken house where the electronic sun never sets and the food flow is continuous in mechanized bird feeders. Computers determine the right portions of soybeans and corn for the birds, and the process is so efficient that it takes only two pounds of feed to produce one pound of poultry. Cattle, on the other hand, take six to eight pounds of feed to produce one pound of meat.

In the poultry houses of the Eastern Shore the grow-out cycle is fifty-six days. On the final day of a chicken's life, a squad of men enter the house, capture the birds, and put them in wire cages which are stacked on flatbed trucks and transported to the processing plants. The chicken houses are hot and smelly and the life of a professional chicken catcher is anything but enviable.

Once they arrive to be slaughtered and packaged, the birds are strung up by their feet on wire loops for their final trip down the processing line. Machines electronically stun the birds and slit their throats. Then they enter a steam bath where the birds are scalded. Mechanical rubber fingers course over the dead birds, plucking out all the feathers that have been loosened by the steam. Along the way inspectors from the state Department of Agriculture look for birds with cancers or other defects such as pin feathers or manure burns. The inspectors must be alert because the birds come along the assembly line at the rate of 148 a minute. The production line is mesmerizing and sometimes the inspectors suffer from "chicken hypnosis."

Next the chicken's feet are cut off and it is beheaded before being given to a worker who uses a vacuum-cleaner device to remove the bird's lungs. The remaining innards are pulled out of the birds by a staff of white-coated women in hard hats. At the end of the line is the chilling vat, a lake of bobbing slaughtered chickens that are being cooled for cutting and wrapping. On the average day a Perdue chicken-processing plant can slaughter and pack 270,000 birds, produce 220 tons of ice, thousands of gallons of chicken fat for industrial use, and tons of animal feed derived from feathers.

In the late 1920s, President Herbert Hoover promised Americans a chicken in every pot. In the 1970s it actually happened; and such "fowl" play happily sustains the city of Salisbury.[9]

✳   ✳   ✳

The poultry industry is only one source of Salisbury's economic growth in recent years. The population of Wicomico County has grown to over 70,000 in part due to the efforts of

Downtown Salisbury is the legal and business hub of Wicomico County. Photograph by Pat Vojtech.

Robert Kiley and the Salisbury-Wicomico Economic Development Organization (SWED). Acting in concert with the Chamber of Commerce and city and county government, Kiley and his development team have sought to bring in small businesses and industries that would make the community immune from wild boom and bust swings of agribusiness on the Eastern Shore. Most of these new businesses that receive generous tax incentives and the support of local government employ less than fifty people. Robert Kiley is an ebullient gray-bearded promoter of the region and at times will take off on a moment's notice in a chartered jet to persuade some distant company to relocate in Salisbury. Kiley's god is the multiplier effect of economic growth and he extrapolates with computerlike accuracy the economic impact of one new $12,500 job on the community. A flourishing new industrial park in the county offers testimony to the success of Kiley's development efforts and those of local government. The growth of the Salisbury-Wicomico area as an economic hub is good for the entire Eastern Shore, Kiley asserts. It gives Eastern Shore youth jobs and a stake in the region. "Twenty years ago we were losing our high school graduates and talented workers to the Baltimore and Washington area," says Kiley. "The region is no longer hemorrhaging from out-migration." Since the inception of SWED the local job force has increased from 23,000 to 41,000 in Wicomico County. Eschewing growth for growth's sake, Kiley and his associates point with pride to the fact that local people have been retained to work in locally created jobs. Says Kiley, "This increases the taxable base in Salisbury at about 10 percent a year while the population grows at a modest 1.2 percent a year."

*   *   *

For most businessmen, the jewel in the crown of local economic development is Salisbury State University. Once a struggling normal institute for teacher training, the school experienced rapid enrollment growth in the 1970s and 1980s. By the fiscal year 1990-1991, Salisbury State employed six hundred people full time with a payroll in excess of $24 million. The school also purchased more than $15 million in goods and services from the surrounding region. Economists at the university's Franklin Perdue School of Business help local entrepreneurs through executive seminars and business degree programs. Furthermore, the university has grown to be an important center for the arts and hosts the Baltimore Symphony during the concert season. Thus the university has been an important magnet for people and industry in Salisbury.

While people in Salisbury might prefer to remain insulated from social problems elsewhere in the nation, they are nonetheless aware that great social changes are taking place in their community, changes not always to their liking. Increasingly there seems to be a divergence between the social reality that conditioned their perceptions about life on the Eastern Shore and today's social facts. Everywhere in Wicomico County the forces of economic growth and real estate development are transforming the landscape and obliterating the mental and physical signposts of people's lives. Overnight, farms become subdivisions and mass retailing outlets bring a kind of neon standardization to the community in taste and social outlook. Says Judge Richard Warren of the District Court in Salisbury: "Salisbury is no longer a small agricultural community where people leave their homes unlocked when they are away. It's developing an urban and suburban lifestyle."

Part of Salisbury's problem and that of other towns on the Eastern Shore is that it was a commercial crossroads. As such, Salisbury did not grow according to any particular plan; it didn't reflect the dream of some wealthy founder or idealistic planner. It just became a sprawling riverfront town. Low interest rates, a low inflation rate, and a strong national economy have contributed to a surge in the building of homes and businesses on the lower Eastern Shore. Also, as the quality of life deteriorates in the metropolitan area, more and more retirees move to Salisbury. They like what seems to them an unhurried pace and the access to two golf courses and proximity to Atlantic beaches.

Meanwhile as the city expands and Wicomico County throbs with newfound economic prosperity, "Main Street" is dying. Downtown Salisbury is a quiet parklike open plaza with empty stores. Those businesses that remain are not enough to make the downtown a major retailing center as it was in the old days. As late as the 1950s the streets of downtown Salisbury were thronged on a Saturday night and people had difficulty walking on the sidewalks. Today on Saturday afternoons there is a funereal quiet to downtown. On the Eastern

Shore, as elsewhere, the automobile and new shopping malls killed Main Street. Roadside commercialism exploded in Salisbury in the 1970s, and Route 13, the main north–south highway through town, became one long strip of franchised food stores, automobile lots, and shoppers' marts. A large enclosed mall on the outskirts of town gave the final coup de grace to Main Street. People had moved from Main Street to the Miracle Mile. It took two decades to happen in Salisbury, but it happened nevertheless. Customers now arrive in cars; and large convenient parking lots became more of a commercial bonus than an attractive shop window. Compared to the mall, Main Street seems tired and tawdry; and you have to pay to park in the city lot if you want to shop. The city is trying to revitalize the downtown with festivals and historic preservation campaigns; and many citizens are unwilling to see Main Street vanquished. The prognosis for the future of downtown Salisbury, however, is not good.

Approaching Salisbury from the north on Route 13 can be dispiriting, for here you see neon strip development run wild. It is a linear suburban marketplace of car lots, motels, garages, car washes, and discount retailers. Through their windshields motorists see that a revolution has occurred on the Eastern Shore. Once motorists who were weary with the endless countryside longed for a diversion, a gas station or a hot dog stand. Now in Salisbury the neon diversion is endless and motorists long for the country. By the 1980s nearly anything could be bought along the roadside of Route 13. Today's drivers see an overwhelming commercial screenplay. Route 13 may well be the story of Salisbury's future. The plot, however, is disturbing to the local well-ordered vision of Main Street. The easygoing commercial life is being overwhelmed by the quick shop, fast-food culture, says George Demko, a local scientist. Salisburians have seen the future and it is Arby's.

Yet to a great extent Salisbury is as much a state of mind as it is a sense of place; and Salisburians carry the ideas and values of the small town with them. Salisbury remains a society of joiners. Men turn out a hundred strong for the Rotary when it meets weekly at the Salisbury Elks Club. The Moose, Raritans, Lions, Kiwanis, Elks, 4-H, Daughters of the American Revolution, and the Knights of Columbus also boast large memberships. The town's Republican and Democratic organizations are as much social clubs as they are vote-getting machines. They attract singles, divorcees, the restless, and the bored as well as the political operatives. Somehow, the town of Salisbury fosters the spirit that says you belong. But it is up to the individual to find out how and where. Thorstein Veblen's classic remark about country towns holds true for Salisbury, for the town does indeed give character to the region.

Meanwhile the small town of Salisbury becomes each year more like the metropolis, if only a small-potatoes version of it. Natives worry that the spirit of community that has been Salisbury's most important resource might be overwhelmed by the big-city problems that continue to emerge in the town. The city now has suburbs, something that amazes long-term residents. Salisbury also has a drug rehabilitation center and active chapters of Alcoholics Anonymous and Parents Without Partners.

Yet Salisbury is still full of caring people who would rather talk face to face than call on the telephone. It is also the home of the Greater Salisbury Committee, an extremely powerful lobbying organization for economic growth and civic improvement. The Greater Salisbury Committee was founded in the 1920s and is one of the oldest economic development organizations in the region. Led by an energetic ex-Army officer named Bob Cook, the Greater Salisbury Committee watches over planning and zoning, follows the employment charts, and casts a well-informed eye on both the town's negative and positive social indicators. Each morning the members of the committee play an intricate game of telephone tag as they check on what is going on. Says one local attorney: "The men of the Greater Salisbury Committee are an ambitious, very political bunch. If things are not going right in Salisbury, they go right to the governor of Maryland."

Meanwhile the town's flourishing library and hospital are monuments to the kind of community solidarity that continues to prevail in Salisbury even though it is a bit ragged at the edges. Bob Hamill's barbershop hums with good-natured gossip—the news here is often more current than the material you read in the town newspaper. The letters to the editor section of the *Salisbury Daily Times* has its share of epistles from right-wing kooks and fanatics. Some are still fighting New Deal liberalism, while others crusade against pornography and humanism in the schools. But the letters also reveal another side of community life: readers write in to thank strangers for helping them when their cars run out of gas on the highway; readers question the materialism of the current age and cite the wisdom of the Bible; and the anniversaries of loved ones both living and dead are remembered with tenderness and poetry. Salisbury is no longer the dreamy dozing Eastern Shore town of a generation ago. Yet for all its problems, it is a good, generous town, the kind of place that people will have etched in their hearts long after the Salisbury they knew has disappeared.

6

Semper Eadem

We have a distinctive way of life down here, a good life that is rich in many things.

—Millard Tawes

The people of Somerset County have always clung tenaciously to cherished traditions and the conventional folk wisdom. The county motto, *semper eadem* (always the same), provides them a standard for judging a hectic and often absurd modern world. Although there have been many changes on the Eastern Shore since World War II things have changed less in Somerset than in most other places.

While many residents find comfort in the traditions and provinciality of Somerset, others worry that the county may be transformed by outside forces. Increasingly country estates and proud old homes that have been in the hands of the same family for generations are being purchased by absentee owners and "foreigners" for summer vacation and retirement use. Although the county has worked to develop tourism, it has encountered problems. Holiday fun-seekers in expensive powerboats run over watermen's crab buoys and snarl trotlines. Tourists swarm to Smith Island and call it "picturesque" without bothering to investigate or understand the island's history and its people. Looking back at over forty years of life and work on Tangier Sound, Walt James reflects that county life of yesteryear seems "like a dream." The Tangier Sound that he knew as a boy does not exist today. When the Deal Island native started out in the 1930s, sailing craft and steamboats

abounded in Somerset waters. The great boats have disappeared, he argues, and the sound has little appeal these days:
"I like to remember it as it as it used to be when things were
done in a slower, more casual manner, the normal sailing time
of a boat between Crisfield and Salisbury (up the Wicomico
River) was about eight hours and people were content then
forty years ago to spend that much time reaching their destination. Today a car can cover the distance between the two
cities in one hour or less."

Although technological innovation has been wondrously
beneficial to the county, James worries that the preoccupation
with "things and gadgets" has allowed the county to stray from
the good life. "That feeling of remoteness once experienced in
the tidewater counties is no more," James mused. "I am glad
I knew it before the modern age took over."[1]

Yet the people of Somerset have always been resilient and
the modern age has not destroyed the county's spirit. The
county still has its great wealth in land and water. Many
residents believe that Somerset is God's own country; and
according to local folklore, "The Lord made Somerset on the
eighth day after resting on the seventh." An example of the
fierce local devotion to the county comes from the tale of a
Mount Vernon village man who had a leg cut off in an automobile accident in Baltimore. Anxious to have his limb buried
on the family homestead, he had the amputated leg properly
boxed and shipped back to Somerset.[2]

This devotion to local life was reflected in the career of
the late Governor Millard Tawes. After a long career in state
politics and eight years as governor of the state during the
stormy 1960s, Governor Tawes came home to Crisfield. His
family had been in the seafood, ice-packing, and banking
business since the late nineteenth century and Tawes returned to the town that had nurtured him. In his small
simple office adorned with political cartoons from his days
as governor, Tawes could be found usually surrounded by
his friends. Close by, a secretary typed more than forty
letters a day that kept Tawes in close communication with
nearly every sector of state politics. Both the mighty and the
humble paid homage "down Somerset" to the squire of
Crisfield. Whether it was naming the baby, helping Junior
get into college, or sounding out Annapolis on a highway
project, Tawes was Somerset's affable public servant. Out-

side Tawes's office an old seafood barrel marked the governor's private parking space. "That old barrel," one native remarked, "it's plain, it's loose, it's easy, it's relaxed, and it does its job. It reminds me of Millard hisself." Townspeople looked at the old barrel and smiled. Here was a man, who for eight years had been the most powerful man in Maryland, back in Crisfield parking his own car and mixing easily with his own people. The heady atmosphere of Annapolis power politics had not diminished the governor's egalitarian spirit.[3]

The spirit of Somerset has also been reflected in community efforts to preserve the county's rich historic legacy. In 1956 Mr. and Mrs. John Jeffries acquired Tunstall Cottage in Princess Anne and began the work of restoring the dilapidated 250-year-old house. It was while they were working on the cottage that they became aware of Princess Anne's museum-like quality, with its federal-period houses and architectural treasures like Teackle Mansion on Prince William Street. Princess Anne, they concluded, should also be refurbished and displayed from time to time. Although the first community open house was a haphazard affair, it did arouse local citizens and brought a few hundred visitors to the town. During the next two years, Mrs. Maude Jeffries became widely known as the town's indefatigable crusader for architectural preservation and enlisted the support of practically every local organization.

In October 1958, the town celebrated the first Old Princess Anne Days. Although the original intent of Old Princess Anne Days was to give residents a chance to show their historic possessions and thus gain more pride in their heritage, the purpose of the event was soon broadened to include the purchase of Teackle Mansion and educational programs in historical preservation. What began simply as the return of Somerset natives to the town of their birth soon developed into a major cultural event on the Eastern Shore. On October 13-14, 1962, nearly five thousand people visited the twenty-two homes and plantations of historical interest on the Old Princess Anne Days Tour. Recently the town has become a regular stopping point on the architectural heritage tour circuit between Annapolis and colonial Williamsburg, and residents of Somerset glory in the fact that the future of Princess Anne lies in its past.

*   *   *

Despite their devotion to preserving the old ways of community life, Somerset Countians are an exceptionally contentious lot. Controversy is the warp and woof of local life; and when they are not arguing among themselves, they are fighting with outsiders. This side of Somerset life is reflected in the old story of a minister who had just arrived from out of state to take up a pulpit in the county. Being naturally curious about his new home, he asked a farmer what kind of crops were raised locally. Said the farmer with a sly grin: "Mister, we raise hell in Somerset County and we get fourteen good crops a year." Boundary squabbles between Somerset farmers are hotly contested and keep Somerset's lawyers well-employed. Arguments over fences, boundary lines, and road maintenance are as emotional and fraught with consequence as are quarrels over Christian biblical exegesis. Some farm families have been fighting over "their lines" for generations. Somerset folks also worry that someone will get ahead of them or "pull a fast one." When the federal government began distributing free surplus food in the county in the early 1960s, the natives argued over who was eligible and who was not. When one Somerset local with a new car drove up to load his surplus cheese, meat, and butter, an outraged native photographed his car and license plate and published it in the local newspaper.

The worst arguments, however, are reserved for up-county-versus-down-county issues. Essentially Somerset is two counties: Up-county is the northern part that includes the county seat at Princess Anne, and down-county is the port of Crisfield and the southern part of Somerset. When it came time to build a new big county high school in Somerset, the meetings of the school board became a crucible of conflict over where the school would be located. School authorities proposed building it in the middle of the county, but this satisfied no one. Local pressure on school board members was intense and finally, in exasperation, the school board decided to build two new high schools—one in Crisfield and one in Princess Anne. Thus feuds of this sort also determine the fate of businesses and industrial plant sites in Somerset. Such squabbles reflect the fact that on many issues involving tax dollars and politics, Somerset is often at war with itself.

*　　*　　*

The one historical consolation is that Somerset has been a feisty argumentative community since the seventeenth century. It all began with the Quakers and Colonel Edmund Scarborough in the 1660s. In those years the royal colony of Virginia embarked on a policy of religious persecution of the large community of Quakers then resident in Accomack County on Virginia's Eastern Shore. Rather than submit to the domination of crown and established church, the Quakers simply packed up and left. According to Virginia authorities at that time, Quakers were an "unreasonable and turbulent sort of people . . . teaching lies, miracles, false visions, prophesies, and doctrines tending to disturb the peace, disorganize society, and destroy all law and government and religion." Settling on the Annemessex River in what is now the area of Crisfield, the Quakers were welcomed into the Maryland Colony by Lord Baltimore as they were needed to push back the frontier and make the southeast corner of the proprietorship economically productive. Quaker religious dissent also translated into political behavior and the new settlers quickly established a reputation for being willful and independent minded.

The Quakers proved, however, to be a minor irritant in Somerset life compared to the notorious Colonel Scarborough. The brother of Charles Scarborough, the court physician to Charles II, Colonel Scarborough was well connected and affluent. After sailing to Virginia, Scarborough became part of that clique of Chesapeake adventurers who sought to carve an empire on the Eastern Shore at the expense of the Calvert proprietary. They cloaked their land hunger in their loyalty to the king and their anti-Catholicism. In a colossal blunder, Maryland Governor Cecil Calvert empowered three commissioners, one of whom was Scarborough, to grant land warrants and administer the oath of allegiance to colonists. Scarborough's only intention was protecting Virginia's interest and the wily soldier created no end of mischief for the Calverts. On the Eastern Shore of Virginia Scarborough had established a reputation as a ruthless Indian fighter and a patriotic Virginian who invaded Maryland's Eastern Shore with a troop of forty horsemen in 1662 to punish Quakers and make the citizens of Somerset pay taxes to Virginia. Scarborough threatened to confiscate the property of any Somerset farmer who refused to acknowledge Virginia authority, a convenient way of advancing his own interests as well. Scarborough was a law unto himself in the Virginia colony and owned several large estates and a fleet of ships. Claiming that Somerset and the lands along the Manokin and Annemessex Rivers were within the colony of Virginia, Scarborough kept the border between the two colonies in turmoil for years. Also, Colonel Scarborough succeeded in stirring up the Nanticoke Indians to fury so that Somerset was literally forced to go it alone, almost as an independent country. When Somerset leaders petitioned Lord Baltimore for help, they were told to "stand on their owne guards." Small wonder, then, that this remote Eastern Shore county would grow accustomed to running its own life and be defiant of outside interference.

The dissenters of Somerset quarreled incessantly with the Calvert family over taxes and the stern uncompromising egalitarian faith of the Presbyterian Church that had been planted in the county by Francis Makemie served as a basis for a rough-hewn political and religious democracy that would accept little direction from British authorities.

Makemie arrived in Somerset sometime in 1683, an ordained twenty-four-year-old Presbyterian missionary from the north of Ireland. Secure in his faith and bound to spread the Presbyterian gospel in the New World, Makemie did not shrink from controversy or battle. Moderates in the colony referred to him as a hard-headed Scotch-Irish zealot; others saw in him an educated man with a divine purpose. Regardless of historical opinion, the record shows that Makemie founded the first Presbyterian community in America and planted churches all along the lower Delmarva Peninsula. Used to religious persecution in his native Ireland, Makemie was more than a match for dissenting Quakers and intolerant Anglicans. In Somerset Makemie made his headquarters near the Pocomoke River and established a church in what is now the village of Rehobeth. Also, he allied himself at times with dissenting planters like Colonel William Stevens to advance his religious interests. Soon Makemie's organization skills bore fruit with churches that referred to themselves as "Makemieland." The crusading cleric was also a good businessman. Makemie derived a good income from tobacco speculation and the shipping of pickled fish and oysters. His family married well and was allied with Colonel Edmund Scarborough's descendants and the powerful slave-owning planter Robert King II.[4]

During Maryland's colonial period nothing irked the people of Somerset County more than having to pay taxes to support the Church of England in their community. And when Reverend Philip Hughes came to Princess Anne to begin the life of an Anglican county parson, he little suspected that he would become a highly controversial political and religious figure on the Eastern Shore. The clergy in Maryland at this time were well provided for, and Hughes wished only to enjoy the comforts of a moderate parish living. Unfortunately, the increasingly bitter quarrels between the colonial governor and the Anglican vestries on the Eastern Shore over the selection of ministers and their salaries would extend into Hughes's personal life and destroy his career. The right of inducting ministers was a valuable instrument of patronage, and Lord Baltimore and his governors were unwilling to surrender it to stubborn parish vestries. Although the complaints of vestries over having dissolute and grasping parsons imposed on them was sometimes well founded, many clergymen of learning and integrity, like Hughes, were simply caught up in the furor of political controversy on the eve of the American Revolution.

An Irish preacher who had served as a chaplain in the British Army during the French and Indian War, Hughes cast his fortunes with colonial America and managed to obtain a parish in Somerset that had an annual income in tobacco, local money, and English currency of about £20, a very handsome sum for the time. Hughes, however, did not count on the stormy reception that would await him on Maryland's Eastern Shore. By the time of the Hughes appointment, the parishes of Worcester and Somerset had had their fill of patronage in the pulpit. They were tired of the drunkards and debtors that Lord Baltimore foisted on them in the name of religion and at this time many Eastern Shore parishes were demanding the right to select their own ministers without the proprietor's approval.

Hughes's first assignment in Worcester Parish in January 1767 was short-lived. The men of the vestry circulated vicious stories that Reverend Hughes loved the rum tankard too much. Even though the parson earned the parish's grudging respect with his soldierly bearing, Governor Horatio Sharpe transferred Hughes to Coventry Parish in December.

Millard Tawes as a young businessman. Photograph from the collection of the author.

Teackle Mansion was built in 1803 by Littleton Dennis Teackle. Well-known banker and merchant and friend of Thomas Jefferson, Teackle lost a fortune in seized cargoes to the Barbary pirates during the Tripolitan Wars. Photograph by Pat Vojtech.

Coventry, a parish of rough, quarrelsome, and independent men, had challenged Lord Baltimore's charter rights on the matter of clerical privilege. As the people were required by law to maintain their churches through payment of taxes in tobacco and currency, they therefore claimed the right to choose their own ministers. This argument struck at the political as well as the religious authority of Lord Baltimore, for it asserted the vestry's power of the purse in colonial affairs. Governor Sharpe hoped that with Hughes installed in the parish, common sense and discipline would replace seditious talk. The men of Coventry Parish, however, thought otherwise.

When Hughes arrived at Rehobeth to receive his induction and prepare the church for its Christmas celebration, he was confronted by the vestry. The parson's induction had to be read aloud in the churchyard because the angry parishioners had bolted the church shut. Undaunted, Hughes later faced an angry mob of two hundred men who opposed his attempt to preach at the chapel at Dividing Creek. The mob taunted the parson with the threat that he would be shot down if he attempted to open the church.

Confronted by a force of "Church Wardens in Arms . . . With Swamp Men and Shingle Makers and the rest of their Banditti," Hughes decided that he would have to be equipped with a Bible and a brace of pistols in order to preach the Lord's word in Coventry Parish. When Hughes announced that he would preach while armed on the pulpit, the vestry knew that the scrappy minister was more than they had bargained for. Throughout the winter and spring of 1767-1768 Hughes preached in empty chapels and deserted meeting places. He received notes threatening his life. Shortly thereafter, the Coventry vestry changed tactics and began to send a volley of protest letters to Governor Horatio Sharpe, claiming that "We would not, by a Servile Submission, Alienate Our Rights and Liberties, and tamely give up our freedom to Monarchy." In a nutshell, this meant that Coventry Parish did not want to pay Reverend Hughes's salary.

Shortly thereafter, Reverend Hughes was assaulted by an angry parishioner in Somerset and threats were made against the parson's wife. Things degenerated to a point where one vestryman ordered Hughes jailed and fined forty shillings for plotting violence against the parishioners. It finally took the armed intervention of Governor Sharpe to restore order in Somerset; and by the spring of 1769 many of Hughes's more vigorous opponents were in jail. Although the governor made certain that Reverend Hughes received his salary, the embattled clergyman quit his post for a more tranquil sinecure in Chestertown. Later, during the Revolution, many Anglican clergymen on Maryland's Eastern Shore suffered the same fate as Reverend Hughes. Hughes's experience, at any rate, is a good illustration of the kind of resentment of outside interference that the people of Somerset showed in their political and religious relationships with Maryland authorities in the late colonial period.[5]

*   *   *

During the American Revolution the marshes and islands of Pocomoke and Tangier Sounds were infested with pirates and lawless renegades who preyed upon Chesapeake Bay plantations and shipping. Such were the depredations of Joseph Wheland and his pirate band on the county's economy that Somerset petitioned Annapolis for permission to construct an armed barge to patrol county waters. Within a short time, this fleet was expanded to four barges owing to the continued depredations of the pirates on the local economy. The local barge flotilla, however, did not fare well against the pirates, and in a major engagement, the revolutionaries were repulsed and the commander, Zedekiah Walley, was killed in a canon fusillade. The haughty Joe Wheland then sailed with his pirate fleet to Tangier Island and thumbed his nose at the patriot ships. Meanwhile Wheland sacked towns and farms on both sides of the Bay; and it was not until well after Cornwallis's defeat at Yorktown that the United States Navy extinguished the nest of pirates that preyed upon Somerset.

While Somerset was rebellious by 1775, the county had a large number of outspoken loyalists like Isaac Atkinson. In February 1777, Annapolis dispatched General Henry Hooper and an armed force to quash a Tory insurrection in the county and restore order. Hooper's mission ended in failure and throughout the country Tories cut down liberty poles and erected the standard of King George III. By 1778 the British army was as popular as the patriot cause and George Dashiell, the head of the Somerset militia, reported that armed partisans who were true to themselves and their constantly changing interests roamed the county. Somerset's Tories were fiercely democratic and saw the Revolution as nothing more than a war to make the rich planters of Somerset even richer. Nevertheless, Somerset did produce two exceptionally able revolutionaries, Samuel Chase and Luther Martin, and these men did give admirable leadership to the patriot cause. Chase signed the Declaration of Independence and went on to become a justice of the United States Supreme Court. A former Somerset school teacher, Martin served as Maryland's attorney general. As a lawyer Luther Martin often collided with Thomas Jefferson over political, personal, and legal issues. Martin was a staunch conservative Federalist and no friend of the kind of yeoman democracy envisioned by Jefferson.

During the War of 1812, British warships once again preyed on Somerset and the lower Chesapeake Bay region. And although the much-troubled residents of Somerset could do little more than pray for their deliverance, they did have a worthy friend and ally in the person of Reverend Joshua Thomas. Coming of age right after the Revolution, this poor Somerset farm boy took to the water and worked as a fisherman and crabber on the Bay. Just before the War of 1812 Joshua Thomas was converted to Methodism; and in his log canoe, named appropriately, *Methodist*, he preached the new gospel to the half-pagan fisherfolk of Tangier, Smith, and Deal islands. When Tangier Island was occupied by the British navy during the war, Joshua Thomas preached to 12,000 king's marines and told them that they would not succeed in taking Baltimore. For the "Parson of the Islands," God was on the side of the Americans; and as fate would have it Baltimore stood firm against the British invasion.[6]

Methodism, with its concern for human freedom and toleration, would leave its mark on the county and for decades Joshua Thomas would serve as the conscience of Somerset. Today at the chapel that marks his resting place on Deal Island, you can find Joshua Thomas's sobering reminder: "Come all my friends as you pass by. Behold the place where I do lie. Once as you so was I. Remember you are born to die."

In the period between the War of 1812 and 1850, Somerset's economy declined. Poor wheat prices and a downturn in the demand for lumber and naval stores contributed to a slow but steady out-migration of the population to newer lands in Kentucky and the West. On the eve of the Civil War, however,

Somerset's fortunes had improved considerably with a resurgence of the demand for flour and barrel staves from merchants and farmers in the Caribbean and in Europe. The new maritime prosperity had an exhilarating effect on Somerset's local economy as ship captains eagerly bought the available farm produce and lumber in the county. Thus as 1860 dawned with fresh promise, many in Somerset hoped that the county was about to enter a new era.

*　　*　　*

Unfortunately the new era that Somerset entered was not one that it wished. During the Civil War, Somerset was ruthlessly occupied by the Union army and its political economy was turned topsy-turvy by the conflict between the states and racial emancipation. Although the Eastern Shore did not become a battleground during the Civil War, the battle for the hearts and minds of the people of Somerset illustrates how the war rent the fabric of much of Eastern Shore society.

On the Eastern Shore during the war, Somerset was known as a hotbed of secessionism. Local slave owners like Edward Long and James Upsher Dennis were militant defenders of the Confederacy and hoped to take the Eastern Shore into Dixie's fold. Also, as members of the Maryland House of Delegates, they were a strong voice for secession in state politics. Tied by slavery and custom to the South, Somerset chafed at the state political bonds that kept it in the Unionist camp. During the election of 1860, Abraham Lincoln received only two votes for the presidency, a fact still much talked about in the county. The chart below gives an accounting of the presidential vote in Somerset:

> *Election of 1860—Somerset County Vote*
> John C. Bell (Constitutional Union)—1,536
> John C. Breckinridge (Southern Democrat)—1,339
> Stephen A. Douglas (Northern Democrat)—89
> Abraham Lincoln (Republican)—2

Secessionists in the community faced the determined opposition of John Crisfield. A wealthy lawyer, business promoter, slaveholder, and member of congress from the first district, Crisfield believed that the romance of southern rights would pale before the cold economic and military realities of an expansive North. Also, Crisfield was a devout patriot who had been one of "the strong Union men" who had gone to

Washington to make a last-ditch effort to save the country from war in February 1861. Crisfield and others in Somerset would soon be overwhelmed by the events of the war, however.

Following the humiliating defeat of the Union army at Bull Run in the summer of 1861, President Lincoln placed the state of Maryland under military occupation. He and his government feared that Maryland would pass an ordinance of secession in the September session of the legislature. Further, the War Department placed Somerset's delegates, Edward Long and James Upshur Dennis, under military surveillance. Both men served on the Maryland House Federal Relations Committee and supported state recognition of the new Confederate government. On September 16, 1861, Dennis and Long were arrested by federal marshals and taken directly to Fort McHenry when it appeared that they might succeed in their plan. Thirty other Confederate sympathizers in the legislature were also jailed. Following his release from Fort McHenry, James U. Dennis was classified by the War Department by the code SSS, indicating a secessionist of the most violent type.[7]

General John A. Dix, commander of the Maryland Department of the Union army, worried that secessionists were "active" and "confident" on the Eastern Shore. According to his intelligence sources, the Eastern Shore of Virginia was a secessionist stronghold that would endanger the counties on the Delmarva Peninsula. Thus, in the fall of 1861, General Dix dispatched several Union regiments to the Eastern Shore to confiscate arms and disperse rebel sympathizers. Most of the soldiers went directly to Somerset to disband a troop of secessionists called the Tyaskin Guards. Confederate sympathizers in Princess Anne and Whitehaven were arrested and interned in Fort McHenry. Occasionally secessionists were shot. George Davis, a Whitehaven farmer who "hurrahed for Beauregard" and the Confederate victory at Bull Run was seriously wounded by a Union officer. Two companies of Union infantry sailed on the military gunboat *Balloon* to Whitehaven and then marched eight miles to Princess Anne where they promptly disarmed the local militia.

To prevent the smuggling of war materials to the enemy, General Dix obtained a small fleet of government steamboats and tugs for use in patrolling the rivers, inlets, and bays of the Eastern Shore. The Union steamer *Tiger*, drawing less than five feet of water and captained by Lieutenant D. C. Constable of the Union navy, was particularly effective in seizing boat-loads of boots, shoes, and liquor that were bound down the Chesapeake Bay for the Confederacy.[8]

Yet, in the winter of 1861-1862, neither the steamer *Balloon* nor the *Tiger* were a match for "the Confederate Schooners" of Deal Island. The *Algonquin*, the *Chesapeake*, and the sloop *Victory* were the fastest and best smuggling vessels on the Bay. These schooners, much to the consternation of Union naval vessels, ran a highly successful freight operation in food, clothing, and liquor from Deal Island to the Rappahannock River in Virginia. The captains of the "Confederate Schooners" knew the Bay well and could elude pursuers in shallow water. Captain Samuel D. Lankford of the sloop *Velma* carried Confederate payrolls, supplies, and troops to Virginia. Many of Somerset's smugglers specialized in one or two staples. The Sterling brothers, for example, smuggled coffee and salt to the Confederacy. Green-leaf Johnson of Rehobeth specialized in boots and shoes. These were high profit items that could be easily transported. George H. Fields, another enterprising Somerset smuggler, earned his livelihood from running the Union blockade of Virginia in his Chesapeake log canoe. This fast sailing boat plied the rivers of coastal Virginia, and Fields ran a floating grocery and hardware store selling everything from hats to lead pencils, pipes, soap, carpenter tools, and phosphorous.[9] These Somerset blockade runners did a flourishing business until 1863 when a fleet of Union gunboats capable of running in shallow water put an end to their trade.

Somerset's response to the Union war effort also had its farcical side. In December 1861, Littleton Long, Hance Lawson, and William J. Porter organized a union infantry company for service in the First Regiment of Maryland's Eastern Shore Infantry. Organized as Company K with Littleton Long as the ranking officer, the militia group was assigned the task of proceeding into Delaware in order to arrest Confederate partisans and confiscate all military weapons and other materials that were being sent to the Confederacy. At that time, Dover was thought to be a hotbed of secessionism. Marching overland to Salisbury, the company took a train to Delmar and thence to Dover. In both towns the men of Company K earned notoriety for their rude behavior to women, insolence to officers, drunkenness, and dangerous discharge of firearms. The liberation of Delaware from Confederate tyranny thus accomplished, Company K returned to Somerset County. Captain Long had an unruly company of farm boys, most of whom had no understanding of the war's purpose. Most treated military service as a holiday. Discipline problems were so severe that the Company was practically unmanageable. Of over one hundred men in Company K, fifty-four either deserted or were dishonorably discharged.[10]

On the Eastern Shore, the chief casualty of the war was Congressmen John Crisfield. In the House of Representatives Crisfield had defended the interests of Maryland's loyal slaveholders against radical Republicans like Owen Lovejoy of Illinois who wanted to strike a blow at the South through racial emancipation. When Lincoln issued the Emancipation Proclamation shortly after the Battle of Antietam, Crisfield and other Somerset leaders denounced it as a paper manifesto and placed themselves squarely against its use as a war measure. Shortly thereafter, the Union army began to recruit blacks for military service, and Somerset found itself being treated by Union soldiers as if it were a conquered province. When Crisfield accused Lincoln on the floor of Congress of using emancipation for selfish political purposes in January 1863, the Eastern Shore congressman became persona non grata at the White House. During the summer of 1863, Henry Winter Davis and other prominent antislavery leaders in Maryland launched a campaign to run candidates to defeat proslavery politicians like Crisfield in the November elections. Antislavery Unionists nominated John A. Creswell of Harford County to oppose Crisfield for Congress. Anxious to assure Crisfield's defeat in the election, Henry Winter Davis asked General Robert Schenck, commander of the Maryland Department, to issue a military order that would virtually guarantee the election to Creswell. Accordingly, Schenck issued General War Order No. 53 which was ostensibly designed to prevent pro-Confederate elements on the Eastern Shore from using the November election to "foist enemies of the United States into power." Schenck also sent soldiers to every political subdivision on the Eastern Shore that had a polling place where specifically appointed marshals could arrest those at the polls whom the soldiers identified as disloyal.

Throughout his congressional campaign Crisfield had suspected that underhanded devices would be used to defeat him. Attempting to speak at Salisbury and other places on the

Eastern Shore, Crisfield encountered hostile crowds of Union soldiers who jeered him. Also, he discovered that the election ballots were printed on colored paper to allow soldiers to follow the voting at the polls. Crisfield and his ticket were placed on a white ballot, while his opponent's name was printed on a yellow ballot. In Somerset, Union troops were ordered to make sure that county residents would only vote the yellow anti-slavery ticket.

On election day, November 4, 1863, a squad of one hundred federal soldiers rode into Princess Anne to enforce War Order No. 53. Armed with carbines, the soldiers surrounded the courthouse, arrested John Pinto, the election judge, and several others who attempted to vote, including the congressman's son, Arthur Crisfield. After fifteen minutes of argument with Congressman Crisfield and other county leaders, the military closed the polls.[11]

John A. Creswell, the pro-emancipation candidate, defeated Crisfield 6,742 to 5,482, and military interference in Kent and Somerset counties determined the election. Shortly after his defeat, Crisfield contested the election in the Maryland legislature but Henry Winter Davis and his radical allies were strong enough to prevent Crisfield from being restored to his congressional seat. When peace finally came, many citizens would long remember how Union troops had waved the yellow ballot and crushed democracy on Maryland's Eastern Shore.

In the postwar era Somerset became a prosperous seafood mecca for the nation. The growing national appetite for oysters drew thousands of watermen to the great oyster beds of Tangier Sound, and overnight the sleepy village of Somers Cove became a watermen's boomtown. When the railroad came to the village, John Crisfield came to the local celebration. According to local history, Crisfield slipped on a dock and fell into the water, thus christening the new town with his name. Before long Crisfield became a sprawling oyster center and its reputation as a tough frontier-style town spread far and wide. Fights in the streets were common, brothels did a thriving business, and men who drank too much in the local saloons could find themselves shanghaied on an oyster schooner and made to turn the dreaded hand windlass that pulled in the dredge basket from its "lick" across the oyster bars. In its heyday Crisfield billed itself as America's seafood capital and sent out millions of bushels of fresh and canned oysters. It also processed millions of bushels of Chesapeake Bay blue crabs and slaughtered and cooked thousands of marsh terrapin, the prized delicacy of Maryland. In the late nineteenth and early twentieth centuries, Crisfield was known as the town of the main chance, where men gambled for fortunes and sometimes won. Even today, long after the oyster boom has passed and the oyster bars of Tangier Sound are largely depleted, Crisfield still champions the rugged individual, a man who can make a fortune through hard work, hard bargaining, and luck.

Crabs have replaced oysters as Crisfield's money crop, and a hard-shelled businessman with a shrewd eye can make a fortune or get badly clawed by his creditors. Processing the soft-shelled crabs (blue crabs that have just molted their shell) in Crisfield offers all the risks and rewards of a lottery. As a delicacy, soft-shell crabs are in demand all over Maryland and beyond. Soft-shells, though, are highly perishable and the supply is highly dependent upon the weather, the quality of the water of the Bay, and one's ability to deal with the Chesapeake Bay watermen who harvest them.

Today, at John T. Handy Company in Crisfield, soft crabs are an industry that has helped breathe new life into the town's depressed seafood industry. A former Perdue Poultry executive, Terry Conway, purchased the small seafood company from a retired packer and set about to make it the number one seafood company in the state. By developing a good working relationship with the Chesapeake watermen and paying great attention to processing, Conway was able to get local financing to build a major freezer plant and assembly line out of what was formerly a "Mom and Pop" kind of business. Conway had no trouble marketing his fresh soft-shells locally but he needed outlets for the thousands of soft-shell crabs that filled his freezers in Crisfield.

In blitzkrieg fashion, Conway hit the fancy restaurants of New Orleans and San Francisco and touted his product. He delivered his frozen soft-shells with fast reliable air service. Then he went on to New York City, and the international food fairs of Spain, Germany, and England. For Conway, the Chesapeake soft-shell game was one of name recognition, and the hard-driving seafood entrepreneur sought to do the same thing for his soft-shell crab products that Frank Perdue did for chicken on the Eastern Shore. Conway struck gold when he went to Japan; the Japanese are the ultimate seafood lovers and they relished soft-shelled crabs with the same enthusiasm as Eastern Shoremen. A six-figure business rapidly ballooned into a multimillion-dollar enterprise. In the end, a Japanese trading company bought Conway out, and the seafood processor found himself one of the richest men in Crisfield. In true Crisfield tradition, Terry Conway had held open a weather eye for the main chance; he gambled and won. For the right man, Crisfield is still a fast-buck town.

Similar fast-buck stories abound in the history of local agriculture; for, in its heyday, Somerset was the fresh fruit and produce capital of the lower Eastern Shore. When Dr. John S. Howk arrived in Somerset from Missouri to assume the pulpit of Rehobeth Presbyterian Church in the spring of 1888, he noticed a strong sweet fragrance in the air. "I got off the train at Westover," he wrote, "and we were driven across the country though fields perfumed with strawberries."[12] A brisk urban demand for fresh fruit and vegetables in the late nineteenth century gave impetus to the strawberry industry in the county, and by 1900 local farmers annually shipped out hundreds of boxcars of strawberries from Marion Station. The strawberry crop quickly became a vital component of Somerset's agricultural prosperity and, in 1917, county farmers produced a record 4,430,040 quarts of the popular fruit. Loaded in 535 boxcars, the crop fetched a tidy profit of $258,940 for area growers. Somerset's famous "strawberry train," operated by the Pennsylvania Railroad, transported the highly perishable crop to produce terminals in Philadelphia, Newark, and Jersey City, New Jersey. The railroad boasted that berries picked in the morning in Somerset were on the supper table in Philadelphia that night. Even during the Depression of the 1930s Somerset would remain one of the top ten strawberry-producing counties in the United States. While traveling through Somerset, Frank Rush, a Maryland poet, vividly described the bustling scene at Marion Station:

> Strawberries! Strawberries, Delmarva Strawberries!
> Where in the world do you see them so fine?
> Truck loads and train-loads, boat-loads and ferries.
> Fortunes, of course, from the low trailing vine.[13]

Tomato farming, though less inclined to stir the poetic muse, occupied an equally important position in Somerset's agricultural economy. Cassius Dashiell, the son of well-known businessman and political figure, Hampden Dashiell, opened the first tomato cannery in the county in 1895. In the following year three more canneries opened—in Princess Anne, King's Creek, and Westover—and farmers received six dollars a ton for their tomatoes. Growers in Revell's Neck were particularly skillful tomato farmers and made that crop as important to the county as the strawberry. By 1929 there were sixty seafood and vegetable canneries in the county, with twenty canneries devoted exclusively to tomatoes, that gave employment to 1,866 people.[14]

The transplanting of young tomato plants from seedbeds to the fields was backbreaking work. During the 1920s and 1930s young boys were paid ten cents an hour to move across a plowed field planting tomato seedlings every four feet. The county's six-thousand-acre tomato crop in those days was usually harvested in August, a hot and humid month during which millions of fierce salt-marsh mosquitoes plagued tomato pickers mercilessly. Pickers received three cents a basket with no credit for bruised tomatoes. As the tomato-laden wagons approached, the sleepy canneries would suddenly be transformed into busy rural factories and the savory aroma of scalded tomatoes would permeate the countryside.

Visitors were fascinated by the workings of a cannery. Tomatoes would be dumped into oblong wire baskets and these would pass through a steam scalding operation to assure easy removal of the skin by peelers. The peelers would sit on long benches at troughlike tables which were sloped to permit the tomato juices to run off and allow the accumulated skins to be deposited outside. Farmers would come in wagons for the deposited peelings and feed them to their hogs. Peelers received a token with the name of the cannery on it for each bucket of skinned tomatoes. Tokens could be exchanged for cash or used as scrip in local grocery stores. The tomatoes were then placed in cans, the lids were soldered, and then the cans were dropped into vats of boiling water for cooking. While none of the Somerset canners could rival Albanus Phillips, the imperious tomato king of Cambridge, operations like Kings Creek Canning Company and Long Brothers of Westover did a prosperous seasonal business. As new machinery was too costly for small operations in Somerset, many local canneries were eventually driven out of business by large automated plants. After World War II the ruins of defunct canneries would be a common sight in Somerset County.

"I'm the last tomato canner in Somerset County," laments Sidney Miller, the owner of Kings Creek Canning Company. Sidney Miller is a local institution among the lunch bunch that regularly frequents the Washington Hotel Inn in Princess Anne. Short, barrel-chested, and myopic, Sidney is known for his droll sense of humor and his knowledge of truck farming on the Eastern Shore. "Ain't many of us old tomato canners left here on the Shore nowadays," he laments over a mid-day drink.

Sidney Miller's father started packing tomatoes at the Kings Creek Cannery in Somerset back in 1916. In those days truck crops were king on the Eastern Shore and a man could make a fortune canning tomatoes for Philadelphia wholesalers. Canned tomatoes were an American staple and every cross-roads country store sold them. When Sidney was a young man, the Kings Creek Cannery packed string beans, peas, and tomatoes. "We even canned pears," laughs Miller. "But there wasn't much of a demand for them and we lost money." In the boom years after World War II, the Kings Creek Cannery employed 750 people during the July-October canning season. "Some years," Sidney recalls, "were right prosperous. One year, back in the 1950s, we did a $2 million gross. You never know when you're going to have a good year. Figure on one really good year out of five."

In a rasping cigarette-cured voice, Sidney Miller reflects cynically on the canning business. "The whole industry has gone to pot. People don't eat canned tomatoes like they used to. And today the production costs are the smallest part of canning's expenses," he adds. "It's the price of steel cans that gets you. We have high-priced steel and the can company passes on the price of steel to us. We, in turn, can't pass on the price of the cans, 'cause if we do, the chain stores won't buy our product. We really get squeezed."

He also grows fresh vegetables, and, like other truck produce growers in Somerset, Sidney Miller depends on mi-grant labor to pick his tomatoes at harvest time. "It's hard honest work," he says, "and people around here don't want to do it. These days people would rather collect welfare than work." Miller and several other growers operate a migrant labor camp near Westover just south of Princess Anne. "The damn camp is a headache," Sidney Miller complains. "Anyway you look at it we are the losers. If the migrants stop up the toilets or kick out the screen windows, the growers get blamed for it. If we evict the violent ones for fighting, they call us ruthless. The migrant laborers have government Legal Aid lawyers, liberal Catholic nuns, and the United States Department of Agriculture on their side. We're just a small family business and every summer we have to contend with all the do-gooders, gamble on the weather and worry whether some crew chief is sneaking in illegal immigrants to pick our tomatoes. Nobody gives a damn about us. If we lose our shirt, we don't get a subsidy from the government like the boys in corn and soybeans do."

Sidney Miller is not afraid of the federal government. "I'm a damn proud businessman," he claims. "I get hassled by the government on immigration and labor matters and I fight back. The migrants have Legal Aid to defend them for free. I have to pay an attorney $100 an hour to defend me and my business. Whether you're right or wrong in a dispute with Legal Aid don't matter, though. The legal costs get you in the end. Most small businesses can't take that much punishment. That's why most of the canneries have closed down." Sidney Miller walks through the open sunlight into the deserted cannery. "We've lost a bundle of money on tomatoes recently. My boy bought into the business and now he's sorry he did. There are just too many problems."

In 1986 Sidney Miller closed Kings Creek Cannery. He and his son sold off their stock and began to look for a buyer for their empty warehouses. An age of tomato canning in Somerset County had come to an end with scarcely little notice or regret. Sidney has a few extra drinks at the Hotel Inn now that he is "tarred and retarred." His son bought a convenience store outside of Princess Anne. "Anyhow," chuckles Sidney Miller, "it don't matter none. You ain't lookin at the last of a dyin' breed. Hell, I'm dead already."

*　　*　　*

Occasionally a well-dressed elderly foreign tourist will come to Princess Anne. In a heavily accented voice he will ask for directions to a nearby farm. "We always know who they are," says one local, "because they're looking for people that have already died. They're the old German POWs and we had a mess of them around here during World War II."

On the afternoon of June 24, 1944, a large unscheduled passenger train stopped at a railroad siding near Westover. While the locomotive hissed impatiently, heavily armed soldiers quickly bounded out and placed themselves strategically around the train. Peering out through the heavy oak slats that had been nailed across the car windows were over eight hundred German prisoners of war destined for internment at Camp Somerset. Lightly clad and suntanned, the Germans were veterans of General Erwin Rommel's famous Afrika Korps.

During World War II over 425,000 Axis prisoners of war were interned in the United States, and of that number 372,000 were German. Following the 1943 surrender of the German Army in North Africa, the Allies found themselves without facilities to handle the mass of POWs, and the only solution was to transport a majority of them to America. Later, after the Normandy invasion, many German POWs from the French theater were also shipped to the United States. Most of these German POW camps were built in the South as mild winters made for more economical operation of the facilities.

In December 1943, state authorities in Annapolis, to their surprise and consternation, were informed by the War Department in Washington that several German POW camps would be located in Maryland. After Annapolis learned that nothing could be done to halt "the Nazi invasion," the militia worked feverishly to convert old National Guard barracks and Civilian Conservation Corps (CCC) camps into prisoner-of-war compounds.

The largest POW installation was located on the western shore at Fort Meade; other smaller facilities were scattered throughout the state. By July 1945, there were over three thousand German prisoners in camps on the Eastern Shore. Camp Somerset, located five miles south of Princess Anne, was the largest of these regional prisons. As the German prisoners marched from the train, they saw close by what was to become their home for the duration of the war, a thirty-five-acre compound surrounded by an eight-foot-high fence with six guard towers. News of the arrival of the captured soldiers from the Afrika Korps spread like wildfire through the rural town of Princess Anne, and many in the community feared that the prisoners were spies who somehow would provide Hitler with information on the American homefront. This was reinforced by the fact that, in the winter of 1943, there had been a number of Nazi submarine sightings off the coast of North Carolina and many Maryland newspapers carried stories of "mystery ships" cruising at night off the coast of Ocean City.

The prisoners had come up from Norfolk after crossing the Atlantic in old French freighters. After several weeks aboard the cramped, lice-ridden vessels, the Germans were happy to arrive at Camp Somerset. "We'd brought in this unwanted Afrika Korps and the whole Nazi control was moved right into our backyard," recalled Maxwell MacKnight, chief of operations for all the camps, and Marylanders, like everyone else in the country, adjusted to the new circumstances.

Given the pressing demands of the Allied war effort, Camp Somerset was an excellent facility for the enlisted men of the Afrika Korps. They were assigned to one-story barracks in groups of thirty-eight. The camp had flush toilets, showers, a library containing 1,300 volumes, mostly in German, and a well-managed dining hall. Each prisoner received rations of 3,400 to 3,700 calories a day and was allowed to purchase three packages of cigarettes and three bottles of beer a week from the prison canteen. To many Somerset residents who bore the emotional and economic scars of the Great Depression, the POW camp was "a country club prison." According to historian Judith Gansberg, "Prisoners wrote their families not to send them food in gift packages, begging them to keep the food for use at home where it was really needed." To men who had been eating meager German army rations in the deserts of North Africa for a year, the quality of the food at Camp Somerset was astonishing. Every week the prisoners received fruit, meat, vegetables, and large amounts of bread; the rations furnished the POWs at Camp Somerset were far superior to the food given American GIs in the South Pacific. Thus, despite the barbed wire, Camp Somerset was a relatively luxurious place in which to spend a war.

The prisoners at Camp Somerset began their day at 5:30 A.M. with reveille, followed by breakfast. After cleaning the barracks and policing the compound, they were sent on work details outside the camp. During 1944-45, prisoners worked as contract labor at eight cents a day for county farmers. The remainder of the camp was sent to work in sawmills, tomato canneries, and warehouses in Princess Anne and Salisbury. While generally good workers, the Germans were unprepared for the difficult task of cutting cordwood in Somerset's thick swampy forests. When several prisoners staged a sit-down to protest against their work environment, the farmers stripped them of their clothes and chained them to a tree in the swamp. After a three-hour ordeal with Somerset's infamous mosquitoes, the Germans turned cooperative. By the spring of 1945, 113 Germans worked in local orchards and 132 for the Somerset Truck Growers Association; others worked at Bountiful Ridge Nursery or cleared right-of-way for the Eastern Public Service Company.

Prisoners were required to wear brown outer garments with the large letters "P.W." stitched on their backs. Colonel Eugene J. FitzGerald, the camp commander, had CCC and militia experience and was fluent in German. FitzGerald and his 163-guard detachment swiftly punished those who broke camp rules. Unlike many of the POW camps in the United States during this period, Camp Somerset was relatively free of "incidents" like the one that happened in Mississippi when a guard opened fire on prisoners because he "hated Nazis." Several of the camp officers also spoke German and served as mediators during prison conflicts. In turn they sent whatever intelligence they were able to glean to the War Department for analysis.

Although the camp contained only enlisted men, it nonetheless included a number of hard-core Nazi party members who were uncooperative and were often placed in the prison brig. The successful administration of Camp Somerset, concluded William McCahon, a State Department representative who visited the camp with the International Red Cross, was based upon FitzGerald's "understanding of German culture and Nazi psychology." Also, FitzGerald established a good working relationship with a young German prisoner of war priest who arrived at the camp directly from Normandy and was respected by the Catholic prisoners.

Although American military authorities were meticulous about following the procedures of the Geneva Convention concerning the physical welfare of the POWs, they nonetheless did not hesitate to introduce anti-Nazi programs in the prison camps. At Camp Somerset, the POWs also were barraged with American movies that stressed democratic themes and emphasized the American way of life. While few prisoners took the films seriously, most watched them because it was a means of improving their English.

Toward the war's end, there were 1,034 prisoners at the camp. When it appeared that the POWs would be repatriated to the Russian sector of occupied Germany, there were several escape attempts. After the Nazi surrender in April 1945, relations between Camp Somerset and the community improved and Princess Anne groups held teas, suppers, and dances for American soldiers working at the compound. The postwar feelings of goodwill extended even to the prisoners as local citizens donated canned goods and chocolate to the camp and worked in the prison library and school to prepare the prisoners for repatriation.

By August 1946, Camp Somerset had sent most of its prisoners home, and military authorities worked with those who remained to close the camp by Christmas. In later years Camp Somerset was converted into a migrant labor camp, and the days that the soldiers of the Afrika Korps spent "behind the wire" became part of the folklore and history of the Eastern Shore.[15]

*   *   *

Today Princess Anne with its historic homes, neatly trimmed yards, and tree-lined streets is much the same village that visitors encountered in 1850. The pace of life accelerates when county court is in session; and at the Washington Hotel Inn, the great-grandsons and grandsons of planters, lawyers, and land speculators gather regularly for lunch. At the rear table in the main dining room retired judge Lloyd "Hot Dog" Simpkins fiddles with his corncob pipe and dispenses jokes and earthy wisdom in the same easy well-mannered way that he once dispensed justice in the courtroom. Farmers still quarrel over land rights and in afternoons lawyer Tony Bruce is usually found in the courthouse researching land titles. On the weekends the "boys" go fishing and afterwards end up at the Harbor Club in Mount Vernon for a round of beers and tequila shooters. Late at night in summer the parking lot at Peaky's Bar and Restaurant in Princess Anne is filled with pickup trucks and the bar is crowded with thirsty softball players.

The principal political and economic decisions that affect county life are still made by a tightly knit elite. The fear of "outsiders" remains strong and most residents admit that the only way to be really accepted is to be born and raised in the county. Some change has come to the county, though. Local boosters have brought in a few small industries, and the state has constructed a maximum-security prison just south of Princess Anne. Popular attitudes toward the prison are divided: some see it as creating new jobs and stimulating economic growth in the county while others worry that the county will become a penal colony for Maryland's criminal refuse.

Yet the land and the people abide. On a sunny late fall afternoon, the Deal Island marsh is ablaze as local hunters burn off the marsh grass to facilitate muskrat trapping. The black smoke curls lazily upward into the brilliant blue sky. At crossroads stores local farmers gather to talk of corn and soybean crops and goose hunting. For generations the people have been tied to the low flat farmlands of the county and the waters of the Chesapeake Bay and no other county is as deeply rooted in tradition as Somerset. The local motto *semper eadem* still holds. As Governor Millard Tawes once put it, "We have a distinctive way of life down here, a good life that is rich in many things."

Part Two

SOUL: Race Relations on the Eastern Shore

7

Slavery

*I am an Eastern Shoreman, with all that name implies.
Eastern Shore corn and Eastern Shore pork gave me my
muscle. I love Maryland and the Eastern Shore.*
—Frederick A. Douglass

Nothing haunts the Eastern Shore of Maryland quite like the specter of Negro slavery. For well over two centuries a racial and labor system prevailed on the Eastern Shore that was based upon the exploitation of blacks and the denial of all aspects of Negro humanity and personality. The "peculiar institution" here had a harshness and vitality to it that exercised a profound influence on race relations in the region long after the Civil War and black emancipation. Today no one can really understand the Eastern Shore without some understanding of slavery, how it evolved in the region, and its impact on both blacks and whites.

In the late antebellum period, Southerners, conscious of the attacks on their way of life by the northern press and abolitionist organizations, tended to refer to black slavery as "our peculiar institution." It was almost as if the sting of human degradation could be mollified with the balm of soft words. Slavery began in the Chesapeake area as an almost unthinking decision to solve the labor supply problem on Eastern Shore tobacco plantations in the latter half of the seventeenth century. By the middle of the eighteenth century slavery would be such an ingrained part of the Eastern Shore social order that people could not envision an alternative standard of personal and economic relationships.[*]

*   *   *

Slavery grew out of the demands of the tobacco plantation economy that evolved in the Chesapeake in the seventeenth century. In the frontier period of the Eastern Shore from 1640 to 1690, settlers confronted a harsh wilderness and a strange climate. Using slash-and-burn agricultural techniques, they cleared fields and planted tobacco, the one cash crop of the New World that could be easily grown, cured, and shipped and sold in England and Europe. Initially, convict laborers, who were transported to the Chesapeake as punishment for various felonies (in disproportionately large numbers as compared to other areas in the colonies), and indentured servants, people who sold all the rights to their labor for a period of up to seven years in exchange for passage to Maryland and a chance to become free yeomen, worked the tobacco fields side by side with their masters. Given the incessant demands of tobacco cultivation and the shortage of labor in the area, white servitude quickly took hold as the plantation labor system.

Many white men and women found themselves transported to Maryland in the seventeenth and eighteenth centuries for petty crimes like pickpocketing and prostitution. Once here, convict laborers had to work for a term of five or more years. Often they were severely exploited by their Eastern Shore masters. Without the traditional English restraints of established family or local legal institutions, the convicts were treated like slaves, often having to wear iron collars around their necks as a badge of their status. Some were branded with hot irons; others were mutilated by harsh masters. Even though many of the convicts had trades, a majority were employed as field workers. In Queen Anne's County, for example, the convict Anthony Tucker was a weaver by trade, but was forced to plow and do plantation work. Notes historian

---

[*] The commodity economy that evolved on the Eastern Shore must be viewed in the larger regional context of what historians refer to as "the Chesapeake." This region included the western shore of Maryland and the tidewater counties of Virginia. The plantation mentality lingered on the Eastern Shore long after the decline of tobacco as a cash crop produced by slaves.

Roger Ekirch: "Most of these convicts were young, male, and experienced troublemakers."[1]

Also, white servitude was linked closely with social and economic conditions in England. The upheavals of the Cromwellian Civil War in the seventeenth century, coupled with the enclosure system and the decline of small-scale peasant agriculture, prompted many English men and women to seek new lives and fortunes in the New World. The realities of the area around the Chesapeake, however, seldom matched the expectations of the "redemptioners," as indentured servants were often called. Like the convicts, most were treated as little better than slaves in the Chesapeake. Randall Revell, for example, carved out a tobacco empire in Somerset County in the 1680s using the sweat of indentured servants on his plantation, Double Purchase. In fact, Revell was constantly involved in litigation to make sure that he received every last measure of work from his redemptioners.[2] Therefore, in the early history of the Chesapeake region, it was sweat labor rather than color that determined the local social economy.

In the late seventeenth century tobacco prices plummeted on the world market due to oversupply and the vagaries of the English imperial system. Chesapeake planters, in turn, sought to stabilize their profits by increasing their production. With tobacco falling to a penny a pound in the early eighteenth century, planters on the Eastern Shore had little recourse but to plant more crops with cheap labor.

After 1690, however, the flow of indentured servants and convicts from England to the Chesapeake Bay country slowed to a trickle. With improvements in the economy and the return of stability to English society following the advent of King William and Queen Mary, most Englishmen and women cast their lot with the fortunes of the mother country. Thus did stable economic and social conditions in England shape the fate of the labor force of the Eastern Shore during the colonial period.

The insatiable demand for labor on Eastern Shore plantations would be met by the English Royal African Company, a slave trading business that evolved out of the Guinea trade of the west African coast in the seventeenth century. British merchants in London and Bristol, ever keen-eyed for profits, and Eastern Shore tobacco planters saw their economic interests converge in the late 1600s. During the early years of the colony, slavery grew slowly on the Eastern Shore, not so much from disinterest in slavery on the part of the white settlers as from the unavailability of Negroes in large numbers. Slaves were a valuable commodity and western shore planters and other farmers in the Chesapeake region took the lion's share of these black cargoes for their tobacco plantations. The first laws regulating slaves in Maryland, however, were enacted as early as 1663. After this date, all Negroes born in the colony were decreed slaves, even if their mothers were free women. This law was rectified in 1681 when the Maryland Assembly passed a special law that decreed that children born of Negroes and free white servant women were free. This legislation was tacit admission of the high rate of interracial sex that took place on the Eastern Shore and elsewhere in the colony. In 1715 the assembly passed an act forbidding magistrates and ministers from marrying any white to "any Negro whatsoever, or Mulatto slave." The one loophole in this law was that a white and a free mulatto could marry. Finally, by 1728, the legislature declared that white women who had children by a free mulatto would have their children bound out as indentured servants for seven years.[3]

The introduction of racial slavery in Maryland left more than its share of economic casualties, most notably the small planters and freeholders of the Chesapeake. Small planters could not afford to purchase slaves who were much more expensive than redemptioners. Within a short time, and certainly by the 1680s, the dominance of small planters in the Chesapeake began to disintegrate. According to historian Allan Kulikoff, the economic base that had supported their ascendancy crumbled as the "loss of white servants revolutionized the social relations of production."[4] Between 1680 and 1740 planters suffered at the hands of an international tobacco market over which they had no control. Most planters on the Eastern Shore at this time earned barely enough to recover the costs of production. With tobacco at a penny a pound, only those with inherited wealth or large landholding could make a profit in the tobacco business.

Blacks began to arrive in significant numbers on the Eastern Shore after 1660. Most were imported in small groups on ships in the Caribbean trade. Significantly, most of these blacks had either been born or seasoned in Barbados or one of the other sugar plantation islands. Most of them were familiar with English customs and the English language.

Between 1690 and 1770, Kulikoff and other historians note, over 100,000 black people were imported into the Chesapeake under the auspices of the Royal African Company slave traders. Almost all came from Africa from the region of the Bight of Biafra or what is now Nigeria. These slaves came from the Ibo, Moko, and Efkin tribes; other tribal groups came from Angola. Black immigration to the Eastern Shore and the Chesapeake country took place in two waves. During the peak period of 1700 to 1739, over 54,000 blacks were imported by slave traders into Maryland and Virginia. A second wave of 42,000 blacks occurred between 1740 and 1770. After 1770 the annual import of African slaves into the Chesapeake dwindled to about 800 a year. According to historians, the slave trade between the Chesapeake and Africa declined after 1770 owing largely to the significant rate of natural increase of seasoned slaves already in the region. Thus did the high birth rate of Eastern Shore slaves make the international traffic in human misery redundant.

But during the peak years of the early eighteenth century, the trade in Africans was indeed profitable for the Royal African Company.[5] Demographers who have studied the subject estimate conservatively that from the time of Christopher Columbus to the end of the American Civil War over fifteen million Africans were uprooted and became part of the slave diaspora that stretched from Brazil to the Caribbean to North America.[6] For transatlantic voyages, the most profitable cargo to the Chesapeake region consisted of two hundred Africans—one hundred able young men, sixty women, thirty boys and ten girls from ten to fourteen years of age. This, writes Allan Kulikoff, was the kind of "Black Cargo" that captains of slaving vessels liked most to handle. It assured a maximum survival of slaves and a maximum rate of return for the Royal African Company.[7]

The increase in Negroes on the Shore was usually accompanied by an increase in black insurrectionary activity. Black uprisings, though on a small scale in the eighteenth century, were frequent and worrisome to white planters. Ship captains who used blacks as deckhands and laborers were occasionally killed or wounded on Eastern Shore waters by their rebellious Negro servants. The introduction of Negroes on the Eastern Shore also greatly complicated the relationship of local whites with the resident Indian population. Most Nanticoke Indians and other tribes of the Eastern Shore did not understand the rather sophisticated caste system that was developing in their midst. Blacks mixed easily with Indians just as white planters and fur traders had done before them. But in the case of black relationships, Indians saw their own status deteriorate and Indian fraternization with Negro slaves may have intensified white hostility toward local aboriginal populations.

It is sufficient to point out that the Eastern Shore in the early eighteenth century would be an especially volatile community. By creating a society of convicts, indentured servants, and slaves, the Calvert proprietors guaranteed that their experiment in the New World would be an exceptionally violent one. That the proprietors recognized problems in the colony with regard to blacks at least is evidenced by the Maryland slave law of 1715. This piece of legislation contained over 135 sections relating to Negro slaves. A rigorous pass system was established and no Negro or other servant was allowed to leave the county without the master's permission. Any Negro who had the temerity to strike a white person was to have his ears "cropt on order of a Justice." Whites had authority to kill any Negro resisting arrest, and severe restrictions were placed on ownership of property by slaves.

Not all blacks on the Eastern Shore in the eighteenth century were slaves, however. There was a population of free Negroes on the Eastern Shore that probably antedated the institution of slavery itself. There are numerous instances of Africans coming to the Chesapeake in English ships in the seventeenth century as personal or indentured servants. The sixty-one free black adults that historian Tom Davidson found living in Somerset in the period 1745-1755 enjoyed a relatively high status in the community. Most were independent farmers and property owners. A majority of these free blacks had parents who were also free. They were descended from mulatto stock or had parents who were manumitted by conscientious planters earlier in the century. A significant number of free blacks were descended from free white women who had been convicted before the court for "inordinate copulation." Some free blacks, like the Johnsons, for example, had emigrated northward from Accomack and Northampton counties on Virginia's Eastern Shore. The descendants of George Johnson owned large amounts of property and enjoyed many of the rights and perquisites of the local white planter class.[8]

*   *   *

Ironically, the status of these early free blacks deteriorated markedly after the American Revolution when large-scale manumissions on the Eastern Shore gave rise to a large class of free blacks. When free blacks were a tiny segment of the free society of the Eastern Shore, they were tolerated. When they became numerous, they were perceived as a threat by the white establishment and closely controlled.

The American Revolution's emphasis on the rights and dignity of man also had a significant impact on the thinking of many Eastern Shoremen about slavery. The Maryland Society for Promoting the Abolition of Slavery and the Relief of Poor Negroes sent its agents to the Shore from its headquarters in Baltimore. And in 1785 the Maryland House of Delegates received petitions for the abolition of slavery from citizens in Queen Anne's, Kent, Caroline, Dorchester, Worcester, and Talbot counties.[9] Antislavery thought was also based on the realities of a changing economy. By the time of the Revolution tobacco was "played out" on the Eastern Shore and most planters had shifted to grain farming. The cycle of wheat and corn placed fewer demands on planters for slaves than tobacco culture.

In Talbot County in the 1780s, Quakers and Methodists manumitted their slaves in such significant numbers that the Anglican Church and its slave-owning vestry became alarmed. The Third Haven Quakers of Easton liberated all of their slaves by the early 1780s and the Methodists were prodded by the great abolitionist, Freeborn Garretson, to liberate their blacks. A former slaveholder himself, Garretson was active in Talbot in 1778 and again in 1783. Garretson was jailed in Dorchester and harassed in Talbot. His Methodist ally, Joseph Hartley, was also imprisoned in the Easton jail for his antislavery views. While the Anglican planters of Talbot could not outlaw manumissions, they did succeed in passing laws making former masters legally responsible for any wrongdoing by their ex-slaves. Abolitionists received harsher treatment, however. The antislavery minister, Warner Mifflin, for example, was tarred and feathered and deported to his home state of Pennsylvania.[10]

Black freedom was frequently debated in the state legislature; and, in fact, the legislature in 1827 seriously considered the statewide abolition of slavery. While many Eastern Shoremen believed that the institution was either an economic hindrance or a moral blight, the delegates from the tidewater counties could not bring themselves to give up slavery. Many Shoremen feared that a large free black population would cause numerous social and racial problems in the region.

The Nat Turner rebellion in Southhampton County, Virginia, in 1831 ultimately hardened Eastern Shore views on slavery. Turner and his band of revolutionary blacks slaughtered several white planters and terrorized the tidewater. After Turner was captured and hanged by the Virginia militia, all that remained of antislavery on the Eastern Shore was a weak commitment to colonizing free blacks in Liberia. Similarly, laws on the punishment of runaway Negroes and those who assisted them became more severe. By 1844 the legislature approved a reward scale of $15 to $50 to any individual who apprehended and brought to jail a runaway slave. Also, anyone on the Shore who assisted a slave to escape risked a five-year prison sentence.[11] In Dorchester County, Charles T. Dixon, a friend of the Baltimore abolitionist William Gunnison, was arrested and dragged off to Cambridge in 1859 for violating an 1835 Maryland statute that forbade the circulation or sale of any literature "having a tendency to create a discontent among and stir up insurrection of the people of colour of this state . . . ."[12]

Slaveholders on the Shore often petitioned the legislature for compensation for the slaves they killed during escape attempts. In 1807 the House of Delegates received a petition from a Somerset planter for compensation for the death of a runaway who drowned in the Pocomoke River during flight. As late as 1856 it was possible for a planter to receive $1,000 from the state for a slave killed while resisting arrest.[13]

Rebellion and escape were common themes of the slave experience on Maryland's Eastern Shore. Proximity to Pennsylvania, Delaware, and New Jersey made more than a few slaves contemplate escape from the drudgery of rural Chesapeake life. Also, abolitionist organizations in Philadelphia regularly infiltrated the farming communities of the Eastern Shore, providing slaves with the means and information for escape.

The most famous conductor on this underground railroad of black freedom was Harriet Tubman. Born in slavery on a Dorchester County plantation around 1821, Harriet Tubman knew well the degradation of Negro servitude. As a young girl she was accidentally smashed in the head with a two-pound farm weight that was hurled at a runaway slave by a slave catcher. This injury would give her serious headaches for the rest of her days. As one of eleven Ross children owned by Edward Brodas, Harriet first challenged her master at the age of about thirteen when she learned that she and her family would be sold to a Cambridge slave trader. While Brodas was probably unimpressed by her entreaty, he nonetheless decided to hire out his slaves on nearby farms rather than sell them. In the 1840s Harriet married John Tubman, a Dorchester free Negro. Despite her marriage to a free black, Harriet's status was far from secure. Finally, in 1849, when Harriet learned that she was going to be sold at auction for work in the deep South, she escaped. Her husband lacked the will to flee northward and he subsequently remarried.

Traveling in Pennsylvania and New York, Tubman was befriended by Quakers and other abolitionists and became active in the antislavery cause. Her knowledge of the Eastern Shore and the black community made her an excellent conductor on the underground railroad. Usually disguised as a ragged farmhand, she would stealthily enter plantations late at night. Her signal for escape was a softly sung "Go Down, Moses, way down to Egypt's land." According to tradition, Tubman led between two hundred and four hundred blacks to freedom during the antebellum period. This achievement, however, lacks historical documentation. Calvin W. Mowbray, a Dorchester historical researcher, argues that Harriet Tubman may not have led more than thirty-nine blacks north to freedom.

Carrying a pistol both to prod nervous slaves onward and to defend herself from slave catchers, Tubman spirited her charges in secret, north, toward freedom. Unable to read and write, she nevertheless displayed remarkable ingenuity in the management of her runaway caravans. She usually began her escapes on Saturday night as the outraged owners would not be able to advertise for their runaways until the following Monday. With the passage of the Fugitive Slave Law of 1850, Tubman preferred to carry her fugitive slaves all the way to Canada, explaining that she could no longer trust the legal authorities in the northern states. After northern antislavery newspapers wrote of her exploits, exasperated Maryland plant-

Frederick A. Douglass, fugitive slave, abolitionist, statesman and son of Talbot County. Courtesy of the Historical Society of Talbot County.

ers placed a $40,000 price on her head, dead or alive. Tubman was a close confidante of the white abolitionist, John Brown, and helped him to plot the raid at Harpers Ferry, Virginia (now in West Virginia).

During the Civil War, Harriet Tubman served as a spy for the Union Army in South Carolina and afterward worked for the resettlement of Negro war refugees in her adopted town, Auburn, New York. After her death in 1913, the citizens of Auburn erected a monument to her memory and her accomplishments as a crusader for black freedom. Harriet Tubman, to this day, remains scarcely mentioned, however, in the annals of Dorchester County history.[14] In assessing her career, it is sufficient to say that Harriet Tubman was a powerful symbol of black freedom. In the last decade there have been numerous pilgrimages to the site of Harriet Tubman's slave home in Bucktown by civil rights groups.

Although slave property on the Eastern Shore was far from secure and many slaves ran away, the great majority of slaves gave little thought to leaving home. They were caught in a web of family and community ties and a cycle of work and religion that made the Eastern Shore of Maryland as dear to them as it was to Shore-proud whites. Furthermore, in many communities where they were known, both free blacks and slaves enjoyed freedom of movement, and many of the laws that regulated their daily life were weakly enforced. It is in this context that one can understand how runaway slaves could return to their masters. In 1854 two escaped Negroes agreed to return from Pennsylvania to their master in Worcester County provided they would not be convicted as runaways and sold out of state. At their master's urging, the state legislature approved a special act of the assembly allowing them to return to their old plantation without fear of punishment.[15]

Lastly, it should be mentioned that most slaves had a constricted view of what kind of world lay beyond the plantation. Frederick Douglass, himself a well-known fugitive slave, understood this difficulty quite well when he discussed the barriers to slave escape. For the slave, Douglass said, escape was a formidable undertaking. The real distance to Pennsylvania was great enough, "but the imagined distance was, to our ignorance, even greater. Every slaveholder seeks to impress his slave with a belief in the boundlessness of slave territory . . . . We all had vague and indistinct notions of the geography of the country."[16] Escape from the Eastern Shore was not easy. Slave catchers resident at Seaford, Delaware, kept a watchful eye for fugitive blacks. And although some blacks escaped by boat to New Jersey, crossing the Delaware Bay in flight from Worcester County to Cape May was a perilous undertaking.

Of the whites who dealt in the capture and kidnapping of slaves, Patty Cannon was the most notorious. Operating from a tavern in Dorchester County with her son-in-law, Joe Johnson, Patty Cannon led a gang that both stole slaves and kidnapped free Negroes for sale in the deep South. Cannon was a bold and violent woman. Often she and her henchmen went to Philadelphia and plied free Negroes of that city with strong drink before shanghaiing them into slavery. Blacks who rebelled against her were murdered. Inasmuch as she was anathema to both slave owner and abolitionist alike, police authorities were always hard on her trail. A sheriff's posse composed of men from Dorchester and Caroline counties and Sussex County, Delaware, finally captured her in 1829. Rather than be hanged in public at the courthouse in Georgetown, Delaware, Patty Cannon committed suicide. According to local legend, at the time of Patty Cannon's capture there were over twenty frightened blacks in chains hidden in the attic of her home waiting to be shipped southward on her infamous underground railroad. Just before her death Cannon confessed to killing eleven persons with her own hand and to having been an accomplice in the murder of a dozen others.[17]

The daily life of slavery in the United States before the Civil War is revealed in a large body of eyewitness accounts, autobiographies, and slave testimony that form an important part of the southern historical record. While actual slave testimony and autobiographical accounts of Negro slaves on Maryland's Eastern Shore are limited, the personal narratives of Frederick Douglass cast a sharp and informative light on what it was like to be a slave. Frederick Douglass's roots went deep into the history of the Eastern Shore. According to writer Dickson Preston, Douglass was probably descended from slaves who had been in Talbot County at the time of first settlement in the 1660s. Significantly, much is known about Douglass's ancestors, the black Bailey family of Talbot, largely because Douglass's master, Aaron Anthony, maintained an elaborate genealogy of his Negro slaves. In sum, Douglass, unlike most slaves in the South, knew of a documented ancestry that took his family back five generations on Maryland's Eastern Shore. Many of the blacks in Talbot County during Douglass's youth came from Barbados and other islands in the Caribbean. They were part of the molasses and timber trade between the islands and the Eastern Shore. Many of these slaves were long removed from any direct contact with African culture. Thus it would be the Eastern Shore rather than African culture that would nurture and develop Frederick Douglass. He, however, had little knowledge about his own ancestry on his paternal side. Until well into middle age, Douglass believed that he had been sired by a union between a white man and his mother. And the fact that he did not know the exact date of his birth troubled him deeply.

As a child the key figure in his life was his white master, Aaron Anthony. A marginal planter who farmed poor acreage on Tuckahoe Creek in Talbot, Anthony could not afford to give his slaves much; and Douglass and his mother were housed in a rough-hewn shack with a chimney made of mud and straw. Douglass's grandmother, Betsy Bailey, was married to a free black man and thus enjoyed more freedom and independence of movement in Talbot than that normally allotted to slaves. It was she, rather than his mother, who played a major role in Douglass's early life.

Aaron Anthony was a stern self-made man who had risen out of poverty, and his strong character and determination to succeed made a profound impression on young Frederick Douglass. A skilled seaman and worker, Aaron Anthony was hired as a ship captain for Colonel Edward Lloyd, the wealthiest planter in Talbot, and would spend most of his career working as either a ship captain or a plantation overseer for the wealthy lord of Wye House. While he worked for the Lloyds, Anthony rented out his slaves and expected them to be worked hard. Furthermore, in the handling of his Negroes, Anthony was an unpredictable master. Often he beat his slaves unmercifully; Dickson Preston writes that Anthony was probably a sexually frustrated, unstable man.

Although he was relatively happy among his slave relatives at both the Anthony plantation and the Lloyd estate, Douglass was deeply troubled by the realities of slavery. He witnessed, as an impressionable boy, the horrible flogging meted out to recalcitrant slaves on the Lloyd plantation. By the time Douglass moved to Baltimore to be the slave of Aaron Anthony's relative, Hugh Auld, the realities of slavery had left an indelible impression upon him. The Lloyds seldom sold their slaves, but they had a reputation for treating them harshly. Also, on the plantation Douglass was forced to scrounge for food as the children were often fed only table scraps. Perhaps it was the escape of his Aunt Jenny and Uncle Noah from the Anthony plantation in 1825 that prompted Douglass to think of freedom while still a small boy. In any event the eighteen months that he spent as a boy-servant to Daniel Lloyd, the son of Colonel Edward Lloyd, gave him a keen awareness of the everyday degradation of slavery.

For a few short years Douglass led a happy life as the servant of Hugh Auld in Baltimore. Working at the Auld home and store at Fells Point, Douglass led a nearly free existence. This life ended bitterly, however, when his legal master, Thomas Auld, reclaimed Douglass in a family dispute with his brother, Hugh Auld. The unhappy teenager was taken back to St. Michaels in the spring of 1833. The sleepy town of St. Michaels was a marked contrast to the vibrant port of Baltimore, and Douglass hated everything he saw, especially the way that blacks were treated in Talbot County. On the plantations of Talbot County white supremacy was the law and blacks who defied their masters felt the sting of the whip. In St. Michaels, uppity blacks who had worked in Baltimore and could read, were classified as "bad niggers." Douglass soon lived up to this reputation by attempting to organize a Sunday-school reading class for slaves.

In frustration, the Aulds rented out Douglass to a white planter. When Douglass refused to do farm work, he was severely whipped. The scars he bore from that beating would symbolize for Douglass the living hell of slavery that he experienced as a youth on the Eastern Shore. Douglass grew increasingly independent and sullen and the exasperated Aulds sent him back to Hugh Auld in Baltimore. After working as a ship caulker for a short while, Douglass escaped by train to New York in September 1838. By his reckoning at that time, Frederick Douglass was twenty years old and ready for a free man's life and a free man's name.

Given his experience as a slave, it is indeed interesting that Douglass would nourish a strong affection for the Eastern Shore all of his life. After the Civil War, Douglass, by then a

world-famous abolitionist, reformer, journalist, and statesman, would visit Talbot County and the Lloyd family. His
memories of fleeting happy experiences on the plantation were
vivid and the landscape and family life of his early days in
Talbot County were often recalled with affectionate nostalgia.
Despite the degradations of the "peculiar institution," Frederick
Douglass believed that he was first and last an Eastern Shoreman.

*   *   *

On the morning of September 6, 1853, Thomas Sudler rode
slowly along the sandy highway in his carriage toward a
solemn and unwelcome duty in Princess Anne. On this day he
had the distasteful task of having to sell one of his deceased
cousin's slaves on the steps of the Somerset County courthouse to settle the estate. There had been problems. Grace,
the thirty-one-year-old slave of the former Eleanor Sudler Hall,
had waged a bitter struggle when she learned that her fate and
that of her eleven-month-old son would be determined by the
auctioneer's hammer. To prevent Grace from escaping, Sudler
had confined her in the Princess Anne jail—a customary
procedure when the settlement of an estate involved slaves.[18]

A few minutes before noon, Sudler arrived at the courthouse where he was met by Edward Wainwright, the town
printer and auctioneer. The black woman and her child were
brought to the courthouse door by the sheriff and the sale
commenced promptly at twelve o'clock.[19] "Selling off Negroes"
was nasty business that put Sudler's conscience in unresolved
conflict with his family obligations. While the slave auction
attracted a crowd of curious onlookers, the actual bidding
proceeded slowly. Many planters were already "slave poor" and
had no use for another female and child. Finally Thomas
Overly, a slave trader for the firm of Woolfolk, Sanders and
Overly, purchased the two blacks. It is most likely that Grace
and her child subsequently went overland in a coffle [a chained
line of walking slaves] to the firm's huge Negro jail in Baltimore
at Eutaw and Camden streets and then were transported by
schooner to New Orleans.[20]

Thomas Overly and Richard Woolfolk enjoyed considerable notoriety in Princess Anne as suppliers of Negroes to the
labor-starved plantations of Louisiana and Mississippi. They
also had a brisk business in transporting slaves to the tobacco

farms of Charles and Prince George's counties. An unprecedented boom in cotton prices in the deep South in the 1850s spurred brisk trading on the New Orleans slave market as thousands of planters became possessed by the "Negro fever." Cotton was king and slave traders advertised, "Top prices paid for likely young Negroes." At his office in Princess Anne, Thomas Overly posted the latest market prices for Negroes on the Richmond and New Orleans exchanges:[21]

Best Men (18-25 years)	$1,200-$1,300
Fair Men (18-25 years)	$950-$1,050
Young Women	$750-$850
Boys (four feet tall)	$375-$400
Girls (four feet tall)	$350-$450

In the 1850s slavery was on the decline in Somerset and the other counties of Maryland's Eastern Shore. Soil erosion and falling commodity prices forced the Shore to yield its Negroes to the western shore of Maryland and other regions of Dixie where slavery enjoyed a more vigorous existence. As historian William Calderhead has pointed out, the Eastern Shore was the only area of the state where blacks were actively traded on a large scale. After deducting costs, a good slave trader could usually make a profit of $60 per slave at auction, a large sum for those days. On the Shore Talbot and Somerset were the leading slave trading counties. In the other counties of the region there were as many manumissions of Negroes as there were slave sales. Only Kent County refused to give up its blacks. Slave traders were not welcome in Chestertown and in the late antebellum period most Kent planters chose to liberate their slaves rather than sell them.[22]

According to the census of 1860, the last count of slaves in the Chesapeake, there were 24,957 slaves in the eight counties of the Eastern Shore (Wicomico County was not created until after the Civil War) and 91,894 whites. Of the total whites, only 4,487 or about five percent of the white population of the Shore owned slaves; thus, slavery on the shore by the 1860s was very much a small-scale institution, which was dominated by an even smaller elite.

Free blacks, however, on the eve of the Civil War were a growing segment of the Eastern Shore population. The census of 1860 listed some 28,277 free blacks living on the Eastern Shore. Many lived in far worse circumstances than those experienced by slaves. From the War of 1812 onward racial emancipation was a frequent occurrence on the Eastern Shore. Many prominent Eastern Shore families like the Handys, Sterlings, and Fontaines were active in the Maryland Colonization Society and worked to colonize emancipated blacks in Liberia, the region known as "Maryland In Africa." Thomas King Carroll, an antislavery planter from Somerset County, was an active leader in the affairs of the colonization society. Attempts to colonize more than a handful of free blacks from the Eastern Shore in Liberia, however, resulted in failure. Most free blacks were attached by birth and culture to the Eastern Shore and were reluctant to leave.

Significantly, the most important force for black liberation on the Eastern Shore was the Methodist Church. Methodists looked upon slaveholding as a wickedness in the eyes of the Lord and labored to keep the white Eastern Shore conscience attuned to the subject of black freedom.

Regardless of their personal convictions, Eastern Shore whites knew well the problems of slaveholding. Blacks were crafty, insolent, and rebellious—not only a source of boastful paternalism but also a source of infinite exasperation. Occasionally an Eastern Shoreman would speak frankly on the frustrations of slaveholding:[23]

> What is slavery worth to us . . . . ?
> Fields; corn; hogs; niggers.
> It takes a big field to raise a little corn;
> the hogs eat up all the corn;
> the niggers eat up all the hogs;
> and what do you have at the end of the year?
> Just what you had to begin with—fields and niggers.
> I'd rather have a string of a dozen herrings than a dozen Negroes!

Yet by the late antebellum period, the tidewater Eastern Shore had been profoundly influenced by slavery, an institution that had been in continuous existence since the mid-seventeenth century. Slavery on the Eastern Shore was as much a system of racial and social control as it was a labor system. It gave planters a measure of control over free Negroes and prevented the lower classes of both races from challenging the power of elite groups in the region. As such, slavery served as a crude regulator of the tidewater's racial and political climate. Racial prejudice and the weight of social custom prompted whites of the Eastern Shore to identify strongly with the ideals and values of the slaveholding South. Also, slaves ultimately were a kind of speculative capital and even those who were critical of the institution knew the latest prices for Negroes on the New Orleans market. Mindful of their investment in blacks, many Eastern Shore slaveholders subscribed to the Slaveholders Insurance Company of Maryland against potential losses from runaways. With a flourishing southern market for corn, sweet potatoes, and pork, many people on the Eastern Shore saw the agricultural destiny of the region aligned with Dixie's. Therefore, despite the decline of slavery in the late antebellum period, proslavery sentiment remained strong on the Eastern Shore.[24]

Slavery on the Eastern Shore had its own special characteristics. As most slaveholders in the region owned five slaves or fewer, slavery was an intensely personal relationship that brought master and slave together daily, often on a close and intimate basis. As late as the 1850s, more than a few slaves on the Shore were but one or two generations removed from the heritage of Africa. While the international traffic in slaves was outlawed by federal statute in 1808, sea captains in the troubled times of the War of 1812 smuggled blacks from West Africa—many from the Guinea Coast and the Senegambia. Also, ocean commerce put the Eastern Shore of Maryland in close contact with the Afro-Caribbean culture of Trinidad, Tobago, Antigua, and Barbados in the antebellum period. Frederick Douglass noted in his youth the presence of many Guinea Negroes on the Eastern Shore with their African dialects and transmogrified English. African folk superstition survived in the isolated rural environment of the Eastern Shore. Conjurers, root doctors, and others versed in the arts of "hoodoo" provided leadership to the slave community of the Eastern Shore.[25]

Most slaves worked as farmhands and unskilled laborers. Many were hired out for cash when their services could provide their masters with extra income. On weekdays after planting or at harvest time, slaves could be seen loading lumber or grain on schooners moored at Salisbury, Oxford, or Cambridge. Some slaves were apprenticed to tradesmen, while others tended large herds of pigs that roamed through the pine forests or dug sweet potatoes for eventual shipment by boat to the Gulf Coast states.

Planters on the Eastern Shore generally permitted slaves to have gardens and small chicken coops; and often blacks swapped eggs and vegetables with area townspeople for coffee, tobacco, and small amounts of cash. In places like Princess Anne, Easton, and Denton, enterprising slaves during holidays made molasses candy and sold it to whites at local churches. Some slaves in good physical condition earned money as prize fighters. The rough crowd of planters' sons that frequented Theodore Dashiell's Somerset Hotel in Princess Anne liked to wager on fist fights involving blacks from surrounding farms. Despite laws against a slave hiring out his own free time, many slaves did so. Thus, in bondage, did many blacks show an entrepreneurial spirit that contradicted the white stereotype of the lazy slave.[26]

When it came to matters of racial control, whites had no illusions about their slaves. There had been "Negro tumults" on the Eastern Shore during the colonial period; and when the British invaded the Chesapeake during both the Revolution and the War of 1812, black runaways and renegades helped the English soldiers to put farms and plantations to the torch. After the Nat Turner insurrection in Virginia in 1831, slave owners took deliberate steps to make certain that blacks would not bring about a racial apocalypse on the Eastern Shore. In Princess Anne, Easton, and other county seats on the Shore church bells rang at 9:00 P.M. in winter and 10:00 P.M. in summer for Negroes to go indoors. Blacks who violated the curfew risked a whipping. Local militia units occasionally patrolled the highways at night and stopped blacks with the intimidating question, "Boy, who do you belong to?" The sale of alcoholic beverages to blacks—free or slave—was generally forbidden on the Eastern Shore.[27]

John Brown's raid at Harpers Ferry in October 1859 tapped a deep vein of fear in Eastern Shore slaveholders. Although captured and convicted in Virginia for conspiracy and racial insurrection, John Brown raised again the nightmarish visions of Nat Turner and the terror of Santo Domingo in the Caribbean when whites were ruthlessly slain by mutinous blacks. Shortly after Brown's capture, a rumor of a black rebellion in Somerset County spread through the community like wildfire. A group of Somerset citizens alerted at church rose from prayers and broke up the benches to provide themselves with weapons. A posse later canvassed the neighborhood and found nothing. At night armed whites searched the houses of several free blacks for weapons. Later a slave believed to be an insurgent was killed by an enraged crowd of whites.[28]

In the last years before the Civil War, Eastern Shore citizens believed themselves to be more afflicted by the curse of "free negroism" than by slavery. In 1860 there were 28,277 free Negroes on the Shore accounting for 53 percent of all blacks in the region.[29] The large size of the free black community constituted a worrisome presence for Eastern Shore whites and local authorities fretted far more about these blacks than about their own slaves. Free blacks constituted the largest single threat of free people to the highly autocratic and paternalistic politics of the Eastern Shore.

Whites especially feared free Negroes' consorting with slaves, implanting the idea of freedom, and helping slaves to abscond or rebel. Also, by experiencing "freedom" they shared one of the white man's proudest possessions and undermined distinctions between whites and blacks. Therefore it is not surprising that the laws regulating the conduct of free Negroes on the Eastern Shore were exceedingly harsh. If free Negroes "got out of their place" they could be and were publicly whipped. Free blacks who were found guilty of minor crimes were banished from the Eastern Shore upon pain of enslavement. Also, those free blacks who crowded local jails could also be whipped and sold into slavery. Such Draconian measures, notes historian Ira Berlin, "were not a response to any real or imagined threat to white dominance."[30] It was just the way in which the Eastern Shore handled its free Negro population, a matter of unthinking but constant racist repression. Slaves on the Eastern Shore were controlled by the Constitution and the laws of Maryland. Free Negroes were ruled by the sheriff's cat-o'-nine-tails.

Thus, given the oppressive social environment of the free Negro, it is surprising to find evidence of the free black community's upward economic climb on the Eastern Shore during the period from 1850 to 1860. In many areas on the Eastern Shore so prosperous did some black watermen become that whites demanded that blacks be legally prohibited from harvesting and selling oysters. Blacks acquired property and many owned their own one-room cabin with fireplace and sleeping loft. Occasionally blacks could acquire great wealth.

The census of 1860 reveals a Mrs. Virginia Underhill, a 70-year-old black "laborer" in Somerset with assets amounting to $19,000 —a fortune by standards of her day. Often blacks worked as farmhands and earned fifty cents a day plus board. Farm work was vigorous and a fifteen-hour day was not uncommon. Also, free blacks were required by law to donate three days of labor a year to their home county for road maintenance. Farm work ceased at noon on Saturday. In the afternoon blacks rested and prepared for long walks to Eastern Shore villages to buy food and clothing from local merchants. It was not uncommon for blacks to walk twelve miles just to buy some sugar and coffee.

Throughout the 1850s the South enjoyed a period of almost continuous economic expansion and often labor scarcity forced Eastern Shore planters to attempt to control and dictate the local free Negro labor force. Planters demanded that blacks sign "iron clad" labor contracts; and free Negro peonage, so familiar in the post–Civil War South, loomed large on the Eastern Shore during the antebellum period. Also, idle blacks were compelled by law to find employment within fifteen days or risk being forcibly hired out to a planter.

Disturbed by the presence of large numbers of free blacks in their midst, delegates from Caroline, Talbot, Worcester, and Somerset counties met in Cambridge in September 1858 to adopt a common plan of action. The delegates feared free blacks and thought them responsible for a wave of barn burnings on the Eastern Shore. Many delegates favored the reenslavement of free blacks. Somerset County representatives passed a resolution at the meeting declaring that "free negroism" and slavery were incompatible and that Negroes should be made to go into slavery or to leave the state. This proslavery militancy was probably in direct response to the growing reluctance of the free black community of the Eastern Shore to acquiesce to the white-inspired contract labor program. In the January session of the state legislature, Somerset delegates supported the Jacobs Bill, a plan to reenslave all blacks who had less than $150 and refused to be hired out on labor contract. Although the bill was defeated in a November statewide referendum, Somerset and other counties supported the bill. Undaunted, Somerset County authorities offered free blacks over eighteen years of age the right to renounce freedom and take masters.[31]

By the eve of the Civil War race relations on Maryland's Eastern Shore had evolved into a settled pattern of repression, violence, and white paranoia about the consequences of black freedom. Slavery, while a declining institution, still enjoyed widespread support in the white community as a political model for race control. On the Eastern Shore where slavery was peripheral to the local economy, the "peculiar institution" commanded a fierce white loyalty, and debate on the institution's future was largely forbidden. Thus two centuries of racial oppression would form the historical framework for a philosophy of white supremacy that would condition the social and political experience of all Eastern Shoremen well into the twentieth century.

8

Freedom's Ferment

De blessed Jesus, he mended the old constitution an sine
and seal it wid his blood; and he open de door and say come
forth . . . .

—Reverend Stephenson Whittington, 1864

Since the Civil War the history of race relations on the
Eastern Shore of Maryland has been a story of struggle
and tragedy. Although the Eastern Shore counties are within
a two-hour drive of the national capital, these communities in
spirit and sense of place have been more like the deep South
when it comes to racial attitudes. Like slavery, segregation and
white supremacy died hard as a sustaining ethos of Chesapeake country life. And it is only since the 1960s that considerable progress has begun to be made in terms of racial
accommodation. To a great extent this accommodation has
been possible only because of the intervention of the federal
government in the area of civil rights on the Eastern Shore and
continuing black militancy in the courthouse, the school-
house, and the community. In order to understand the evolution of civil rights disputes on the Eastern Shore, we must first
look at the Civil War and its aftermath. A host of racial
problems emerged in the region at this time.

During the Civil War the prospect of racial emancipation
deeply disturbed many leaders on Maryland's Eastern Shore.
Emancipation, they feared, would result in the loss of millions
of dollars in property and would raise the issue of black
equality in the region. Attempting to strike a psychological

137

blow at the Confederacy, President Lincoln asked the loyal slave states to abolish the institution with the help of federal compensation. The offer went forth as a war measure that would save money and lives by shortening the conflict.

In March of 1862, President Lincoln sent for Congressman John Crisfield, the leader of the First Congressional District on Maryland's Eastern Shore, to sound out the Maryland delegation on the idea of emancipation. During his talk with Crisfield, Lincoln spoke about the terrible war affecting the nation and how inevitably slaves came to the army camps as refugees. The radical group in Congress, he claimed, tried to protect the Negro fugitives while slaveholders complained that their property rights were denied. Lincoln's comments prompted Crisfield to ask the president whether it would be an act of cruelty toward blacks to emancipate the slaves. The choice, Crisfield asserted, was "between slavery on the one hand, and degradation, poverty, suffering and ultimate extinction on the other."[1]

Although he disagreed with Crisfield on emancipation, Lincoln respected him. A man of courage and unquestioned patriotism, Crisfield was an articulate spokesman for the border states that Lincoln was so loathe to alienate during the war. Shortly after Lincoln signed the bill for compensated emancipation in the District of Columbia, he made a peace overture to the Maryland congressional delegation that would allow it to have a major voice in the process of emancipation in Maryland. This overture was rejected. Finally in July 1862, after the passage of the Second Confiscation Act, which forbade the army from chasing runaway slaves and sanctioned the enlistment of Negro soldiers, Lincoln again met with Crisfield. Lincoln assured Crisfield that he would guarantee Maryland slave owners $300 for each emancipated slave and colonize the freed Negroes in Latin America at government expense. "You had better come to an agreement," Lincoln warned Crisfield, "Niggers will never be higher."[2] Crisfield, however, remained intransigent. Thus by placing himself squarely against emancipation, Crisfield lost an opportunity to direct the process of black liberation in Maryland in a manner that would disrupt as little as possible the social, political, and economic life of the state. Conditioned to maintaining a racial caste system that had been in continuous existence for over two centuries, Crisfield and other Eastern

Shore slaveholders stood immobile as the winds of social change swirled about them.

When President Lincoln issued the Emancipation Proclamation, which freed blacks in the Confederacy as a war measure, Eastern Shore planters denounced the measure as a "paper manifesto." In Congress John Crisfield attacked the president for his contempt for the Constitution and worried now whether an "ignorant and savage army" of blacks would now embark on "indiscriminate butchery" in the South.[3] Although the Emancipation Proclamation freed slaves only in those states in rebellion against the federal government, slavery was doomed in Maryland. Throughout 1862 and 1863 on the Eastern Shore, the exodus of fugitive slaves from Maryland plantations continued with increasing tempo. By the summer of 1863, the Union army was pulling blacks off Eastern Shore farms and putting them into uniform. Lincoln's decision to allow free Negroes to enlist in the Union army was prompted by the all-consuming manpower needs of the army during the critical summer of 1863 when military casualties reached record proportions. And, given the widespread resistance to the draft in the North, Lincoln viewed blacks as the best available source of men for the Union military machine.

In July 1863, Colonel William Birney and a large detachment of federal troops arrived on the Eastern Shore. Birney was the son of the prominent abolitionist, James G. Birney, and his task was to recruit blacks in the region for a Negro regiment in the state. Sharing his father's hatred of slavery, Birney made little distinction as to whether free blacks or fugitive slaves joined his regiment. Birney saw his position as a military commander as an excellent means of striking a blow at slavery and the tidewater elite who controlled the Maryland legislature. Colonel Birney's men conducted enlistment raids on the Eastern Shore to get slaves to desert the plantations. A steamer with an officer and armed guard on board would sail into one of the many rivers that flowed into the Chesapeake Bay and blacks would slip away into the night. The steamer would weigh anchor and head toward a camp in a different part of the state. During that summer over two hundred blacks from Somerset and Worcester Counties fled to Snow Hill to board a boat they called "Jesus" (*The John Tracy*) that would take them to "Paradise." On October 31, 1863, that same steamer sailed up the Pocomoke River and docked at Snow Hill. On board the steamer were a Negro brass band, Colonel Birney, and some Negro soldiers. The black soldiers paraded the streets of Snow Hill with fixed bayonets while blacks flocked to the boat. Late in October 1863, 140 slaves left Princess Anne in Somerset County to enlist in the Union army and boarded the steamer *Meigs* in the Pocomoke River. Of those slaves, six belonged to John Crisfield.[4]

Ironically, many white planters bowed to reality and manumitted their slaves on condition that they would join the army as substitutes for the sons of the planters. While Eastern Shoremen for the most part were loyal to the Union, that loyalty did not include being drafted into the army. Far better, they reasoned, to have black soldiers serve in their place. In Somerset County alone in 1864, over 270 slaves were manumitted on the condition of their enlistment in the Union army. Most of these slaves joined the 9th and 19th Regiments of Colored Troops of Maryland. These black sons of the Eastern Shore would be engaged in some of the bloodiest fighting of the war at Petersburg, Virginia, in 1864. Later they would be part of the occupation force that governed Richmond after the Confederate surrender in 1865. After the war, Somerset and other counties on the Eastern Shore paid enlistment bonuses of $100 to $300 to its combat-hardened black veterans.[5]

* * *

Of the numerous social and economic adjustments confronting the Eastern Shore in the Civil War era, none would be so painful as emancipation. Fearful that both the old free blacks and the new freedmen would either become an unreliable labor force or desert the region, Eastern Shore whites resorted to an apprenticeship system that, until outlawed by the Maryland Constitution of 1867, was a *sub-rosa* continuation of slavery.[6] During the antebellum period, state law had permitted county Orphans Courts to bind out children of free blacks who were destitute or public wards. After emancipation, the Somerset County Orphans Court and other Eastern Shore courts used this authority to bind out blacks under age twenty-one to local farmers. White leaders in the county rationalized the apprenticeship system for blacks on the grounds that the unskilled and illiterate freedmen were both a public charge and a burden to the taxpayer. Apprenticeship, they argued, upheld local custom and gave the region a dependable labor supply, an important concern for former slave owners.[7]

During a trip to Easton in November 1864, Samuel A. Harrison, a Talbot native, remarked that local planters were wasting no time placing blacks under apprenticeship. The Orphans Court of Talbot County was crowded with "a large number of our citizens," he wrote. "And I understand that the negro children were generally, indeed universally, bound to their former masters." Further, by binding out the children, the planters could generally count on the fact that the black parents of the apprentices would be unwilling to desert their children and would work in the local community for one of the former masters.[8]

An examination of the Orphans Court apprenticeships in the Maryland Hall of Records reveals that between 1864 and 1874 over 536 blacks were bound out in Somerset County. Many blacks fled the county to avoid being coerced into involuntary servitude. On the Eastern Shore blacks protested to the United States Army and the Freedmen's Bureau that the county governments were attempting to revive slavery. While the Freedmen's Bureau was too preoccupied with the enormous problems of postwar adjustment throughout the South to give the Eastern Shore much supervision, it did intervene in behalf of William Tilghman after he appealed to General O. O. Howard to rescue his son from an unscrupulous white.[9] Similar cases were on the Freedmen's Bureau Complaint Docket for Queen Anne's, Kent, and Cecil counties. At the height in 1867, about 3,281 black children were apprenticed in the state. Furthermore, adult freedmen found themselves assigned by law in Kent, Dorchester, Queen Anne's, and Talbot counties to provide four days unpaid work per year on the county roads. Forced labor was a carryover from slavery and was used to harass and control the freedmen.[10]

Eastern Shore blacks feared the justices of the peace as these men could apprehend "rogues," "vagrants," and other "idle and dissolute persons" who had no visible means of support and bind them out at hard labor for three months. Similarly, black convicts could be leased out at hard labor to local planters. Throughout Maryland in the postwar period about 6,000 blacks were bound out as convicts.[11]

As in most areas of the postbellum South, on the Eastern Shore freedmen responded to racial and economic oppression by turning to the church. In the critical years after emancipation, the black churches served as important social and political centers for the advancement of the race. The most heartening development for blacks on the Eastern Shore at this time was the founding of the Delaware Conference for Colored Methodists in 1864. Except for the episcopacy itself, blacks dominated the ecclesiastical management of the organization and the conference proved to be a fertile training ground for black ministers and lay leaders on the Eastern Shore. By 1886 there were 15,334 blacks in the conference and blacks owned church property worth $250,000. In Somerset County, for example, blacks, by 1886, had succeeded in constructing a large Methodist church in Princess Anne, which became the nucleus for black political activity, and the Delaware Conference established Princess Anne Academy, a manual training school for blacks out of which grew the University of Maryland, Eastern Shore.[12]

*   *   *

Economic developments often transform the lives of individuals; and changes in the Eastern Shore agricultural economy in the postwar years profoundly influenced the lives of blacks. With the expansion of corn and wheat production on the American Great Plains, Eastern Shore grain farmers could not compete on the national market. Instead, they turned to orchard products; and by 1868 the *Maryland Farmer* reported that the Eastern Shore was well on its way to being the "fruit garden of America."[13]

The emergence of the orchard industry on the Eastern Shore between 1865 and 1880 was widely reported in Eastern newspapers. Visitors like Charles Hopper reported that Queen Anne's County "was practically covered with peach orchards . . . ." Local fruit canneries hummed with activity. "Such music I have never heard as made by the great concourse of colored peach workers," Hopper also noted. It would be work in the orchard and seafood industries of the Eastern Shore that would provide postemancipation blacks with some measure of economic stability and give them a certain amount of freedom to work out their own destinies. Further, with the port of Baltimore burgeoning as an industrial metropolis by 1880, migration off the Shore was an alternative to working in agriculture.[14]

Old tidewater planting families saw the new economic order for blacks differently, however. As early as 1868 the Maryland Superintendent of Labor and Agriculture told the legislature that "our African laborers have ceased to be reliable or profitable . . . ." The only alternative to the black labor force, he reported, was to extend "encouragement and aid to European immigration . . . ."[15] In truth, the black labor force was shrinking in the postemancipation years. Even with the franchise of the Fifteenth Amendment to the United States Constitution and the right to engage in politics, many blacks left the region. The phenomenon of blacks "voting with their feet" was not lost on the *Salisbury Advertiser*, which reported in 1873 that large numbers of Negroes were leaving the Eastern Shore counties to seek homes in Philadelphia.[16]

Given the stresses and strains of racial adjustment on the Eastern Shore in the postbellum period, blacks prevailed in a number of ways. The Republican Party, once a pariah faction on the Eastern Shore before the war because of its antislavery ideology, now made public overtures to Negro voters, and many black Republicans who became active in the party were given patronage appointments as customs inspectors, clerks in the post offices, and justices of the peace. Many local blacks held good jobs in the flourishing rail and steamboat businesses of the Chesapeake as well. According to the census of 1880, a large class of black artisans worked in the numerous shipyards of Dorchester, Talbot, Somerset, and Wicomico counties.[17]

During the period from 1890 to 1917, however, race relations began to deteriorate on the Eastern Shore. Large numbers of black immigrants from other states in the deep South came to the Eastern Shore in response to advertisements published by cannery owners and farmers. Although these blacks came into the Chesapeake region because of a general cheap labor shortage that prevailed, xenophobic whites tended to treat them as a potentially dangerous class. Local blacks were quickly placed in the same category. Also, the 1890s were years of great economic uncertainty for Eastern Shore farmers. The shock waves of the nationwide panic of 1893 reverberated throughout Maryland's Eastern Shore and a poor corn crop the following year hurt many farmers. And when local agriculture was depressed, farmers vented their anger on blacks. Also, despite having their freedom most blacks were unable to gain ownership of land. For all the tidewater counties on both sides of Chesapeake Bay, only 1,078 blacks are listed by the 1870 census as owning land. The average value of land holdings for this group was around $350. Most blacks were trapped in a white-dominated subsistence wage system. As late as 1880 in Kent County, for example, the census schedule listed only fifty-one black farmers and only thirty-four of them owned their own land. Kent County at that time had 7,205 black citizens.[18]

In state politics, the problems of urbanization and industrial growth commanded the energies of legislators, and agricultural regions like the Eastern Shore were left to their own devices. As state Republicans equated the political control of Baltimore with the survival of the party, they de-emphasized their support of blacks in the rural counties. The Republican Party's change of emphasis was keenly felt in Somerset County and a short sketch of local politics can serve as a microcosm of the emerging racism on the Eastern Shore and the state at this time. From 1870 to 1885 blacks composed the strongest voting bloc in the local Republican organization. Blacks consistently voted for Abraham Lincoln Dryden, a prominent white Republican, and sent him to the state legislature for several terms. The Dryden family commanded a strong black and white coalition of Republicans in the county, and Dryden's father, Littleton Dryden, served twelve years as deputy United States marshall and United States commissioner for the Eastern Shore. While in power the Drydens resisted attempts to disenfranchise blacks and made sure that blacks got patronage appointments in the Baltimore Customs House. Supporting the Drydens was a group of outspoken Princess Anne blacks led by Henry Ballard, Isaac Cottman, and George Pollit. These local farmers were among the first blacks to vote in the county after the passage of the Fifteenth Amendment. In 1894 Lincoln Dryden ran for Congress against Joshua Miles, a conservative Democrat, and was defeated. The evidence suggests that Dryden's defeat resulted from a schism within the local Republican Party. Many white Republicans disliked working with blacks and looked for leadership from men like Edward F. Duer. At the Civil War's end, Duer had been active as justice of the peace apprenticing blacks, and now, eager to advance his own fortunes, Duer launched a "whites only" movement and sought to have his party reflect the new interests of the state Republican organization.[19]

Somerset blacks were angered by the Republican de-emphasis of civil rights and switched their allegiance to the Democrats. In 1885 the Democratic Party soundly defeated the Republicans in county elections and the *Salisbury Advertiser* reported that the victory was due to "the great inroads which the Democrats made on the colored vote." Blacks, however, were uncomfortable in the party of the old slaveocracy and, in the 1890s, formed their own splinter organization, "the Colored Independent Republicans."[20]

The 1890s also witnessed a resurgence of racial hysteria on the Eastern Shore. The source of this hysteria was grounded in the large number of tramps and hoboes in the region at this time. Although many of these tramps were white and occasionally worked in the oyster packinghouses, most whites thought of this tramp population as a black menace. As in most cases of social hysteria, the threat of blacks was more imagined than real. Cases of violence involving blacks, however, were widely covered in Eastern Shore newspapers. In June 1894, for example, Edward Carver, a white constable, was murdered in a country store in Westover, Maryland, by a gang of blacks from Virginia who had been picking strawberries for area planters. Both Carver and the black farm workers had been drinking heavily and a fistfight ensued. During the brawl, Carver was fatally slashed with a razor. A posse from Princess Anne soon rounded up ten of the blacks and interned them in the Somerset County jail. On the evening of June 9, an angry mob of whites overpowered the jailer and grabbed Isaac Kemp, the reputed leader of the gang. Thrown out of jail, Kemp faced an impromptu firing squad and died in a hail of bullets.

Two black lynchings also took place in Somerset during these years, and both followed a similar pattern. A black was accused either of assaulting a white man or attempting to rape a white woman. In 1897 William Andrew was lynched in Princess Anne after reportedly attacking Mrs. Benjamin T. Kelly; and James Reed, accused of murdering a white policeman, was lynched in Crisfield in 1907.[21]

By 1904 a new kind of racially repressive system had been installed on the Eastern Shore. In response to changing economic conditions and the growing popularity of political and scientific racism articulated in Southern newspapers and in the state legislatures of the old slaveholding states, Maryland blacks were forced to confront a movement to disfranchise them and take away what few rights they had. In addition to the growing respectability of white violence as a means of race control on the Shore, blacks were forced to use "Jim Crow" facilities on steamboats and passenger trains. In hotels and other facilities that had never been formally segregated, the new spirit of "separate but equal" prevailed. Unfortunately for Eastern Shore blacks, separate was never equal. Thus it is hardly surprising that after the turn of the century, the Eastern Shore lost over twenty percent of its black adult male and female population. Many left messages with their family that simply said, "Gone To Chester." The great shipyards in Chester, Pennsylvania, had a voracious appetite for the Eastern Shore's leaven of black workers. Even though disfranchisement failed in the state, most blacks never returned, preferring employment and the impersonality of urban life to the social hell of Maryland's Eastern Shore.

*   *   *

From the turn of the century until the Great Crash of 1929, blacks on the Eastern Shore were influenced primarily by the cycle of economic life in the tomato and fruit canneries and the seafood packinghouses of Crisfield, Cambridge, Oxford, and Denton. Even before the Great Depression of the 1930s, Maryland's Eastern Shore was one of the most rural and impoverished regions of the state. The Chesapeake Bay and primitive highways isolated the Eastern Shore from Annapolis and metropolitan centers, and few on the Shore at this time spoke out against violence directed at blacks. Conservative in politics and provincial in outlook, the white population of the Eastern Shore was proud of the region's plantation heritage and defended violence as a necessary means of "keeping niggers in their place."

With the onset of the Depression, struggling blacks and whites competed for jobs on truck farms, in canneries and sawmills, and by 1933 the economic situation for blacks and poor whites generally had become desperate. Wages for blacks in local sawmills fell to twenty-five cents a day and there was strong prejudice against giving blacks relief of any kind. Those few blacks who received flour from the local Red Cross had to perform domestic service in white families to pay for it. The widespread unemployment of both whites and blacks on the

Black watermen tonging oysters on the Wicomico River in 1938. Courtesy of the Library of Congress.

Eastern Shore caused great concern and a Baltimore relief worker who visited the region worried that "we have . . . restless men that have got to be put to work—soon!"[22]

The Depression also had a devastating impact on the Eastern Shore's small class of struggling black teachers in the segregated public school systems. In Maryland during the 1930s white janitors received higher salaries than most black school teachers who were college graduates and certified professionals. And throughout the Depression the state maintained different salary scales for white and black teachers. A white teacher on the Eastern Shore in the 1930s annually earned an average of about $900 compared to the black teacher average of $423. This black salary, poor as it was, however, was a king's ransom compared to what few economic alternatives prevailed on the Shore for black professionals at this time. Black school teachers on the Shore were an anomaly. Most were educated at the normal institute of Princess Anne Academy in Somerset County and were expected to maintain their credentials despite the fact that they were kept out of white institutions of higher learning and libraries. Given the economic and social pressures generated by the Depression, these professionals were powerless to speak out against the oppressiveness of life in the region at that time. Black teachers on the Shore in the 1930s functioned with the odds stacked against them and it is not surprising that few were able to achieve leadership roles in these tidewater communities.[23]

During hard times on the Eastern Shore, the Negro was usually made the scapegoat for the region's economic problems. Vera Fulton, a visitor to the Eastern Shore during the 1930s, summed up the matter bluntly when she wrote that during periods of prolonged unemployment there was no issue in these counties but "racial hatred." When bread is scarce, she claimed, "lynchings provide highly satisfactory circuses."[24] Also, the historic isolation of the Eastern Shore from the rest of the state gave the region a belated frontier environment where men often took the law into their own hands. On the Eastern Shore and in the South generally, it was believed that, unless a Negro was lynched now and then, white women living on solitary farms would be in danger. Central to southern racial beliefs at this time was the assumption that whites had unlimited rights to persecute and occasionally murder black criminals. Also, for the most part, lynchings provided people an emotional escape from the economically dreary and unilluminating life of isolated rural communities. The one baffling aspect of southern lynchings, wrote Arthur F. Raper in his classic study, *The Tragedy Of Lynching*, was that the mob was seldom content with the death of the victim. The mobsters often tortured, mutilated, and burned their victims. "One is forced to the conclusion," Raper asserted, "that their deeper motivation is not just for the punishment of the accused as for an opportunity to participate in protracted brutalities."[25]

In December 1931, the alleged murder of Daniel J. Elliott, a white lumber merchant in the city of Salisbury in Wicomico County by Matt Williams, a black former employee, raised a storm of indignation on the Eastern Shore. Although Williams was speedily apprehended by the local police and hospitalized for "self-inflicted wounds," local demagogues screamed for vengeance. Shortly thereafter, a mob dragged Williams from his hospital bed and lynched him. His body was subsequently carried to Salisbury's black neighborhood and burned.[26]

The Williams lynching prompted a national protest as civil liberties groups, civil rights organizations, and churchmen publicized the murder and demanded the apprehension of Williams's killers. Broadus Mitchell, a professor of political economy at Johns Hopkins University who investigated the lynching for the American Federation of Churches, urged federal intervention as the only means of protecting the civil liberties of blacks on the Eastern Shore. H. L. Mencken, in his column in *The* [Baltimore] *Sun*, attacked the Eastern Shore as a depraved civilization "wherein there are no competent police, little save a simian self-seeking in public office, no apparent intelligence on the bench, and no courage and decency in the local press." Characterizing the Eastern Shore as an "Alsatia of Morons," the combative journalist argued that Williams's lynching was the result of social degeneration that had allowed "ninth rate" men to come to power.[27]

The Eastern Shore wasted little time retaliating against Mencken and *The Sun*. In one day Salisbury merchants cancelled $150,000 worth of business from Baltimore firms that advertised in that newspaper. Farmers tore up their *Sun* subscriptions and drivers of *Sun* news trucks were molested. Salisbury spent so much time denouncing Mencken that the local courts delayed bringing the accused lynchers to trial. In the end, a local grand jury found no one guilty of Williams's murder.[28]

A similar crime occurred that year in neighboring Worcester County. Green Davis, a white truck gardener with a small farm near Ocean City, his wife, and children were murdered in their sleep; and Euel Lee, a Negro who was known to have quarreled with Davis over wages, was arrested and charged with the crime. Lee was a sixty-year-old wino with a long arrest record. Intimidated by the police, Lee promptly confessed that "the Devil and Whiskey" made him do it. After being jailed in Snow Hill, Lee was visited by Bernard Ades, a Baltimore attorney representing the International Labor Defense, a Socialist organization currently waging an antilynching and black civil rights campaign in the South. Lee quickly changed his plea to innocent and Ades requested a change of venue to Towson on the western shore. Upon leaving the jail, Ades and his associates were attacked by an angry crowd and his car was wrecked. No one in Snow Hill would repair his car and Ades was warned not to return to the Eastern Shore.

The Euel Lee case dragged on for two years because Bernard Ades, a talented and courageous lawyer, was able to capitalize upon gross errors made by Maryland judges and tied the case up in complicated litigation. Also, with the case moved to the Baltimore metropolitan area, the Euel Lee affair became a cause celèbre for the Socialist Party of Maryland, the National Association for the Advancement of Colored People (NAACP), and the Urban League. Convinced of his innocence, these organizations battled for Lee all the way to the United States Supreme Court.

The court denied Lee's appeal and Governor Albert Ritchie ordered the lower court's verdict of death by hanging to be administered. A last-ditch effort to obtain a state pardon for Lee was refused by the governor. In signing Lee's death sentence, Governor Ritchie wrote, "I consider the propaganda that he is innocent to be without the slightest basis in fact." Ades and Henry Williams, a black attorney for the Communist Party, which was also defending Lee, charged a frame-up; rallies and demonstrations in support of the condemned man were staged all over Baltimore.

The Eastern Shore was outraged by the protracted defense of the Negro criminal by "Communist Jew lawyers." By allowing Euel Lee to be removed to Baltimore, the Eastern

Shore had become the object of ridicule and the punishment of the murderer had been delayed for two years. As men gathered in country stores in the evening across the Eastern Shore, they vowed that there would be no more Euel Lee cases. The next time they would take matters into their own hands. And it was during the dramatic conclusion of the Euel Lee case that the Armwood lynching occurred in Princess Anne.

In late September 1933, John Richardson, a white Somerset County farmer, and George Armwood, a twenty-eight-year-old black in his brother's employ, schemed to rob Mrs. Mary Denston. The seventy-two-year-old white woman was reported to carry large sums of money on her person and often walked alone on the dirt road that connected her house with her daughter's farm. The robbery was to be a simple affair. Armwood would lurk in the woods until Mrs. Denston passed; then he would jump out, grab Mrs. Denston, and steal the money. To avoid identification, Armwood was to wear a large woolen cap pulled down over his eyes. After the robbery, Armwood and Richardson would divide the money. As Armwood was slow-witted, Richardson rehearsed the plan at some length with him.

On October 16 at 11:00 A.M., Armwood attacked Mrs. Denston as she passed a clump of trees near her home. The old woman proved to be more spry than Armwood anticipated and during the scuffle the Negro succeeded only in tearing off her dress to get at the money in her bodice before he panicked and fled into the woods. A short time later the half-naked and terrified woman was discovered by a state roads employee who gave her some clothing and notified the sheriff. After calming down, Mrs. Denston identified her attacker, claiming that she would recognize Armwood's face "among a thousand." Armwood's cap, which was found at the scene of the crime, corroborated her testimony. Rumors of the Denston "rape" spread throughout the county and hysterical women gave currency to the wild tale that Armwood had chewed off both of Mrs. Denston's breasts.[29]

County Sheriff Luther Dougherty and Lieutenant Ruxton Ridgely of the state police quickly organized an armed posse of 2,000 men and combed Somerset and Worcester counties for the fugitive. The highway between Princess Anne and Salisbury was also jammed with posse men in cars hunting Armwood. "Armed men," reported the Baltimore *Sun*, "stood

about stores and filling stations and congregated about policemen whenever they stopped." Armwood, meanwhile, had fled
to the Richardson farm and begged John Richardson and his
brother to save him. A small boy, however, spotted Armwood
near Red Hill, Virginia, just across Maryland's border with
Virginia's Eastern Shore, and quickly alerted the police. Within
an hour Deputy Sheriff Norman Dryden of Somerset County
drove up to the farm with two armed men and arrested the
terrified Negro.[30]

Fearing mob violence in Princess Anne, Dryden and his
men took Armwood to jail in Salisbury by way of Snow Hill. At
Salisbury, Armwood was turned over to the state police and
placed under a heavy guard. The men and their prisoner had
been in the jail scarcely three minutes before an angry crowd
gathered outside. City authorities feared that they would be
unable to protect the Negro and urged the state police to take
Armwood out of Salisbury. As the mob outside the jail grew
increasingly unruly, Captain Edwin Johnson of the state police
called Governor Ritchie's office and asked for Armwood's removal to Baltimore. Without waiting for clearance from Ritchie,
the police rushed their prisoner to Elkton in distant Cecil
County. Finally Ritchie telephoned Johnson and the police
transferred Armwood from Elkton to the Baltimore City jail.[31]

In Princess Anne, local law enforcement officials were
under considerable pressure to guarantee that the Armwood
case would not follow the pattern of the Euel Lee trial. Both
State's Attorney John B. Robins and Judge Robert F. Duer of
the First Circuit Court demanded that Armwood be returned
to Somerset County and at 10:15 P.M. on October 17, Sheriff
Luther Dougherty removed Armwood from the Baltimore jail.
Later that night a caravan of five police cars escorted the
chained prisoner back to Princess Anne. While in Baltimore,
Armwood had confessed to the assault and was photographed
and fingerprinted. His white accomplice, John Richardson,
was charged with being an accessory to the fact and remained
in the Baltimore jail. The caravan arrived in Princess Anne with
its weary prisoner at 3:30 A.M. With Armwood secure in the
Somerset County jail, State's Attorney Robins told newspaper
reporters that his chief wish was "to see justice done as soon
as possible." The people of the county were satisfied and would
remain satisfied, Robins claimed, "if there was no undue delay
in the trial of Armwood." On the afternoon of October 18,

Governor Ritchie telephoned Princess Anne and both Robins and Judge Duer assured him that Armwood would be safe in the local jail. Robins predicted trouble only if state police tried to take him from the county.[32]

Visitors, curiosity seekers, and reporters from Baltimore newspapers thronged Princess Anne. By four o'clock in the afternoon small groups of men stood on street corners and talked excitedly of the rumor that five hundred Shoremen from Accomack County, Virginia, were preparing to drive to Princess Anne and lynch Armwood. At first, Captain Johnson later testified, the crowd that assembled in front of the jail appeared to be "a friendly gathering." By 7:30 P.M., however, the mood had turned ugly as men began yelling, "Let's lynch that nigger!" As darkness fell, Captain Johnson ordered three police cars in position to focus headlights on the crowd. At 7:45 P.M. men began throwing stones at the police and as the crowd advanced, the police lobbed six canisters of tear gas into the mob and retreated to the front door of the jail. Fearful that the state police would be unable to control the situation, Captain Johnson requested assistance from the local American Legion unit. The legionnaires, however, informed the police that the laws of their organization forbade their protecting Negroes during riots.[33]

At eight o'clock Judge Duer, accompanied by his friend, George W. Jarmon, made an impassioned appeal to the mob to let the Negro remain in jail and promised that the grand jury would be convened and that the trial would begin promptly. In his appeal Judge Duer said, "I know nearly all of you." Duer's speech, though, annoyed several men in the crowd who yelled out, "What about Euel Lee? We ain't gonna have no Euel Lee in Somerset County!" Shouted another: "Yeah! and Bernard Ades will defend him. To Hell with Ades!" After speaking at length to several members of the crowd, Duer cautioned the men, "Remember, I place you upon your honor." Replied the men, "All right, Judge, go home, we'll attend to the matter." After Duer and George Jarmon left the jail to attend a dinner party, a *Sun* reporter rushed to telephone Governor Ritchie that the crowd in Princess Anne had increased to about 2,000 and was growing more violent. At 8:30 P.M someone set off the town fire alarm which further excited the mob.[34]

Soon the crowd began to hurl "an avalanche of bricks and stones" at the police. Captain Johnson was struck in the face by a brick and knocked unconscious. The crowd cursed the state police and warned them that they had guns, and, if the policemen started shooting, they would shoot back. "That crowd at Princess Anne was sober," a witness reported. "They weren't farmhands in overalls." At nine o'clock a mobsman yelled, "Come on, let's get him," and the crowd rushed the jail. Five policemen were beaten to the ground and others were swept aside by the fury of the townsmen who used a heavy oak battering ram to smash three doors and reach the cell of the terrified prisoner. Throughout the intense struggle in front of the jail, the police did not fire one shot in an attempt to disperse the mob. "It was futile for us to use our arms," Captain Johnson later testified. "We were overwhelmingly outnumbered and we were overpowered." After the jail was forced, Sheriff Dougherty rushed up to the second floor and pleaded with the mob not to take Armwood from his jail. Norman Dryden, the frightened jail warden, turned his keys over to the mob leaders. "There wasn't anything else I could do," he said. "I was just too scared that they were going to get the wrong man."[35]

Armwood put up a desperate resistance in his cell and was only semiconscious when the mob carried him out of the jail. The mob carried Armwood a short distance before it stopped to figure out what to do with him. One mobsman took a knife and severed an ear from Armwood's head while several others stabbed him in the neck and face. As the mob howled and cheered, a rope was placed around Armwood's neck and twenty men dragged him to death down the gravel street to the main business section. The mob planned to hang the Negro on the courthouse lawn, but someone suggested Judge Duer's home and the body was dragged the full length of Main Street to the Duer residence. As there was no suitable tree in Duer's yard, the crowd decided on a tree in front of a neighbor's house. The mob quickly jerked up the body of George Armwood and left it hanging for ten minutes. "Here's what we do on the Eastern Shore," the mob cried. The dead black was then cut down and the mob dragged Armwood's body to the front of the courthouse where it was stripped naked, doused with gasoline, and set afire while the mob howled excitedly.

By 11:30 P.M the streets of Princess Anne were deserted. The shades were drawn at Judge Duer's residence and no one answered the bell. Both Sheriff Dougherty and State's Attorney Robins had fled the town to avoid newspaper reporters. Around midnight the town garbage truck hauled

Armwood's charred body to a nearby lumberyard where it was left to be claimed by an undertaker.[36] When the *Sun* reporter left Princess Anne the next day, he wrote that everything was "business as usual. There wasn't anything crestfallen about the people you saw on the street, you'd think that nothing had happened at all."[37]

The Armwood lynching intensified the storm of national protest over lynchings in the South at this time. (In 1933 the year of Armwood's murder, there were twenty-one lynchings in the United States.) Former President Herbert Hoover issued a public denunciation of lynchings in the South and urged Congress to use its authority to curb racial violence. In New York City, Dr. Samuel Calvert, general secretary of the Federal Council of Churches of Christ, sent a letter to every major newspaper in the country in which he stated, "I have no hesitation in saying my feeling of utter horror at the atrocious lynching in Princess Anne expresses the [opinion of the] Council of Churches as a whole." Roger Baldwin, the national president of the American Civil Liberties Union, offered a $1,000 reward for evidence leading to the arrest of any member of the lynch mob. Baldwin also urged the intervention of the federal Department of Justice in the case.[38] In New York, Washington, and Baltimore, protesting citizens' groups demanded the criminal prosecution of Duer and Robins. And the Socialist Party of Maryland adopted a resolution calling for the impeachment of Governor Ritchie and the trial of Robins and Duer for second-degree manslaughter.

The *Sun* was also exceptionally vigorous in its denunciation of the lynching, the Eastern Shore, and Governor Ritchie. Ritchie, claimed the *Sun*, took too many chances with Armwood and at a critical moment the state police lost their nerve. Writing in his *Sun* column, H. L. Mencken concluded that it was hopeless to expect any positive changes on the Eastern Shore. The good people with talent and brains had left and the "riffraff" stayed behind. Antilynching bills, Mencken predicted, would never pass the state legislature. "The only way to clean out the area is to reduce its representation in the legislature and let Baltimore take the lead," he wrote.[39] While protest over Armwood's death raged in Baltimore, Princess Anne prepared to celebrate Founders' Day. Among the floats being prepared for the local parade was "a pageant depicting seventy years of Negro progress on the Delmarva Peninsula."[40]

Although blacks resident in the jail at the time of the lynching had seen Armwood's killers, they refused to testify. Most said that they were too frightened at the time to recognize anyone. Also, both Sheriff Dougherty and Deputy Dryden swore that they did not recognize anyone even though the state troopers in sworn affidavits identified Irving Adkins, William Thompson, and Pete "Big Boy" Smith of Princess Anne; William P. Hearn and Shelburn Lester of Salisbury; and Jack "Walloper" Sterling of Crisfield as leaders of the lynch mob. Despite evidence supplied by the attorney general of Maryland, the Somerset County Grand Jury refused to indict the men and State's Attorney Robins informed Attorney General Preston Lane that he would not arrest the accused lynchers.

Frustrated by Somerset's intransigence, Governor Ritchie called out the state militia and had the mob leaders arrested and taken to the armory in Salisbury in the early hours of November 28. "The state government," Ritchie declared, "cannot stand by and permit a State's Attorney to decline to arrest people who are reliably charged with crime, and, as long as neither he nor the judge would act, it became my duty to . . . cause the arrests to be made."[41]

When word got out that the mobsmen were being held in Salisbury, a large crowd surrounded the armory. To get the prisoners to awaiting army trucks, the militia had to attack the crowd with tear gas and fixed bayonets. As the convoy with its prisoners roared away, the crowd showered the trucks with bottles and bricks. Trucks carrying Baltimore newspapers were seized by angry townsmen and their contents flung into the Wicomico River.

Hard on the heels of the state militia came Sheriff Luther Dougherty of Somerset County with a writ of habeas corpus issued by Judge Duer that demanded the return of the prisoners from the Baltimore City jail to Princess Anne. Neither the governor nor the attorney general was informed of Judge Duer's action, and the four men were whisked back to the Eastern Shore before the state had time to organize its case. Governor Ritchie was furious and in a news conference accused Judge Duer of using a "technicality" to release the men before the state could present its evidence.

On November 29 the accused lynchers were brought before Judge John R. Pattison in Princess Anne. When the judge found that State's Attorney Robins had filed no charges against the men, he dismissed the case. A few days later the grand jury failed to return an indictment against the accused lynchers and the Armwood case was closed by county authorities.

For Attorney General Preston Lane and Governor Ritchie, the case had ended in frustration and disappointment. Lane, by going to Salisbury with the militia to arrest the lynchers, had risked his life and his career to have Armwood's killers brought to trial. Fully aware of the political and racial repercussions of the case, Governor Ritchie was steadfastly determined to suppress mob violence and lynching in Maryland. In the final analysis, there was no way short of declaring martial law in the First Judicial Circuit of the Eastern Shore and suspending civil government that Ritchie could have overridden county officials. State's Attorney Robins frustrated the state's case against the lynchers at every turn with delays, legal casuistry, and sentimental appeals to county rights.

Although the discharge of the mobsmen helped to cool the inflamed feelings of farmers and townsmen of the Eastern Shore, there was great resentment against Governor Ritchie. Throughout the Shore, residents placed large white initials, N.R.A.! on their cars and trucks—"Never Ritchie Again!" Shore legislators also talked of creating a new state in the Union, "Delmarva" out of the Eastern Shore of Delaware, Maryland, and Virginia.[42] In 1934 Ritchie was soundly defeated in the state gubernatorial election. While it is difficult to pinpoint the exact reasons for his defeat, the Armwood case was certainly a contributing factor in his loss of votes on the Eastern Shore.

With the onset of World War II in 1941, most Eastern Shoremen turned their back on the region's troubled racial past, preferring to concentrate on defending American democracy overseas. The hate and bitterness that to a great extent had characterized race relations in the region since Emancipation, however, remained a festering wound that would trouble the Eastern Shore when a new postwar generation sought to resolve the problems of racial segregation and prejudice in the 1960s.

9

The Struggle for Equality

If America don't come around, we going to burn it down, Brother.

—H. Rap Brown

T he Jim Crow racism that had prevailed in the region for decades weakened considerably after World War II as America sought to demonstrate to the world that it was a citadel of democracy and egalitarian sentiment. In 1954, the Supreme Court in *Brown* v. *Board of Education of Topeka* struck down racially segregated schools; and state lawmakers in Annapolis sought to quicken the pace of school desegregation and racial accommodation in Maryland.

In the 1960s blacks in the South made a social revolution in their fight against segregation. The fruit that this revolution bore on the Eastern Shore was not really what many blacks expected, however. On the Eastern Shore marches gave way to frustration; and the white moderates stood silently on the sidelines, frustrating the hopes of blacks on the Shore for biracial coalitions to end segregation. Despite the decision of the Supreme Court in 1954, all nine counties of the Eastern Shore retained racially segregated school systems. It would not be until 1968 that the last impediments of racial segregation would be removed from education on the shore. In 1960 Talbot took the lead in integrating its elementary schools, but Caroline, Dorchester, Kent, Queen Anne's, Somerset, Wicomico, and Worcester kept their schools segregated.[1]

Early in June 1963, racial discontent, which had been seething and boiling for nearly two years on the Eastern Shore, erupted in Cambridge. In retrospect it is strange that Cambridge became the crucible of racial violence on the Eastern Shore in the 1960s. In terms of segregation, Cambridge was no different from dozens of other southern towns in the tidewater. Although the town suffered from a black unemployment rate of 27 percent, nine new factories had relocated in Cambridge and hired integrated work forces. Also, blacks sat on the town council and on the county Board of Education. Yet Cambridge was very much a rural backwater where whites expected blacks to know their place. Race Street, a main thoroughfare of the town, divided the white district from the black community, creating in effect two social universes with one separate and unequal. Blacks were frequently taunted by whites and risked a beating or worse if they tried to enter white bars or restaurants.

Perhaps the answer to the question of the Cambridge riots lay in the gaunt, tall frame of a feisty black woman named Gloria Richardson. A product of the St. Clair family in Cambridge and member of the local black elite, Richardson had had a sheltered childhood and had gone on to college at Howard University. Her grandfather had served on the city council and her father was a wealthy funeral director. When Richardson returned to Cambridge after a failed marriage, she found it impossible to get a teaching job in the county school system. Finally after working a short time in a factory, she was fired for "lack of manual dexterity." Meanwhile Richardson assumed leadership of a large number of alienated Cambridge blacks who were eager to challenge the city of Cambridge in the name of racial justice.[2]

Throughout the South generally, the racial protests of the spring and summer of 1963 exceeded in intensity anything that preceded them. In 1963, according to the Southern Regional Council, there were 930 public protest demonstrations in 115 cities in 11 states; 10 deaths; and 35 bombings. That summer when racial integration appeared to be slowly taking hold in the South and with segregation on the defensive in the courts and in the legislatures, the mood of many southern blacks changed from accommodation to a violent militancy that surprised even their leaders. It was not that change was not taking place. Rather, it was that improvement in the status of blacks in the South was not taking place fast enough.

159

For Gloria Richardson and her Cambridge Nonviolent Action Committee the issue was decades of black class injury on the Eastern Shore. Richardson and her followers demanded the integration of all restaurants and motels in the city, the creation of jobs for blacks in state and private agencies, and large-scale construction of low-income housing for blacks. In June 1963 black protesters clashed violently with rowdy whites who were bent on trouble. Soon the corner of Pine and Washington streets became a battleground that resounded to the noise of hurled bricks, whizzing bottles, and occasional gunfire. The situation deteriorated so rapidly on the streets of Cambridge that city authorities asked Governor Millard Tawes to send in the National Guard to restore order. Justice Department agents were dispatched by Attorney General Robert Kennedy to the scene; President John F. Kennedy referred to the riot in Cambridge in a television address that stressed conciliation and racial tolerance. There was to be little racial tolerance on either side during that hot summer in Cambridge, however.[3]

Throughout the month of June 1963, jeeps bearing armed soldiers patrolled the streets of Cambridge. At night firebombs and stones were hurled and the crack of gunfire resounded in the Negro Second Ward. Defying police orders, Gloria Richardson linked arms with Reverend Enez Grubb and Dwight Cromwell and led processions of black protestors down Pine Street to the steps of the Dorchester County Courthouse to hold prayer vigils and sing "We Shall Overcome." Within the black community Richardson was known as "Glorious Gloria," the woman who stood her ground before the police and the National Guard in an effort to open the door for black equality.

The National Guardsmen were as bewildered as anyone else by the violence and felt especially vulnerable because they had no ammunition for their weapons, only bayonets and tear gas.

When the violence ebbed, Governor Tawes summoned Cambridge Mayor Calvin Mowbray, Gloria Richardson, Reginald Robinson, a twenty-two-year-old organizer for the Student Non-Violent Coordinating Committee (SNCC), and Philip Savage and Stanley Branche of the NAACP to his office in Annapolis to work out a settlement. As a native Eastern Shoreman and one who had supported moderate plans of racial accommodation in the state, Governor Tawes was extremely embarrassed by the Cambridge riot and vowed to work out a biracial plan even if it took round-the-clock meetings. The black leaders outlined their demands for better jobs, housing, education, and equal accommodations legislation. Prodded by the governor, the town's establishment agreed to integrate the last four grades of high school, hire a black in the state employment office, pass a public accommodations law, and name a biracial commission to work on Cambridge's other racial problems. In return, blacks were to observe a year's moratorium on demonstrations. As one local official put it to the national media, "We surrendered." NAACP officials were so pleased with the outcome that they recalled Branche and Savage back to the national office.

After the riot, school integration continued and blacks were hired in state offices and businesses. On July 8, 1963, the NAACP field representatives left town, believing their work done. The National Guard was also removed. Within an hour of the guard's departure, however, Gloria Richardson led a demonstration down Race Street to Dizzyland, a restaurant whose owner Robert Fehsenfeld was a well-known segregationist. Encouraged by a band of cheering whites Fehsenfeld broke a raw egg on the head of Eddie Dickerson, a white integrationist, and poured water on him. Black protestors and whites exchanged angry taunts and the incident reignited Cambridge's race war. Guns crackled through the night and six whites were wounded. Mobs roamed the streets looking for trouble. Fires were set and firemen refused to enter the second ward for fear of their personal safety. The two hundred-man state police force was soon overwhelmed by the violence, and by July 12 the guardsmen armed with rifles and tear gas were back in Cambridge. The militia promptly imposed a seven o'clock business closing on the town; liquor stores were shut and all streets were to be cleared by nine o'clock. In short, Cambridge was an American town under military occupation. Guardsmen manned an outpost on the Choptank River Bridge. All cars entering Cambridge from Talbot were searched. This time, when peace was finally restored, the National Guard remained in Cambridge.[4]

During the winter, the black revolt settled down and there was relative peace on the Eastern Shore until George Wallace, Alabama's fiery segregationist governor, flew to Maryland to file as a Democrat in Maryland's presidential primary in the spring of 1964. Although many Marylanders thought of Wallace as nothing more than an anti-Negro redneck, others were impressed by his reasoned appeals to law and his arguments against what he called the pernicious growth of federal power, especially as it was embodied in the civil rights bill, then pending in Congress. Wallace spoke to an overflow crowd at Glen Burnie and even got a polite reception at Johns Hopkins University. The trouble began when he announced he would address a white group in Cambridge, the symbol and principal battleground of the Negro revolt in Maryland. As the architect of the civil rights push in Cambridge, Gloria Richardson vowed that she would stage a counter-rally in Cambridge and invited radical black leaders from SNCC and the Nation of Islam. If Wallace was going to ignite white passions, Richardson would do likewise with the blacks.

The National Guard, which had been stationed in Cambridge since June 1963, was strengthened with additional units for the Wallace rally and the black rally, both of which were to be held on the same night, a week before the May 19, 1964, presidential primary. The blacks rallied and immediately began marching through Cambridge toward the Wallace meeting. At the edge of the town's black district, the marchers were confronted by the National Guard and told to turn back. The blacks sat down in the street and refused to move even after they were told Wallace had delivered his speech and was gone. In the Maryland primary held the following week, Wallace got an unusually large white vote on the Eastern Shore and elsewhere. Only a huge turnout of black voters in Baltimore kept Maryland from nominating Wallace at the Democratic National Convention.[5]

By May 25, 1964, the racial tension in Cambridge again went over the edge and troops were forced to disperse demonstrators with tear gas and bayonets. According to Edmund Mester, Governor Tawes's aide on racial negotiations, "There has been a great splintering among the Negro leadership. There is no one to deal with. The crowds are very difficult to control and white groups are becoming very ugly."

Disorder had reached the point in Cambridge where General Milton Reckord, commander of the militia, considered giving live ammunition to the troops. Black crowds attacked whites through the tear gas with bottles and rocks and National Guard officers were forced to use their pistols to fire over the heads of the blacks to disperse them. Although enlisted men had no ammunition, officers had loaded pistols to use if the situation got totally out of control.[6] Ultimately the guardsmen had to clear angry whites off Race Street in a shoulder-to-shoulder charge of fixed bayonets.

Throughout the controversy, Cambridge authorities were angry at what they called the indecision and lack of firmness on the part of General George M. Gelston and the National Guard in dealing with this serious racial disturbance. Likewise the authorities felt overwhelmed by the chorus of black demands for improvement in their lives in Cambridge. Blacks wanted recreational facilities, summer day camps, and immediate low-income housing. Blacks even wanted a city-maintained drag strip so that they could race their cars there instead of against one another on Pine and High streets. Although the town of Cambridge believed that it had bargained with the civil rights groups in good faith, many blacks thought the city was just stalling with words and smiles rather than concrete actions.[7] Meanwhile, State's Attorney C. Burnam Mace appealed to whites not to let themselves fall into the trap of becoming angered by the blacks. "The idea of these outside agitators is to inflame the whites," Mace said. Further, he pointed out that most of these blacks had little stake in the community.[8]

When the violence erupted in Cambridge again in the summer of 1964, Gloria Richardson went into seclusion. She did not even campaign for the voters' ratification of the public accommodations law that she had worked so hard for. Many blacks were angered by her aloofness insofar as Gloria Richardson had been the one person able to forge a successful coalition out of Cambridge's disparate black protest groups. Richardson subsequently left Dorchester to pursue her private career.

In October 1964, the Cambridge Racial Commission, chaired by Clarence Miles, a respected Queen Anne's county lawyer and native of Dorchester, issued a report that recommended withdrawal of the National Guard, more progress toward the integration of the public schools, and more public housing for blacks. According to Miles, "The lack of constant and gainful employment was one of the principal factors contributing to racial discord." Miles said, "It is wishful thinking to suggest that new industries or employers be attracted because the majority of the unemployed of both races are lacking in the requisite skills to meet the challenges and responsibilities of better job opportunities."[9] Dorchester County with its depressed economy held little prospect for the social and economic advancement of unskilled blacks *or* whites.

While many preferred to put violence and racial discord behind them, the Student Non-Violent Coordinating Committee continued to be a vehicle for black discontent in Cambridge. As the field representatives of SNCC saw it, black demands in Cambridge had not been met; therefore, the Student Non-Violent Co-ordinating Committee vowed that there would be more black militancy in the town. Race relations in Cambridge, to a very large extent, would be shaped and conditioned by SNCC; and local leadership of the civil rights movement would be co-opted by a fierce black revolutionary from Howard University named Hubert "Rap" Brown.

When the Student Non-Violent Coordinating Committee chose its national officers in 1967, H. Rap Brown was a most unlikely choice. SNCC prided itself on choosing officers who, the staff felt, would exercise restraint in public statements and emphasize the development of effective urban programs. H. Rap Brown and many of his SNCC colleagues, however, believed in carrying guns. Many SNCC workers, like Brown and Stokely Carmichael were eager to offer their support to violent blacks out of a desire to become spokesmen for a nationwide black rebellion over which they had little control. According to Clayborne Carson, a historian of the Student Non-Violent Coordinating Committee, "despite their awareness of the consequences of their rhetoric, SNCC militants refused to allow the threat of external attacks to prevent them from carrying out their self-assigned role of preparing blacks for the impending social revolution."[10]

The most controversial incident involving H. Rap Brown occurred after he accepted an invitation from the Cambridge Action Federation, composed of members of the SNCC affiliate in Cambridge and black youngsters who were upset by a resurgence of the National States Rights Party and the Ku Klux Klan on the Eastern Shore. While black guerilla warfare flared in Detroit and other cities, Brown prepared a forty-minute speech that he would give in Cambridge on the night of July 24, 1967 to several hundred black residents. When H. Rap Brown arrived in Cambridge, the white power structure was

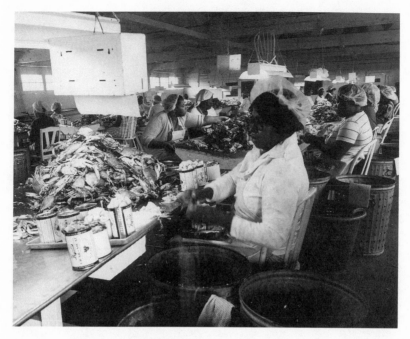

Crab pickers at a Crisfield packinghouse. Photograph by Orlando Wooten.

ready for him. The police chief, Brice G. Kinnamon, and State's Attorney William B. Yates equipped two black police officers with a tape recorder and sent them in to monitor Brown's speech. From that speech stemmed all of Brown's subsequent difficulties with the law.

In his speech to Cambridge blacks, H. Rap Brown stressed the basic themes of racial pride and racial assertiveness, but he went further than other SNCC organizers by saying that it was necessary for blacks to take up arms against white society. Said Brown: "If America don't come around, we going to burn it down, Brother. We are going to burn it down if we do not get our share of it." Brown added that blacks were facing genocide, lived in ghettoes, and were being drafted to fight an imperialist war in Vietnam. He also urged blacks to take over the white-owned stores in Cambridge. "You've got to own some of them stores. I don't care if you have to burn him down and run him out." Brown added that the only thing that the white man respected was money. "When you tear down his store you hit his religion."[11]

While no violence took place during Brown's speech, an hour later gunshots were traded between black residents and police. In his report on the rioting, Chief of Police Brice Kinnamon said that after his speech Brown led a mob armed with guns down Elm Street toward the business district, shooting as they advanced. "Our officers stopped them with gunfire after being fired upon. And we later understood that Brown was hit." [Actually Brown was ambushed by an unknown assailant.]

Later that night, several stores were set ablaze by black arsonists and a black elementary school was also burned. While shops and homes burned, several anxious blacks implored the firemen to come into the black section to quell the blaze. The firemen refused. They were under orders to protect the main business section of the town. As Police Chief Kinnamon later stated: "I placed human life above property and also felt that the fire equipment could be decoyed into the area while the arsonists attempted to burn and loot the business district."At the insistence of Attorney General Francis Burch, who was in Cambridge at that time, a solitary fire engine with the helmeted attorney general and several black people on board entered the strife-torn Second Ward to extinguish several fires.

By morning, seventeen buildings were smoldering ruins, and Governor Spiro Agnew had called out the National Guard.

This time there was no hesitation on the part of the fully armed four hundred guardsmen and their commander. It marked a sharp contrast from the racial disturbances of 1963 when guardsmen carried no ammunition and used tear gas only as a last resort.

Despite lack of evidence, the state charged Brown with arson and the FBI entered the case and arrested Brown in Washington. In the weeks that followed, H. Rap Brown's legal problems multiplied tenfold. He was charged with carrying a gun across state lines into New York and violating bond to attend a Black Panther rally in California. When he returned to New York, the court raised his bond to $100,000 and he spent a month in jail. Throughout Brown's legal travail, he was defended by the glamorous attorney and self-proclaimed legal expert on black revolutionaries, William Kunstler. Keeping the courts at bay and H. Rap Brown out of jail on bond, Kunstler sought a sympathetic portrayal of Brown in the media.

After several tense days Cambridge began to function with some degree of normality. Policeman Russell Wroten who had been blasted with a shotgun and seriously wounded while driving his squad car in the Second Ward was hailed as a local hero. And Senator Fred Malkus accused both the state police and the militia of not doing enough to forestall H. Rap Brown when they knew he was coming to Cambridge. Added Police Chief Kinnamon: "I am firm in my opinion that this eruption was a well-planned Communist attempt to overthrow the city government which amounts to treason. If these riots are not stopped, they will eventually lead to the destruction of our government."[12]

H. Rap Brown eventually went to prison but not for the Cambridge riots. (He was jailed for a 1971 attempted robbery of a New York tavern.) It took nearly six years to prosecute him as Brown spent a large part of that time underground as a fugitive. Finally he stood trial in Ellicott City, Maryland, in November 1973 and Dorchester County State's Attorney William B. Yates rose to say, "The state enters a *nolo pros* to all counts of the indictment."[13] Many people were surprised that a man who had caused so much damage and suffering in Cambridge should walk away on a *nolo pros* count. The indictment, however, was nearly seven years old and Yates and Cambridge authorities wished to spare their town further publicity.[14]

The Cambridge *Daily Banner* added a final postscript to the H. Rap Brown affair: "1967 was a watershed year in

Cambridge's recent history. Between 1963 and 1967 improvement in race relations came grudgingly. Since that time the going has been easier if only because the prospect of disaster is not a choice the city cares to make anymore."[15]

*   *   *

While violence flared in Cambridge, Somerset County experienced its own racial crisis. During the winter of 1964 Negro students from Maryland State College led by John Wilson demanded an end to segregated public facilities in the county. Black student demonstrations were met by white violence and in January-February 1964, the state police armed with dogs and fire hoses brought racial calm to Princess Anne. The state of Maryland, however, complied with the federal Civil Rights Act of 1964 by passing its own public accommodations law; and the restaurants and public facilities were racially integrated within a year. The desegregation of public schools took a little longer; and there was considerable apprehension among both black and white parents that there would be violence in the schools. Beginning with the senior high schools in 1968, Somerset's schools were integrated without incident. By 1972 all of the county's schools were integrated and blacks were employed at all levels in the system. Heavily dependent upon federal funds for its rural school system, Somerset chose the path of integration rather than risk the loss of federal monies and law suits from the Justice Department. Significantly, during this time, the town of Princess Anne resisted the attempts of segregationist fanatics to come to town and inflame racial feelings. When the American Nazi Party sought to stage a pro-white rally in Princess Anne, the town's biracial committee led by local lawyer, Alexander Jones, sued in the courts and prevented what surely would have been an explosive racial confrontation.

Looking back at the changes that have taken place in the Somerset school system and the community, Superintendent of Schools De Wayne Whittington notes a "profound change" in race relations. Whittington knows whereof he speaks because he is the county's first, and the Eastern Shore's only, black school superintendent. When he was selected for the position in 1988 after over thirty years service in the county schools, the choice hardly caused a ripple in Somerset County. Citizens were more concerned with taxes and school budgets than with the racial identity of a school leader.

Some arguments and problems can't be solved by recourse to constitutional doctrine and Somerset's high unemployment rate during the 1970s plagued local efforts at social and economic uplift. One small local development, however, heralded the fact that there would be no more bitter racial confrontations in the county. In the 1970s significant numbers of white students began to attend the historically black campus of the University of Maryland, Eastern Shore. As part of the state's desegregation of higher education efforts, Maryland State College in Princess Anne was incorporated into the University of Maryland system as a full-fledged accredited campus.

The University of Maryland, Eastern Shore, was a product of the Jim Crow racism of the South in the late nineteenth century. Founded by the Methodist Conference of Delaware in 1886, the school evolved in accordance with the separate but equal philosophy of race then in vogue in the South. Until World War II, the school was little more than an industrial and agricultural training institute with a small normal school for the training of black teachers. After the war, though, what had once been Princess Anne Academy became a four-year pre-dominantly black institution renamed Maryland State College. The school was an encapsulated black world on the other side of the railroad tracks and was known more for its championship football teams than for its academic programs.[16]

All this began to change in the 1970s when the Maryland Board of Regents appointed Dr. Archie L. Buffkins to serve as the chancellor of the University of Maryland, Eastern Shore. A mercurial administrator with a doctorate from Columbia and experience as an official in the University of Maine system, Buffkins sought to bridge both the white and black worlds in building what he termed "a multi-racial university." Buffkins courted, cajoled, and confronted both the black and white communities, often antagonizing both. After three years, Buffkins resigned in frustration and later took a position as an arts administrator at the Kennedy Center in Washington. Buffkins did succeed, however, in recruiting talented faculty and students and establishing centers of excellence in research on the campus.

His successor, Dr. William P. Hytche, was a conservative, politically adroit black mathematics professor who had risen in the campus hierarchy and had survived the wave of black militancy on the campus in the 1960s that had sent men like former campus head Dr. John T. Williams into retirement. Dr. Hytche was also mindful of his own encounters with racism in his native Oklahoma and was careful to learn from the experiences of both Williams and Buffkins. Dr. Hytche continued to build bridges of cooperation with the white community and within a year after assuming office the tireless math professor scored a significant breakthrough when community leaders led by Abe Spinak, a science administrator at the NASA facility at Wallops Island, Virginia, agreed to serve on a blue-ribbon campus advisory committee. Dr. Hytche soon became a familiar figure in the corridors of political power in Annapolis; and, capitalizing on the strong support of President John Toll and the University Board of Regents, the new chancellor was able to win appropriations to upgrade the instructional and research components of the university.

When educational planners and politicians toyed with the idea of either closing the institution for financial reasons or merging it with a predominantly white state teachers' college in Salisbury in the mid-1970s, Hytche and his school fought back. "They have tried to make us a number of things," Hytche told the media and his political allies in Annapolis. "They have had every idea under the sun—from turning this place into a chicken farm or a prison. But this place will be, I vow, what it has always been, a place of educational opportunity for the youth of the Eastern Shore and the state of Maryland." In the end Hytche and the University of Maryland, Eastern Shore, prevailed. It had become an important institution of higher education and its research programs were widely known in national and international scientific and academic circles. It was also the most racially integrated school in the state. And within the circuit of historically black land grant colleges and universities of the South, the University of Maryland, Eastern Shore, was widely known as a "model institution." The school had the solid support of the Eastern Shore business community and Somerset County and there would be no turning back the racial clock to either the despair or the violence of past times.

*   *   *

Unlike Cambridge and Princess Anne, Salisbury escaped most of the tumult and violence of racial discord during the 1960s.

At that time Salisbury was as racially segregated as any southern town. Blacks were either treated with amused tolerance or good-natured contempt. Yet, by 1961, many of Salisbury's leaders had concluded that racial segregation could no longer be maintained. It was socially explosive and bad for business. Civic leaders reasoned that enlightened conservativism leading to racial integration would ultimately keep Wicomico County a quiet peaceful place. A biracial commission led by John W. T. Webb, a local attorney, and fifteen prominent white and black citizens persuaded local restaurants to integrate. Ten Salisbury restaurants agreed to open their facilities to all. The action was taken quietly and not reported in the press until April 11, 1961. "Other areas of public accommodation fell quickly into line," wrote local historian George Corddry. Theaters and motels integrated without incident, and John Webb declared happily, "It is now possible for Negroes in this community to obtain the same high-class accommodations as whites." Webb added that there were many problems that remained in the community to trouble race relations, such as poverty and the lack of jobs for black youth, but he and the commission were optimistic. Added Corddry: "By going about their work quietly and opening facilities to blacks without fanfare, little opposition was encountered from the whites. Although initially skeptical, the NAACP eventually supported the work of the commission enthusiastically."[17] The following year, the Sidney Hollander Foundation gave its coveted recognition award to Chairman Webb and the Salisbury Bi-Racial Commission for "its efforts in reducing discrimination and promoting equal opportunity."

In 1963 when Cambridge had to call out the National Guard to restore racial peace in that troubled town, recorded *Life* Magazine, Salisbury remained peaceful.[18] Professor Charles H. Chipman, William Hull, Dr. Elmer Purnell, and Reverend Charles H. Mack had immediate access to the white establishment and the white and black leadership had a clear understanding of each other's needs and problems. It was an odd coalition of liberal whites in the town and conservative blacks; and the blacks were often denounced by radical civil rights activists as "Handkerchief Heads and Uncle Toms."

A whirlwind of racial discord swept across the Eastern Shore in the 1960s, and it was difficult to keep the racial peace in Salisbury. Race relations finally reached the breaking point in May 1968 when a Negro deaf mute named Daniel Henry was shot and killed outside a Salisbury police station by police detective Jerry Mason. Although the detective was suspended from the force and charged with manslaughter, young blacks went on a rampage in the town. Two buildings were burned and countless windows broken before Mayor Dallas Truitt summoned eight hundred National Guardsmen and four hundred state troopers to quell the violence. After the riot, Detective Mason was acquitted because evidence showed that Daniel Henry had committed a crime and the detective had no knowledge that the black was deaf. The grand jury, which contained six black members, exonerated Mason and he was restored to active duty on the Salisbury Police Force.

Relative racial peace came to Salisbury, and, in the years that followed, local blacks became increasingly involved in town and county politics. A black, Emerson Holloway, was elected to the Wicomico County Council and blacks soon were serving on the county school board and city council. Blacks led by Billy Jean Jackson and Rudolph Cane formed a political action committee called New Directions; and when the town's civil rights establishment hosted an elegant catered luncheon in the Salisbury Civic Center for leaders in local government, business, and education, it was an announcement that black power—responsible, conservative, and ambitious—had finally come of age in Salisbury. Even the town's fiery black civil rights advocate, Reverend Chappelle Mills, joined the town racial consensus and worked to win government housing for the city's poor.

Today race relations on the Eastern Shore are better than they have ever been in the history of the region. A growing black middle class in the counties of Talbot, Dorchester, Somerset, and Wicomico is playing an increasingly important leadership role in local community life. Business and civic groups have forged bonds of biracial partnership in working toward the economic development of the region. As the economy of the Eastern Shore continues to expand and diversify, the confining racial strictures of rural life seem destined for oblivion. If the mood today in race relations on the Eastern Shore seems upbeat, however, one should be reminded that it was not always that way.

Part Three

SEA: Maritime Society

10

Waterland

In such a country, existence is likely to show amphibious habits.

—Varley Lang

T he Eastern Shore is an intricate pattern of coves, necks, countless creeks, and meandering rivers. All are nurtured by the mighty waters of the Chesapeake Bay. The flatness of the landscape fools the eye—the land seems as waterlocked as the water seems landlocked. The rivers of the Eastern shore are lazy and flow gently with the tides. In the words of Paul Wilstach: "Land and water fondle each other like caressing lovers, and their embraces have the welding intimacy of lovers' embraces."[1] Some areas of the Eastern Shore, like the southern part of Dorchester County, are so inundated that it is easy to understand why the region produced a people of amphibious habits. In many localities of Dorchester, Somerset, and Worcester counties there are fifty acres of water to every acre of land.

The rivers of the Eastern Shore are all navigable in their lower courses. The Choptank and Miles are fairly deep and give admittance to large ships for at least twenty miles from their mouth. The channel of the Wicomico River in its lower course is fourteen feet deep and provides easy access to the many scows and tugboats that carry oil and fertilizer upriver to Salisbury. The Chester River has a mudbank just below Chestertown that admits only vessels of thirteen-foot draft. The shallower Annemessex and Manokin offer access only to vessels of eight- or nine-foot draft. Only the Pocomoke River is entirely navigable for large Bay craft. Its mysterious forested black waters are as intriguing to boaters and yachtsmen today as they were when the English captains first sighted the great cypress swamps of the Pocomoke in the colonial period.

The endless creeks and rivers of the Eastern Shore stimulated the development of an important minor industry in the region, ferryboats. Until recently nearly every community had its ferries that struggled against high tides and weather to carry livestock, farmers, and produce across tidewater barriers. Two kinds of ferryboats were in use on the Eastern Shore. One was a flat-bottomed scow, pulled by rope, used primarily on the rivers. The rope crossed the river and was secured on the opposite shore. The decendents of this ferry are still in use in Wicomico County and elsewhere. The course of these small three-car ferries is guided by a steel cable secured through a block attached to the ferry's port side. An outboard motor attached to the starboard side provides the motion.

The second kind of ferry was the packet sloop used for traversing the Chesapeake. The main packet boat went regularly from Annapolis to Rock Hall. Packets carried freight as well as passengers and were often referred to as "water stages." Packets also regularly sailed between Oxford and Annapolis, St. Michaels, and Wye Landing. Packet service on the Bay was profitable until the Civil War disrupted commerce on the Chesapeake. Afterwards, the steamboats put the packet ships out of business. With the exception of the packet boats, ferries were free in Maryland and they still are in many places. Ferry men got 7,000 pounds of tobacco from the state in the early days and now they are salaried employees of the counties.

Since the days when it played a vital role in the development of Virginia and Maryland as a waterway for the colonial trade in tobacco, the Chesapeake Bay has served a remarkable diversity of needs. It is the source of a $100-million-a-year fish and shellfish business for Maryland alone; and it is a popular hunting ground for sport fishermen and duck hunters. The Chesapeake has some of the finest sailing waters anywhere along the East Coast. The Bay is also important as a shipping lane for Baltimore Harbor, which is visited by thousands of commercial craft each year.

At present Chesapeake Bay provides some of the best and most heavily used waterfowl wintering habitat remaining in the Atlantic flyway. The Canada goose is attracted to the corn fields of the Eastern Shore, and the American widgeon flocks to the Susquehanna Flats. The Bay country is home for muskrat, raccoon, white-tailed deer, rails, snipe, and hosts of shorebirds and songbirds. According to a National Estuary Study conducted by the Fish and Wildlife Service, an estimated 550,000 ducks and 350,000 geese winter in Bay Country.[2]

The Bay extends 195 miles from the mouth of the Susquehanna River to Cape Charles and Cape Henry, which mark the gateway to the Atlantic Ocean. For 10,000 years the Bay has been the drowned estuary of the powerful Susquehanna, the largest river in the eastern United States, which rolls down through New York and Pennsylvania to supply over half the Bay's daily inflow of fresh water. The Bay is shallow with a mean depth of twenty-eight feet and its marshy areas (wetlands) have been the spawning grounds for most of the finfish population. In the shallow marsh waters, rich grasses provide the beginning of the Chesapeake life cycle.

Planters in the early colonial period learned how to harness the energies of the Chesapeake waterland. They built tide-driven grist mills to grind their corn and wheat into flour. These tide mills were unique. The mill was built beside a "narrow" where the tide ran swiftly. Then its great wheel was sunk in the water and the ebb and flow of the tide kept it continually in motion. The tide mills were located near marshes and were often manned with slave labor. When the mills were not in use, the black slaves probed the marsh with long iron rods for terrapins. Scarcely any part of the vast Chesapeake waterland was without its rich bounty.

*   *   *

In this land of water highways and water commerce, steamboats were the central part of community life. The first steamboat appeared on the Bay in 1813. The *Chesapeake* was commanded by Captain Edward Trippe of Dorchester County, and it was 137 feet long and 6 to 8 feet in depth. Its paddle wheels measured 10 feet in diameter. The boat also had a forward mast to take advantage of the wind. Ironically, the *Chesapeake* began excursion trips on the Bay just as the British fleet was advancing on Baltimore during the War of 1812. On June 19, 1813, the passengers on the Baltimore to Rock Hall excursion paid 75 cents each way to get a close look at British warships. The steamboat came close enough to the British fleet for its passengers to judge the cut of the fleet's sails and to use their spyglasses to see the armed marines on board.

By the turn of the twentieth century, steamboating was a way of life on the Chesapeake. Women, for example, would board the *B.S. Ford* at Chestertown and go shopping in Baltimore. Captain Woodhull, the genial gray-haired captain, was a trusted Bay pilot and popular with Eastern Shore families. As the boat got close to the wharf, a couple of deckhands tossed the mooring lines ashore where they were slipped over big steel cleats. The ship's purser with his black metal box went ashore to sell tickets while the deckhands brought freight aboard. Men gravitated toward the stern of the boat where there was a bar with sawdust on the floor. As the boat cruised the Bay, the men drank and played poker and chewed plugs of Brown Mule Tobacco and filled the brass spittoons on the lower deck.[3] In the heyday years between 1880 and 1915, some fifty steamboats regularly plied the waters of the Chesapeake and connected remote rural areas in tidewater Maryland and Virginia with Baltimore, Annapolis, and Washington.

The *Emma Giles* was not the biggest or fanciest steamboat on Chesapeake waters, but there were those who loved her. Launched in Baltimore in 1887, the boat was named after the five-year-old daughter of Baltimore financier, Edward Giles. Like many steamboats the *Emma Giles* carried freight and day-tripping excursionists to places as remote as Taylor's Island in Dorchester or as popular as Tolchester Beach in Kent.

For nearly half a century the *Emma Giles* cruised the waters of the Little Choptank, the Miles, and the Chester rivers on the Eastern Shore and the rivers of Anne Arundel County on the western shore. It served canneries, seafood packinghouses, and farms as well as connecting isolated landings with the hectic commercial life of Baltimore. In addition to peaches and fertilizer, the boat carried cattle, sheep, and chickens which often gave it a unique aroma. Even when fully loaded, the *Emma Giles* drew only seven feet of water and could traverse many Eastern Shore creeks. When the steamboat came around the bend, a holiday atmosphere ensued. Excitement grew when the *Emma Giles* "hit the wharf, the great wheels backing and sending a surge of foam under the pier . . . the tumult of singing stevedores, bleating sheep, and creaking wagons at the gang plank; the wonder invoked by this palatial apparition . . . from that other world, the great city."[4] Unlike the steamboats of the Mississippi, which were flimsy, cheaply built affairs, Chesapeake steamboats were well engineered and built to last. Although the *Emma Giles* ended her career as a passenger steamboat in 1936, she was still afloat as a barge as late as 1951.

Although the industry had its profitable years, the steamboat business was always a precarious venture, and the boat companies were hostage to the weather and other socioeconomic forces beyond their control. The coming of paved highways and trucks in Maryland in the 1920s began the demise of the steamboat. The Great Depression of the 1930s finished it.

Not surprisingly, this Chesapeake waterland spawned its own distinctive sailing craft. The pungy schooner, a direct descendant of the Virginia pilot schooner and the Baltimore Clipper, was built only on the Chesapeake. It was a common schooner of the local freight and oyster trade for at least fifty years prior to 1880. In addition to its work on the Bay, it had a part in the Bahamas fruit trade and the transport of oysters to Cape Cod where oysters had disappeared. In his *Cape Cod* essays Thoreau mentions that about 60,000 bushels of southern oysters were brought to Wellfleet each year by pungy boats in the 1840s.

Unfortunately, the pungy boats did not fare well in the intensely competitive world of oyster dredging on the nineteenth century Chesapeake. The boats were too deep-drafted to maneuver well in shallow waters over oyster bars; and oyster captains opted for the less expensive and less complicated shallow-draft skipjacks. By the 1970s most of the old pungy boats were abandoned derelicts. The *Mildred Addison* was found abandoned in a cove off Spa Creek, sails still bent; *The James A. Whiting* on the beach in the Coan River in Virginia. Near Rock Hall, the *Plan* lay sunk in shallow water while the *Wave* owned by Captain John Crouch was still functioning and painted in the traditional pungy colors—pink and green. Pungy boats were always light pink from the waterline up to the wales or final twenty-four inches of the hull. This last part was painted in dark bottle green. The light monkey rail was painted white. The origin and use of the word "pungy" still remain something of a mystery.

Pungies were more weatherly than centerboard schooners. Boats in this class had three lower sails and two top sails.

Harvesting oyster spat in the Little Choptank. Photograph by Pat Vojtech.

Some pungy boats were seventy-three feet long and sixty-nine gross tons. Pungies were double masted and, after dredging for oysters, they were used in the active freight trade on the Bay and elsewhere. One of the last pungies, *The Amanda F. Lewis* of Coan River, was converted into a powerboat and sold in Haiti after World War II.

The heyday of the pungy boats was also a time of the flourishing Atlantic coastal trade. Many watermen left their tranquil coves and harbors and ventured forth on the high seas of the Atlantic in freighting schooners in search of wealth and adventure. As the men hoisted the sails of triple-masted schooners, they often sang the old Chesapeake chantey:

> To Cuba's coast we're bound me boys,
> Weigh me boys for Cuba!
> The capt'n set the sail,
> For we're running down to Cuba!

Captain Leonard Tawes of Crisfield was but one of many "coasting captains" who piloted schooners filled with lumber, sweet potatoes, fertilizer, and molasses down the Atlantic coast for the Caribbean. Between 1868 and 1920 Captain Tawes kept a diary of his life at sea. It is a chronicle of adversity, rowdy drunken crews, humorous accidents with barrels of molasses, and change on Chesapeake Bay. The old-time Bay captains were trained in land sightings when they sailed up the Bay at night. When the Coast Guard installed navigation lights on the Bay after 1915, the old captains found them a nuisance as they altered the Chesapeake night scape.[5]

While the pungy schooner has disappeared from the waters of the Eastern Shore, the skipjack prevails. This shallow-draft, centerboarded craft made its appearance on the Bay late in the nineteenth century. Single-masted and highly maneuverable, the skipjack became the oyster dredge boat par excellence; and by the turn of the century there were over a thousand such vessels "lickin the bars" with a dredge scoop that pulled the oysters up off the Bay bottom. Today dredging oysters with powerboats is illegal. Power dredges, as they are called, are too efficient and would quickly decimate the limited supply of oysters that remain in the Bay. Oyster dredging is principally conducted under sail and the future of this small fleet of skipjacks is currently at great risk. Declining oyster yields plus the added infestation of the oyster parasite MSX, which makes the bivalve milky and inedible, have spelled economic disaster for the handful of skipjacks that remain in this once-proud fleet.

There are few jobs physically harder than working on a skipjack oyster dredge. Besides being out in the winter weather, exposed to the full force of wind and water, the men must stay stooped over on a pitching deck as they dig into the pile of shell and debris that the dredge brings up from the bottom. If they are lucky, they will sort out some legal-sized oysters from the pile of wet dead shell, rocks, and sea muck in front of them. When the skipjacks race off Deal Island on Labor Day, the boats are full of pretty girls, politicians, and visitors to the region. But when the ocean spray turns to ice on the rigging and the skipjack is pitching into a howling wind, there are no pretty girls or Baltimore travel writers on board. Yet, it is when the skipjack is slogging it out in the winter weather in search of oysters that the realities of life as a Chesapeake waterman can be experienced. When times are good, a mate on a skipjack can earn well over a hundred dollars a day. He can also come down with rheumatism, and heart problems, get injured by the powerful dredge winder, or even drown in a stormy sea. A good skipjack captain can earn, after expenses, as much as a thousand dollars a week. But it takes great skill and knowledge honed from a lifetime of experience to dredge oysters. Some captains, like Pete Switzer of Tilghman's Island, are artful sailors and shrewd oystermen. Their skill is reflected in comfortable well-appointed houses and solid bank accounts. "This is a rough business and you got to be good at it if you want to survive," says Switzer. This skipjack captain is proud of the fact that he can confront the powerful Chesapeake and wrest a living from it. "We don't play it safe in the rivers and tong oysters," Switzer adds.

Everybody loves to photograph a skipjack. In newspapers we see pictures of some of the weather-beaten faces of old captains, read how they are a "dying breed," and that the skipjack fleet is constantly "dwindling." All this romanticizing about the only commercial oyster sailing fleet in North America is far from the vision most dredgehands have of their work. To them it is just hard, cold, backbreaking work.

The term "waterman" was used in sixteenth-century England to describe waterborne taxi men who plied their trade on the Thames. A hundred years later, the English came to a new country, settling on the shores of the Chesapeake. The landed classes made their homes on firm ground, but the watermen laid claim to the wetlands of the Bay, reaping a rich harvest of fish, crabs, oysters, and clams. These settlers' descendants still live here. "You make a living but you work all the time," is a popular watermen's saying and it sums up their lives.

Living the rugged life of a Chesapeake Bay waterman guarantees a ruddy complexion and powerful arm and back muscles as well as calloused hands—but it's not likely to make you healthy. Doctors who tend to watermen have found that they are no healthier than today's flabby metropolitan business executive. Watermen are just as prone to weight problems, high blood pressure, and heart attacks as today's harried businessman. Dr. William Long, a Crisfield physician, discovered a higher incidence of diabetes and cancer in watermen than in the land-based working population of the Eastern Shore.

Yet for all the hardship, watermen endure. Perhaps it is some atavistic impulse that brings them into constant struggle with nature and prompts them to survive the challenges of Chesapeake Bay. Otherwise it is hard to explain why watermen keep going out on the Bay season after season, especially when the Bay's seafood bounty is declining. Eastern Shore poet Gilbert Byron summed it up best when he wrote:

> From Chesapeake men I come,
> These men a sun-tanned, quiet breed,
> With eyes of English blue and faces
> Lined with many a watch of sunlit waters;
> These men with cautious mouths and lazy stride.
> Grizzled chinned, hip-booted, oil-skinned men;
> These men, they fear the Chesapeake,
> And yet they would not leave her.[6]

Every Eastern Shore waterman is a rich repository of oral history about "the old days" and the waterman's craft. In fact, until his recent death, retired Crisfield waterman, Alex Kellam, enjoyed a second career as a revered Chesapeake Bay storyteller. The Smithsonian Institution in Washington dubbed him "an important resource for Chesapeake folklore." What follows are some vignettes culled from Kellam and other Chesapeake men.

In the days before World War I, when oysters were sometimes a glut on the market in the early season, shrewd watermen took hundreds of bushels of oysters and secretly deposited them in coves and creeks in water with sufficient tidal flows. When oysters grew scarce later in the season, the bedded oysters were taken up and placed on the market. They called this "oysters in the bank."[7]

Tilghman Island in the 1890s was a relatively stable world of simple hardworking people. Watermen built houses with porches on all sides to catch the summer breeze. The island also had cannery packinghouses, restaurants, and summer boardinghouses, blacksmith shops, and several first-rate boatyards. There were no policemen on the island as Tilghman folk were a law unto themselves. The big man of Tilghman in the 1890s was William Stanley Covington, a Tilghman dredger and packer. Covington kept thirty shuckers busy in his packinghouse and sent his buy boat to purchase oysters from watermen on the Nanticoke River and Eastern Bay. The Tilghman packer shipped oysters in twenty-gallon barrels on the steamboat *Joppa* to Baltimore. He also had a store constructed on a mound of oyster shells where workmen brought their hardware, clothing, tobacco, dry beans, salt codfish, and flour. Covington, furthermore, sold four to five barrels of corned beef pickled in brine every week.[8]

In the winter of 1917-18, both the county waters and those of the Chesapeake Bay froze so hard that trucks could be driven over the surface. Tilghman Island tongers cut holes in the ice to get oysters. Also during the big freeze of January-February 1918, Smith Island was isolated for seven weeks. Folks then were used to the ice jams and had extra stores of wood, flour, and coal. The stranded Smith Islanders, however, were down to one meal a day before a ship finally got through.

During bad winters the Chesapeake continues to freeze over. From Deal Island on a cold crisp winter day, one can hear the loud groaning of thousands of ice floes. Occasionally, daring watermen will venture out on the ice armed only with long probing poles and their wits "to see if it's cold enough to walk to Smith or Tangier island." Such a feat was actually accomplished in the 1930s when a relief expedition left Crisfield by foot with food for Tangier Island. Unfortunately, a state trooper named Sergeant Hunter, who led the men, fell through a patch of soft ice and perished.

During Prohibition, some watermen worked for bootleggers, earning a half-gallon of whiskey for a shift at unloading an illegal liquor cargo on the Potomac River. Captain Will Smith, Alex Kellam recalled, caught 36½ gallons of white mule in his oyster dredge one morning. It had been thrown overboard by nervous smugglers when a police boat approached. "We have no idea what the good God-faring Smith Islander did with the booze," quipped Kellam, "but being a waterman he probably sold it."[9]

For the watering communities of the Chesapeake in the 1940s and 1950s, life was simple. Watermen ate a diet of stewed hardheads (croaker fish), black-eyed peas, navy beans, and salt pork. They also consumed large amounts of playcake, a crude bread made of water and flour and a bit of yeast spread out in a pan. The finished product was hard and flat like hardtack. Regular yeast bread was rare on the Chesapeake until after World War II. Oysters, crabs, and market fish were seldom used. Oysters were something you traded or sold but did not eat.

Schoolteachers in watermen's communities in the years between the world wars were tough-minded spinsters. Though they came from the community, most had too much education or too much sense to marry a waterman. The "old maid schoolteachers" were stern and iron willed and determined to pound some knowledge into their pupils' heads. They knew they would only have the boys until their twelfth birthday and then they would leave school to follow the water.

A waterman's life is so hard that sometimes it can be funny. Donnie Cummings of Tilghman Island laughs when he recalls the time he nearly drowned in the Bay. In the winter of 1977 the Chesapeake iced over, and Cummings and a friend took a truck out onto the ice to cut holes and dredge for oysters. The ice gave way and the pickup began immediately to sink. If his partner had not pulled him to safety, Cummings would have gone to an icy grave. Looking back on the experience, Cummings laughs, "I am one of the onliest ones ever sunk a pickup in the middle of the Bay."

By far the most interesting perspective on the current life of the watermen of Maryland's Eastern Shore is that of Varley Lang. A retired oyster tonger with years of experience on the Miles River, Lang is the only man who has written an authentic account of daily life on the Chesapeake from a waterman's perspective. He is also the only Chesapeake waterman with a Ph.D. from Johns Hopkins University. His book, *Follow the*

Water, is an intriguing tale of how an English literature professor teaching in a state university in New York grew disenchanted with his loutish semiliterate students and sought a new career. As fate would have it, Lang inherited a small piece of land from his parents near Tunis Mills in Talbot County where he had spent his boyhood, and the academician decided to start tonging for oysters.

Becoming a Chesapeake waterman was no easy feat for an already middle-aged ex–college professor. At first the other watermen were deeply suspicious of him. It was unheard of at the time for an outsider to become a waterman. Starting from scratch, Lang learned how to navigate a tong boat and slowly and painfully mastered the art of using oyster rakes. "It was a good thing my wife and I had some savings," he later recalled in an interview. "Otherwise we would have starved to death in those first years. It took time for me to get enough skill to get the oysters up or to learn how to find them on the bars." Lang was a congenial, decidedly unpushy sort and gradually the watermen took to him. They shared their skills and secrets with him and took him and his wife into their fold. After two years on the water, Varley Lang could tong oysters with the best of the Miles River watermen and his new career of "following the water" would sustain him for over twenty-five years. Often his wife served as his shipmate and helper, and the Langs were a familiar sight on the Miles and its tributaries.

In his book, Lang reflects on the attractions of a waterman's life. "In his work," says Lang, "the waterman is delivered from the rat's maze of uncertainty. The villains and the heroes of his story are concise and unambiguous; the issues are cleanly cut. Either he has the courage to endure, or he has not."[10] From his life on the water Lang learned that the only true virtues an individual should have are knowledge and physical strength; for you cannot survive as a waterman without either. But it was the defiant individualism of oystering and crabbing that appealed most to Lang and his wife. Slowly over the years they built a way of life that was dependent only on Lang's skill and the Bay country's providence.

In the 1950s when this "young" gray-haired waterman reached maturity as an oyster tonger, the life of a Chesapeake waterman was far different from what it is now. There were almost five thousand oyster tongers on the Chesapeake in those days, Lang recalls. Theirs was a highly self-sufficient local economy. Watermen didn't have a whole lot and didn't want a whole lot. They just enjoyed themselves and worked as they pleased. "If while tonging for oysters, a school of bluefish would come in," says Lang, "we'd drop everything and go after the blues. It was a hard life but a fairly easygoing life." Back then a waterman was insulated from the marketplace by his family, friends, and the Bay's bounty. There were always oysters, clams, fish, and goose, and, for most watermen, bartering was a time-honored practice.

Now, reflecting in retirement, Lang believes that way of life has passed. Nowadays the watermen are just as caught up in the consumer culture as anyone else. They want the TVs, the new boats, the fancy pickup trucks, and all the trappings of modern material culture. As a result, there is not as much time for the easy life out on the water. Today's waterman pursues a life that is far more regimented and far more expensive. If today's waterman is to make a dollar, he doesn't have time to chase a school of bluefish or go hunting geese. Lang regrets that today's waterman is too caught up in debt and too caught up in the status comforts of metropolitan life.[11]

Lang, however, still has faith in the Chesapeake watermen. Watermen, he says, "are the most opinionated, cocksure, critical, conservative, and independent group of men I have ever encountered . . . . They may very well be the last living specimens of an almost extinct species, except in political theory: the independent, the individual man."[12]

Today on the Chesapeake poor conservation practices and pollution place the watermen's future at grave risk. The Chesapeake Bay is a good example of what ecologist Garrett Hardin has called the "tragedy of the commons." Unlike private ownership of the source of production, a commons invites exploitation by all those who are competing for its benefits. Yet, take away the commons and the Chesapeake waterman disappears into corporate enterprises sufficiently capitalized to undertake private mariculture. The development of a private oyster industry in Maryland may lead to the destruction of the traditional oyster trade, and Chesapeake watermen are not about to consent to their own extinction. On land watermen are God-fearing pillars of respectability and are careful to comply with laws affecting public and private property. Yet they view public fishing areas as their own to use or ruin as they see fit. As Lionel Bennett, a Crisfield lawyer, once put it, "If a waterman found the last oyster in Chesapeake Bay, he'd sell it."

While watermen continue to fight the idea of scientifically managed leased oyster beds in Chesapeake Bay, Max Chambers has a dream. This ambitious marine specialist envisions the mass production of oysters in the Chesapeake in the future, and the transformation of an expensive gourmet item into a cheap source of protein for the man on the street. "I want to bring the oyster back to the harvest yields of the nineteenth century," Chambers says. In the 1880s it was possible to take 10 to 15 million bushels annually out of the Chesapeake. Now even during good times in the modern age the Bay yields only 2.5 million bushels. Chambers believes that without scientific management, that is, oyster farming, the yield will continue to decrease. "Despite pollution there is a lot of clean water left in Chesapeake Bay; and the oyster is an animal that we don't have to house, feed, or water."

Chambers' buoyant optimism comes after surviving a tough decade of trial-and-error experience. He first got into the business of opening an oyster hatchery because a marine scientist told him that he could make money at it. Yet Max discovered that it was another thing entirely to put the idea into production and turn a profit. To survive Chambers has had to become a jack-of-all-trades, a scientist, a farmer, and a first-class scrounger. "A number of people," he adds, "thought that all you had to do to grow oysters commercially was to buy some fancy expensive equipment. They all went bankrupt."

Working at his bayside hatchery near Upper Fairmount in Somerset County, Chambers places Chesapeake oysters in large tanks in April and heats the water to summer temperature for about a month. During this time, he feeds the oysters algae to fatten them. While natural oysters spawn in July, Chambers's crop of oysters spawn in late April. "I sort of get a jump on nature," he laughs. Max then scoops the microscopic fertilized oysters or spat and takes them to another tank containing strong net bags filled with oyster shells. Within a short time the spat attaches to the shell; and when the spat reaches small fingernail size on the shell, Chambers removes his bags onto pallets in the Bay and lets nature do the remainder of the care and feeding.

Chambers sells his crop by counting the number of spat sticking to one shell and multiplying that by the total number of shell in each bag. He currently receives $3.50 per thousand spat. Using 100 adult oysters Chambers can produce 3.5 million spat. With commercial methods, argues Chambers, it would be very easy to grow 1,000 bushels per acre of Chesapeake bottom. "They get that much in Washington and British Columbia," he grumbles. "But here in Maryland watermen don't want oyster farms on the Chesapeake. I guess they fear it would turn their way of life into factory work."

Max Chambers is one of only fifty individuals in the country who operate successful oyster hatcheries. It has been a long hard battle to become self-sufficient, he reflects. "The only reason I am making it is because I have stuck with it. I could have made more money doing something else, but oyster farming was an important goal for me. Who knows? I might help to open a whole new food technology in this country."

*　　*　　*

State and federal governments have always been more interested in the Chesapeake Bay for commercial and military purposes than for conservation and environmental management. In 1789, during its first session, the United States Congress passed an act that provided for the erection of a lighthouse at the entrance of Chesapeake Bay. That lighthouse has grown into a multimillion-dollar coastal navigation business, but there is little more agreement on comprehensive resource policy today than there was in 1789. In 1822 John C. Calhoun, a South Carolina slaveholder serving as United States Secretary of War, proposed that the Chesapeake Bay be developed for military purposes. He envisioned a string of Chesapeake fortifications, among which would be Fort Monroe, Virginia, and he proposed that the fledgling Chesapeake & Delaware Canal be surveyed by the Army Corps of Engineers to determine its future navigability for gunboats. Similarly, Calhoun asked Congress to approve funds for surveying canal routes to link the Susquehanna River with Baltimore. Despite Calhoun's bold report, President James Monroe approved only limited federal authority in the Chesapeake.

It was not until the 1920s that Maryland made a genuine attempt at managing the resources of Chesapeake Bay. By then the Potomac River was beginning to suffer from sewage pollution from the city of Washington D.C.; and Maryland Governor Philip Goldsborough became alarmed that raw sewage floating into the Bay would ruin the oyster beds. The real pioneer for Bay conservation, however, was Dr. Reginald V. Truitt, founder of the Chesapeake Biological Laboratory at Solomons Island. A politically well-connected marine scientist at the University of Maryland, Dr. Truitt fought for culling laws and reseeding of oyster beds. Often he had to battle watermen who were bitterly opposed to any regulation of their business. Truitt also participated in the establishment of a marine science laboratory in Dorchester County at Horn Point.

Truitt was the son of a Chincoteague Bay oyster packer, and Worcester County was always dear to his heart. In the 1930s Truitt became concerned with the social and economic future of his home county and formed a "Committee of 45 County Leaders" to discuss planning and zoning. In 1937 he approached Congressman Thomas Goldsborough with the idea of naming Assateague Island a national park. The movement lost, however, because the county feared the loss of tax revenues. Dr. Truitt continued to be Assateague's genteel unpaid lobbyist and worked behind the scenes to have the state acquire land on the island for a park. In the 1950s the island became embroiled in political controversy as many people had purchased property on Assateague and feared state expropriation. A fierce storm in 1962, however, destroyed most of the dwellings on Assateague and put in serious doubt any plans for future commercial development of the island. When Congress passed the necessary legislation in 1965 to create Assateague Island National Seashore, Dr. Truitt's dream of preserving an unspoiled barrier island for future generations had come true.

*   *   *

But both the watermen and the conservationists may be fighting a losing battle as pollution of the Bay brings the estuary to the ragged edge of destruction. The Chesapeake Bay is a lot like the man who has worked most of his life in a shipyard breathing asbestos. He only appears healthy. Many of the Bay's most important species, aquatic plants, soft-shell clams, oysters, blue crabs, white perch, shad, menhaden, and rockfish are at or close to their lowest levels of recorded abundance. As Joseph Mihursky, a research professor at the

Chesapeake Biological Laboratories in Solomons, once said of the Bay, "The thing that frightens me is that all these diverse species somehow have fallen into low ebbs in sychronization. Doesn't that tell you something?"[13]

If you look at the Chesapeake from an entrepreneur's point of view, all you can say is that "it is one Hell of a way to run a business." All the interactions—soil, land development, and fisheries are looked at in a piecemeal way. How many look at the Bay's problems from a fisheries point of view? Municipalities in Virginia, Maryland, and Pennsylvania daily discharge 400 million gallons of untreated sewage all of which ends up in the Chesapeake. Not only is this sewage toxic to fish life but it also encourages the growth of an ugly type of algae that causes eutrophication, or gradual oxygen depletion.

In terms of pollution, the Chesapeake Bay began to lose its pristine state late in the colonial period when large amounts of silt flowed into the Bay from eroded tobacco farms on both the western shore and the Eastern Shore. Later, after the Civil War, the American timber industry organized on a grand scale; and the great timberlands of the Susquehanna Valley were soon turned into millions of board feet of lumber to satisfy a growing country's insatiable appetite for building materials. With the timberlands of the Susquehanna cut over, nothing was left to contain the raging floods of the Susquehanna River which deposited millions of tons of silt and debris in the Bay. Later, coal mines polluted the streams with sulphur and other toxic wastes and these in turn also found their way to the Chesapeake. As late as 1979, environmentalists discovered an abandoned coal mine in Luzerne County, Pennsylvania, into which a million gallons of toxic chemicals and oil had been poured by a chemical waste company. The mine was leaking a thousand gallons a day into the Susquehanna River.[14]

By far the most serious recent environmental disaster on the Chesapeake occurred in 1973 when two former employees of Allied Chemical Corporation, Virgil A. Hundtofte and William P. Moore, set up a company in Hopewell, Virginia, to make Kepone, a powerful pesticide akin to DDT. The trouble with Kepone was not so much how it was used but how it was dumped into the Chesapeake Bay as waste. At their company, Life Science Products Company, Hundtofte, Moore, and their workers dumped large amounts of Kepone into the James

River. The result was that the entire Chesapeake fishery was imperiled. When ingested or inhaled by humans, Kepone attacks the central nervous system, causing shaking and loss of mental capacity. In laboratory animals, it causes cancer. Kepone is extremely persistent once it enters the environment, meaning that it does not easily break down in nature.

It was not until July 1975 that Virginia health authorities shut down the Kepone plant at Hopewell. By that time the James River had become seriously contaminated with the chemical, and authorities both in Virginia and Maryland worried that Kepone would spread throughout the Bay with the tidal flow and enter many of the lower reaches of the rivers that empty into the Bay. Shortly after the plant closing, scientists from the Maryland Department of Natural Resources discovered that bluefish found in the Bay were heavily contaminated with Kepone and that other species in the lower Bay were beginning to pick up the pesticide.

The Kepone scare had a disastrous impact on the Chesapeake's fifty-million-dollar-a-year fishing industry as people began to avoid any fish from the Bay. Commercial bluefishing all but stopped. Seafood Houses like Family Fish Houses Inc., a chain of twenty-one seafood restaurants, assured their customers in expensive media advertisements that the fish they served in their restaurants was taken in the Atantic Ocean and not the Bay.

In May 1976, the state of Virginia charged Allied Chemical (who had a contract and manufacturing agreement with Hundtofte and Moore, the owners of Life Science Products Company) with 940 counts of violating water-pollution laws. Life Science Products Company and the town of Hopewell were charged with over 1,000 counts. Hundtofte and Moore pleaded guilty to 153 counts of violating pollution laws.[15]

Fortunately, Kepone did not spread up the Bay in the way that scientists had feared. It has, however, entered the sediment strata of Bay bottom in the lower Chesapeake. Some scientists considered dredging up the contaminated bottom areas and depositing the spoil on land in order to guarantee that the water would not suffer from further contamination. Others favored strict industrial discharge laws. Waiting on time and tide to ease the problem, scientists were unable to calculate what the final impact of Kepone on the region will be.

The Kepone crisis, oil spills, and other pollution problems on the Chesapeake reflected a serious deficiency on the part of both Maryland and Virginia governments to prevent environmental hazards from entering Chesapeake waters. Dr. Max Eisenberg, a scientist for Maryland's Kepone Task Force, summed up the dilemma in terms that were hardly comforting. Eisenberg believes that Kepone, like mercury, which still turns up in fish, may come to be accepted in small amounts as inevitable. "As far as we know, we can live with Kepone as the problem exists now," he said. "But our lifestyle has become one where we are bombarded with one chemical after another—and unfortunately the cumulative effects of them are not known."[16]

While the gloomy chronicles of the death of Chesapeake Bay appear regularly in newspapers, and scientists issue disturbing forecasts, the Bay still has a few optimists who are impressed with the resilience of the estuary. Says Chesapeake writer Tom Horton, the question should be, "Why haven't we been able to ruin the Bay yet?" Horton believes the saving grace of the Bay is that it is composed of four-fifths ocean water. Thus the tides and currents from the Atlantic enable the Bay to flush itself. Also a lot of the pollution is trapped in areas like Baltimore Harbor or the Patapsco River before it can get out into the Bay and do damage to the ecosystem. Further, the mud at the bottom of the Bay has a great capacity to soak up toxic substances. Even under the best of conditions, notes Bay expert Jerry Schubel, conditions in estuaries are tough. The species that inhabit estuaries have to be able to adapt to droughts, floods, changes in salinity, and variations in food supply. The Chesapeake Bay crab, for example, has survived and has proven resistant to even the most devastating pollution of the marine habitat. Surprisingly, crabs caught in Baltimore harbor are just as clean and edible as those harvested off Tilghman Island. Finally, adds Tom Horton, you have to give the mosquito and the jellyfish their due. Without these two infamous creatures to retard tourism and real estate development in counties like Somerset and Dorchester, the region would suffer a far higher rate of pollution.[17]

Besides, when the advent of summer begins to stir our blood with thoughts of vacations and weekend retreats on the Eastern Shore, who of us wishes to dwell on gloomy prognostications about the future of the Chesapeake? The skies and shimmering waters of the Eastern Shore seem prettier than ever and our only thought is how to survive the weekend traffic of Route 50.

*   *   *

If you want to get away from towns cluttered with plastic and tacky gift stands and franchise food restaurants and the glut of summer people, go to Smith Island, located in the middle of Chesapeake Bay off the port of Crisfield. The watermen here have lived over three hundred years without the need for any organized government. The guiding force in these people's lives is the Methodist religion, and about as fast a social scene as you will see will be a bunch of men playing dominoes down at the grocery store. On Smith Island you can catch a glimpse of watermen's society as it enters its golden age. All it takes is a forty-minute boat ride on the *Island Belle*, the *Captain Jason* or any of the several other tour boats out of Crisfield.

There are two views about life on Smith Island and perhaps what is needed is the perspective of each to achieve a full understanding of the place. First of all, travel writers have tended to romanticize the island out of all proportion. Recently two journalists writing for *The Washington Post* referred to Smith Island as "a patch of misty marsh afloat in the Chesapeake Bay, a few vibrant brush strokes painted on a blue mirror of sky and water." It is a place where life hasn't changed much in several centuries, where "time passes in and out like the tide." It is an island of crabbers and gentle fisherfolk, a place where "women demurely avert their eyes from strangers."[18]

Such paeans to Smith Island probably tell more about the impersonal metropolitan background of the writers than the realities of this community of watermen. Granted, the island can be beautiful on a brilliant summer day. Most of the abandoned cars which once constituted a major eyesore on the island have been removed and the island today is far tidier than it has been in recent history. Like seafaring communities everywhere on the Atlantic coast, the natives have discovered that tourists like to come and gawk at them as well as spend money on boat tours, knickknacks, and souvenirs. The islanders have capitalized on the romantic image of the watermen to present themselves to outsiders and to gain tourist dollars. The people are quick to give tours of their crab sheds and talk of the history of the island.

The other perception of the island is less flattering. First, the island is losing people. Metropolitan life is seductive and its promise of material abundance is well-known even in places as remote as Smith Island. The community's youth are leaving for the mainland. Television is the culprit. It offers vistas to the young on Smith island that were scarcely even dreamt of on the island a generation ago. It conjures wants, desires, and needs of a consumer culture that can only be fulfilled on the mainland. Unlike Tangier Island, Virginia, which educates its youth on the island from first grade through high school, Smith sends its children daily to the mainland on a schoolboat to be educated in the Crisfield schools. While Smith Islanders have always been uneasy about having their children schooled on the mainland, that unease has increased with the availability of illegal drugs and alcohol for the young in Crisfield and the general loosening of social and institutional restraints in Crisfield and elsewhere on the Eastern Shore. In the past, Smith Island's population has fluctuated between 650 and 750 residents. It now is in the 500s. In the future it may well go into a demographic crisis as the island produces fewer offspring to work and sustain the community. Smith Island may well come to be the Eastern Shore's only floating retirement community.

Smith Island life has its share of tensions. A small group of historically inbred people, most of whom have the name of Tyler, Bradshaw, or Evans come together in the social pressure cooker of island life. On Smith Island the only "newspaper" of significance is the seafood packinghouse where women pick crabs and exchange gossip about every facet of island life. Even tourists spending the night at Frances Kitching's motel get discussed in the packinghouse. Fortunately a staunch Methodist religiosity helps individuals to survive the pressures of "the right tight isle." Outsiders, though, have a rough time dealing with island life; and while a few have come to settle, they are mostly summer people. And very few people from the mainland can either tolerate or understand the rigorous public introspection and personal self-evaluation that is part of a weekly service or prayer meeting at the Ewell Methodist Church.

All this will probably change as the island becomes more of a tourist attraction and less a seafaring community. But for the moment at least, Smith Island is one of the most tightly knit communities on the Eastern Shore of Maryland. People do not lock their doors and deals are still concluded on a handshake. People keep their money in home safes rather than in mainland banks. This kind of community solidarity, however, does have its price in terms of conformity and the restraints of tradition that those from both on and off the island are increasingly unwilling to pay. Ultimately the Smith Island that you see when you disembark from the boat at Ewell may be a community that exists only in your own mind. To understand the essence of this community, bring a well-thumbed Bible, leave your beer at home (the sale of alcohol is prohibited on the island), stay for a year, and be prepared to work harder than you have ever had to in your life. Then, if you are lucky you may find the real Smith Island.

*   *   *

In summertime on the Eastern Shore, eating seafood becomes something akin to a religious enthusiasm; and the reigning deity is the Chesapeake blue crab. By July 4 when the crabs begin to get plentiful and cheap, dozens of Eastern Shore communities sponsor crab feasts. Both the Democratic and Republican Parties count on the Chesapeake Blue crab as the staple that will draw politicians and party members alike to their fund-raising events. It is always best to go to crab feasts in old clothes because in the enthusiasm of attacking a pile of steaming crimson red hard crustaceans, crab fat and crab parts tend to fly everywhere. Also the Old Bay Seasoning that gives the crabs their eye-watering delectability tends to get on one's clothes.

There is nothing dainty about the ritual of twisting legs, cracking shells, and prying loose the crab in search of succulent pieces of white meat. While most Eastern Shoremen pick their crabs effortlessly with the aid of a small knife, outsiders approach their pile of steamed crabs with the kind of grim determination and controlled exploration that surgeons reserve for the coronary bypass. You don't pick and save your crabmeat. You eat it as you go along. Also eating crabs is an excellent excuse to guzzle large amounts of beer. Though everyone on the Shore has his favorite way and locale for crab eating, most admit that it is hard to beat eating crabs at a picnic table in the backyard while tuning into a Baltimore Orioles game on a Sunday afternoon. In the kitchen occasionally a crab will miss the steaming pot when you dump him in and go scurrying across the floor to the squealing delight of small children. The embattled crustacean will find a remote corner of the kitchen for his last stand, and it takes practice to be able to retrieve him for the pot without getting pinched. A Chesapeake Bay blue crab is a pesky critter and one pinch from his powerful claw can draw blood.

If the Chesapeake Bay blue crab is a summer passion on the Eastern Shore, muskrat is a joyous winter's delight. Winter time means muskrat suppers in Maryland's Chesapeake Bay country. "Folks around here can't get enough of it during the season and we cook it up every Friday," says Bobby Murphey, owner of the Hotel Inn in Princess Anne. "When it comes to eating muskrat," he laughs, "that's when we separate real Eastern Shoremen from everyone else."

Perhaps it is the muskrat's name that reduces its appeal to non-native diners. Also in these days of franchised food diets, most of us suffer from diminished food curiosity. Can you picture McDonald's selling Muskrat Nuggets? Anyhow, one winter I came to terms with muskrat suppers quite by accident. On a cold gray February day I met my old crony, L. Q. Powell, for lunch at the Hotel Inn. While we waited for service, Powell went into a rapturous monologue about the big catch of muskrat pelts his grandson had trapped on the Somerset County marsh. When Murphey came to our table, he caught me in a distracted moment. "Muskrat's real nice today," he said. "Let me fix you a plate." With hardly a thought I nodded yes. Seconds later out strode Bobby from the kitchen with a steaming platter of meat cooked in a thick broth of sage and other spices with generous helpings of freshly boiled collard greens, hominy, and corn bread. Screwing up my courage, I dug in. I was surprised by the rich flavor of the meat which reminded me of stewed rabbit. "That's why we call it marsh hare," chortled L. Q. Powell. "You eat that regular and you'll be on your way to becoming an Eastern Shoreman."

Since that time I have become a muskrat devotee, though I keep this culinary conviction to myself when I am mixing with my city friends. They who wax poetic over snails in garlic would look down their noses at my primitive muskrat enthusiasm.

During the cold winter months of January and February, muskrat becomes a passion with Eastern Shore farmers and fisherfolk. At about thirty cents a pound, there is nothing more tasty or economical than muskrat. Restaurants in Salisbury are usually jammed during their muskrat luncheon specials.

Muskrat is also a favorite dish for fund-raising suppers at local churches on the Eastern Shore. The short season keeps interest high. Come spring, muskrats start moving around more on the marsh and get ready to breed. All that muskrat fever makes their meat too strong to eat.

Eating muskrat, however, is just a start. With 475,000 acres of Chesapeake marshland, Maryland is the rival of Louisiana for the title of muskrat capital of America. In a good year, muskrat trappers will harvest anywhere from 18,000 to 20,000 pounds of muskrat meat. Most of it is thrown away because it is really the fur pelt that the trapper wants. A good black muskrat pelt will bring anywhere from $4 to $8 from a fur buyer, and the trapping of these animals adds nearly $2 million to the state's economy. According to Maryland fur buyers like Morgan K. Bennett, the fashion world likes muskrat fur because it is light and buoyant and traps pockets of air that insulate against the cold. Thus trapping translates into something more than loose change, and many an Eastern Shore housewife owes that new freezer or satellite dish to those marsh denizens. The average trapper catches between four hundred and six hundred "rats" a year.

Most farmers who trap have a patchwork of nail "rat stretchers" in their attics to dry out the pelts. In Maryland trappers use Conibear body gripping traps for water trapping on the marsh. They place them in the runs or pathways of the muskrats. When the trap springs, the muskrat's neck is broken and death is immediate. The toothed trap so hated by animal rights advocates has been illegal in the state for years.

In skeleton and body build a muskrat is like an overgrown mouse with webbed hind feet and a flattened swimming tail. Muskrats flourish in Eastern Shore marshes and are prolific breeders. They are also very industrious animals; and if they don't inherit the earth because of their labor, it is not because they are unwilling to try. A trained eye can easily spot their cone-shaped lodges on the marsh. In fact, if you drive across the stretch of marsh from Vienna to Elliott's Island in Dorchester, you'll swear that the muskrats have built a marshland metropolis. Muskrats feed on marsh grass, cattails, and root stocks, and flourish in a variety of environments. Man has been trapping them for such a long time that he has entered the muskrat's habitat as a predator and has become part of the marsh life cycle.

For years, trappers have burned off marsh grass to clear the way for trapping; indirectly this has led to the growth in the spring of better grass, which the muskrats prefer. Though small, muskrats can be extraordinarily feisty. Find a live muskrat caught in a trap or corner one on dry land and you are liable to have four pounds of Hell on your hands.

In the 1920s French fur farmers attempted to domesticate American muskrats for their pelts. The matter quickly got out of hand as the animals escaped and proliferated across Europe. Today in many European countries muskrats are considered a menace as they undermine farm dikes and earthen works. Nations like Germany employ full-time "rat catchers" to keep the muskrat population down.

If the muskrat receives bad press in Europe, he is adored by the hundreds of American fur trappers who annually descend on Dorchester County, Maryland, for the North American Muskrat Skinning Championship. "You grab a muskrat, slashing once above the tail," says one expert. "Then you pull the hide off in one piece, like a nightgown, and make two quick knife cuts to the head to separate the pelt from the carcass." The object is to set the fastest time for skinning five muskrats. Usually the winner is Dorchester's own Wylie Abbott, a veteran marsh man. Abbott has been skinning muskrats since he was ten years old. Out on the marsh he is his own boss and plans to stay that way.

As many a trapper will tell you, going for muskrat out on the marsh is not for the faint-hearted. Walking on the spongy marsh is hard work. As you approach water, thick mud sucks at your boots. Occasionally you'll step into a hole and icy water will come in over the tops of your hip boots to torture you. Also the task of hauling a pack load of muskrats across the slippery marsh is exhausting. After slogging through the marsh for a couple of hours, you'll be ready to enjoy a couple of cans of beer and a hot meal and then tumble into a warm bed to rest.

In winter there is a stillness to the marsh that enables a man to concentrate on his thoughts wonderfully. The smell of sea and old salt grass is faintly pleasant and occasionally one can see turkey buzzards circling lazily over stands of pine where the land begins. When the spring comes the marsh will be alive with color and birdlife. The mosquitoes will be out, too, and men will leave the marsh to its original inhabitants. Muskrats will feast contentedly on cattail roots unaware of the desires and appetites of man.

11

Gold Coast

Wealth is not without its advantages.
        —John Kenneth Galbraith, *The Affluent Society*

F or over three centuries Talbot County has been the Gold
Coast of Maryland's Eastern Shore. Wealth has mattered
a great deal in Talbot's history, and the county has always been
dominated by an affluent squirearchy. It bears the name of one
of England's wealthiest seventeenth century families. The
Talbots were troublesome supporters of James I and fanatical
Catholics. From their Irish estates the Talbots caused no end
of mischief for the Crown by supporting the position of Irish
Catholics against the English government. When Talbot County was created in 1662, it bore the name of Lady Grace Talbot,
sister of the second Lord Baltimore and wife of Sir Robert
Talbot. Thus was Talbot part of the romantic tapestry of
Catholic wealth and intrigue in Jacobean England.[1] The tobacco aristocracy that emerged in Talbot, however, would be as
troublesome to Lord Baltimore as the Catholic aristocrats were
to the House of Commons. While they had money, they disliked
paying quitrent to Lord Baltimore and did everything they
could both legally and illegally to avoid doing so.

The wealth that emerged in Talbot was rough cut out of
a frontier environment. The early settlers had to put up with
pestilential swarms of insects, hailstorms, and lawlessness.
Cattle, hogs, and horses ran wild; and while Talbot enacted a
death penalty to curb lawlessness, it was seldom enforced
except in extreme cases. Aside from murderers, it was reserved

mainly for horse thieves and burglars; the loss of a man's horse or his material possessions was to the colonial mind the equivalent of death itself.

During Talbot's century-long tobacco era, servants were in short supply. By 1690 there were more Negro slaves from West Africa in Talbot than English servants. In 1712, for example, there were 492 Negroes among 4,178 whites or 11 percent of the population. By 1790 Talbot's 4,777 Negroes composed 45 percent of the total population.[2] Talbot planters produced the less fragrant Orinoco tobacco, which was a low-quality leaf more popular with the French than with the English. But it sold well and planters plowed their profits back into more land and slaves. Given the fluctuations of tobacco on the world commodity market and the soaring price of land in Talbot during the colonial period, many farmers of the county were unable to rise above a mere grubbing for a living. Increasingly Talbot's rich bought up the land and in Talbot's golden colonial age the county had a disturbingly large number of landless peasants. As historian David Skaggs has noted of Talbot and elsewhere, "Maryland was hardly the land of op- portunity depicted for colonial America."[3] To rise in Talbot County by 1750 one had to marry advantageously or build wealth in shipping, merchandise, or boatbuilding, activities that were generally out of the reach of small planters. On the eve of the American Revolution, Talbot was a society of inter- married cousins, aunts, and uncles that were incestuously intertwined in a web of power and money. Lloyds, Tilghmans, Goldsboroughs, Hollydays, Haywards, Trippes, and Nicolls played a fascinating elite game of marital ring-around-the- rosy.

Talbot's gentry had panache. Its members were so well- connected by birth, marriage, and business that scarcely any aspect of Maryland's social and economic life escaped them. To see the gentry of Talbot during the period 1750 to 1865 is to see men and women enjoying a life-style that in many respects was on the same plane as that enjoyed by many members of the British gentry of the same era. They lived well, dined sumptuously, rode to the hounds, and got hilariously drunk on grand occasions. They supported the Revolution with some reluctance and complained bitterly when British war sloops on the Chesapeake interfered with their winter social life in Baltimore. They produced leaders of integrity, like

William Paca, and slick careerists, like Tench Tilghman, who joined a silk stocking Light Infantry Company of Philadelphia during the Revolution in order to make the right connections. Polished, likeable, efficient, and aristocratic, Tench Tilghman secured a post as an aide on General George Washington's staff. Tilghman died young and is known for little save the fact that he carried the message on horseback to the Continental Congress in Philadelphia that Cornwallis had surrendered at Yorktown.

Samuel Chamberlaine is a good illustration of the kind of gentry that enjoyed power in Talbot County in the late colonial period. Chamberlaine arrived in Oxford in 1721 after serving several years as a seaman on the ship *Elizabeth* out of Liverpool. Having little but good looks, seamanship, and a head for keeping a ledger, he shrewdly married Mary Ungle, the daughter of one of Oxford's wealthiest merchants. His marriage into the Ungle family eased the newcomer's entry into Talbot society. Shortly thereafter, Chamberlaine worked as a factor for Foster Cunliffe & Sons, and both marriage and success in business and land speculation got him an appointment by the proprietary government as a justice of the peace. His wife died in 1726 and a few years later Chamberlaine married Henrietta Maria Lloyd, the orphaned daughter of James Lloyd, the merchant and planter. In 1733, thanks to money from his first wife and his second wife's dowry, Chamberlaine owned seventeen Negro slaves and over 2,600 acres of land. When he died in 1770 his estate included 4,169 acres of land and money and property worth £5,717 sterling. Chamberlaine's career was hardly unusual. A man with a good business sense and a knack for making good marriages could rise in the gentry. The Gold Coast in the colonial period was not all that snooty about a person's background and breeding. All it took to join the gentry was money—preferably in large amounts. As a postscript on Chamberlaine's career, his sons followed a similar Talbot pattern of fortune-wedding by taking brides in the wealthy Tilghman and Goldsborough families.

Talbot's gentry was as much a mercantile class as it was a planter oligarchy. Families like the Hollydays and Goldsboroughs made their money from the practice of law and from land speculation. Often they grew wealthy not from planting tobacco, per se, but from trading in it. They served as brokers between the rich mercantile houses of Liverpool and Bristol and smaller planters on the Eastern Shore. Also, whenever possible these men sought lucrative positions in the customs office which gave them a good salary and advance knowledge of business conditions in England. The gentry did not shun any type of business—from fish mongering to slave trading—as long as it held the prospect of a profit.

Merchant-planters like William Sharp built imposing homes on the water and elaborate outbuildings to store grain and hang tobacco. Most often their land was rented out to tenant farmers or small planters who owned a few slaves. In the mid–eighteenth century Talbot County had about thirty families whose wealth exceeded £2,700 each. Colonial historians claim that this was the level of wealth that separated the common sort from the better sort on the Eastern Shore at that time. These families controlled about 45 percent of all the property in the county while the bottom third of whites in the county held only two percent of the land and wealth. "In this contrast between poor and rich," writes historian Paul Clemens, "Talbot resembled England and the plantation colonies to the South."[4] Most small Talbot planters earned from £15 to £20 a year. A poor tenant farmer in colonial Talbot was lucky to have £3 at the end of a harvest. As large land owners consolidated their wealth and intermarried, it became harder and harder for those without considerable property to rise in local society, regardless of their talent. Between 1662 and 1750, or less than a hundred years, an oligarchy whose ancestors were indentured servants, common seamen, timber cutters, herdsmen, and office clerks and bastard offspring of royal officials had become as snobbish as the French aristocracy.

The Lloyd family stood at the pinnacle of this Gold Coast squirearchy. For over two centuries the Lloyds ruled over Talbot County and the Eastern Shore and lived on estates that rivaled English dukedoms. The first Edward Lloyd, a shrewd Welshman, acquired a large tract on the Eastern Shore for his work in returning the proprietorship to Lord Baltimore after it had been seized briefly by the Puritan faction in England during the 1640s. Lloyd established an estate on the Wye River and then went back to England to lead the gentlemanly life of absentee landlord. His grandson, Edward Lloyd II, worked the family holdings, traded slaves, and immersed himself in politics. The third Lloyd inherited the biggest fortune in America upon the death of his half-uncle, Richard Bennett III, one of the shrewdest promoters, planters, and speculators to emerge in the New World.

The Lloyds built elaborate manor houses and Wye House still stands in Talbot County today as a symbol of that lost world of the eighteenth and nineteenth century Eastern Shore gentry. While the Lloyds were good at making advantageous marriages and inheriting money, they were also good at making money as well. They invested in land, slaves, and transoceanic vessels. When tobacco faltered on the international market, they became wheat farmers; their orchards turned out a seemingly endless supply of porter and brandy. Their lavish entertainments had but one object—the furthering of Lloyd interests in Annapolis, Baltimore, and Philadelphia.

When the British burnt Wye House during the Revolution, the Lloyds built an even more imposing structure. There was a magic spell about Wye House—its orangery (a building for growing exotic fruits), its imposing lawns and hedges patterned after Versailles, and the manor house with its double wings for library and office—that few could resist. The Lloyds loved horse racing, and Edward Lloyd (1744-1796) owned the famous horse Nancy Bywell, which won the Annapolis Jockey Club purse of 100 guineas. His son Edward Lloyd IV (1779-1834), who later became governor of Maryland and a United States senator, loved cockfighting so much in his youth that he was called by Eastern Shoremen "Lord Cock De Doodle Do."

The Lloyds dressed their house slaves in green livery and when their imposing barge with its dozen rowing slaves ventured forth on the waters of the Chesapeake, a canon on board boomed with the noise of their approach. Those were the days when pharaoh did indeed live on the Wye. Young Francis Scott Key romped here and had sense enough to marry into the family.

The centerpiece, however, was Edward Lloyd III. Dressed in silk breeches, a buff-lapelled waistcoat, white silk hose, and black shoes buckled in silver, Lloyd was accompanied by a black page who carried his master's snuffbox. When "Edward the Magnificent," as his friends called him, was seated in his barge, the slaves fired six volleys from their blunderbusses to signal that Mr. Lloyd was on the water. Even by the time of the Revolution, Wye plantation was a showpiece. Enormous wrought-iron gates imported from Italy were a famous county landmark. The Lloyds even installed a fake moat at the end of the road to their plantation to add feudal splendor to their landscape.

The Lloyd Memorandum Book in the Maryland Historical Society lists family holdings in 1781: 11,844 acres of land, 271 slaves, 162 horses, 524 head of cattle, 783 sheep, 413 hogs, 130,000 pounds of tobacco, 200 barrels of Indian corn, a schooner of 6 tons, and silver and property worth over £56,000 sterling. Few English lords could approach in their own domain the munificence of the Lloyds.

Surprisingly, the Lloyds did not dissipate the family fortune like many antebellum planters. Rather they held on to their wealth for nine generations before the male line of the family was exhausted and female descendants married into wealthy families of corporate America in the twentieth century. Until emancipation, the Lloyds were one of the largest slave-holding families in America. The Lloyds seldom sold their slaves as they were part of the family empire that the Lloyds ruled seemingly by divine right. Employing overseers known for harsh discipline, the Lloyds were known as stern slave masters. After the American Revolution, blacks on the Lloyd plantation sang a short ditty about Colonel Edward Lloyd: "God Almighty never intended that any man should own a thousand niggers, but Colonel Lloyd has nine hundred and ninety nine."

By the time of the Civil War, the Lloyd family, in addition to its Eastern Shore holdings, owned plantations in Mississippi, Louisiana, and Arkansas. The Lloyd plantations were exceptionally well run by the Lloyds themselves, and the central farm in Talbot was like a city with its forges, carpenter shops, gristmill, smokehouse, icehouse, numerous storage sheds, and over 180 slaves. Colonel Edward Lloyd V during the late antebellum period was one of the most gracious hosts in America and few people could match the richness and elegance of his French crystal, liveried servants, and delicious Eastern Shore cooking. The Wye House that Frederick Douglass saw as a slave resident there in 1824 was a great house overflowing with handsome well-dressed men and women.[5] It was a many-meadowed plantation with fields of wheat and private deer parks. Sheep grazed on the lawn and black servants moved silently among the visitors and served mint juleps. A private schooner awaited at the dock in readiness to take 150 tons of grain to southern Europe or Mediterranean ports or to take several families to Baltimore for a grand ball.

While there were some Marylanders who were wealthier than the Lloyds of Wye House, few of them lived as well and none lived better. Today's coupon-clipping gentry on the Gold Coast hardly come close to the luxury and sense of absolute mastery in Talbot county that the Lloyds once enjoyed. This is the vision of the old Gold Coast that continues both to haunt and to intrigue Talbot County today.

*   *   *

Today's Talbot County is truly an enjoyable place, especially when you do not have to earn a living there. Its secluded plantations, quiet coves, and navigable rivers make it a sailor's and hunter's delight. All it takes is money, for land is expensive and job opportunities are few. For the émigré rich who have been moving into Talbot County since the end of the nineteenth century this has never been a problem. When the affluent set of Philadelphia and New York first discovered Talbot in the 1880s, they found an enchanting region of decaying manor houses, stunning land and waterscapes, and obedient Negroes. The old tidewater aristocracy by this time was broke, having lost a fortune in racial emancipation and declining world grain prices. Land agents in Easton, like William Halstean, advertised prime lands at bargain prices. One could buy a manor house with servants' quarters and two hundred acres of land with waterfront footage for $12,000. Large tracts of prime farmland could be snapped up for $30 an acre. Halstean was far from modest when he advertised Talbot. Said this energetic promoter: "If you value health, good soil, climate, markets, schools, churches, railroads, navigation, fruits in profusion, crabs, clams, terrapins, wild fowl, and all other salt water luxuries, don't fail to visit Talbot County, Md. before you buy a home for your family."[6]

Here then was a chance to live as a country squire and to savor an aristocratic life-style that was becoming impossible to enjoy in the congested immigrant-ridden industrial cities of the North. Railroads on the Eastern Shore made it possible to take weekend trips from Philadelphia and Wilmington to Easton and other tidewater towns and soon the nouveau riche of America's industrial and financial order began to summer and holiday at their plantations in Talbot County. Economically depressed but historically rich Talbot appreciated the arrivistes and gave them what they so urgently craved—legitimacy.

Talbot County did not become famous as the Gold Coast of the Eastern Shore until around 1912 when rich sportsmen like Sidney Schuyler of New Jersey and Coleman DuPont from Wilmington and a host of Pennsylvania millionaires like J. Ramsey Speer (who caused Talbot County to be jokingly referred to as "little Pittsburgh") put the region on the blue-chip map. By the end of the 1920s the wealthy residents of Talbot could fill an Eastern Shore edition of *Who's Who*. Talbot also attracted wealthy eccentrics like "The Mad Stewarts." Jacqueline and Glenn Stewart were independently wealthy and built a stucco Moorish-style castle on a point of land opposite St. Michaels. The castle had walls three feet thick, a three-story tower, and an oak-and-steel-plate door. Glenn Stewart slept with a loaded pistol and wore a patch over one eye. One day in 1935 Stewart stepped on his yacht *Centaur*, and sailed for Nassau. He never returned, though his widow waited for him at the pink castle until her death in 1964. When appraisers valued the estate, in addition to the property, they found $160,000 in gold coin, bushel baskets of jewelry, a 1931 Duesenberg convertible, and an elegant Steinway piano.

Hollywood soon followed in discovering the Eastern Shore. In the 1930s, Gary Cooper and the famous actress, Fay Wray, came to Talbot to act in a movie called *First Kiss*. The film dealt with the highly improbable story of a young burly oysterman of the Eastern Shore falling madly in love with an upper-crust socialite. The film company hired eighteen watermen and commandeered twenty-five schooners and skipjacks. While the film was of little consequence other than being Gary Cooper's first feature role, it did put Talbot on the map as a proper locale, not only for "society," but also for the Hollywood dream merchants as well.

Neither depression nor war stemmed the tide of the swell set into Talbot County. Among the arrivals were heavyweight champion Gene Tunney, Kimberly-Clark's John R. Kimberly, Jr., IBM's Thomas J. Watson, Jr., New York financier August Belmont, Coca Cola's Lee Tailey, Caterpillar tractor magnate Percy A. Ransome, and numerous members of the DuPont family. By the 1960s Talbot had the singular reputation of having more millionaires per capita than any county in Maryland. Soon politicians and government officials, like George McGovern, bought secluded Talbot hideaways, and a host of lesser millionaires flocked to Talbot County. Lucky tourists occasionally encountered baseball owner, Bill Veeck, at the bar of the Tidewater Inn at Easton, rubbed shoulders with August Belmont at a Chesapeake dog show, or caught a glimpse of famous newscaster Walter Cronkite on a yacht in the Miles River.[7] Hollywood stars such as Phil Harris, Bing Crosby, and Robert Mitchum also flocked to the Gold Coast.

Known for their elegant parties and passionate interest in local philanthropy, these affluent outsiders constituted the new gentry of Talbot County. As they lived in expensive homes on necks of land that jutted out into the creeks and rivers of the county, they were referred to by local farmers as the "Peach Blossom Creek Crowd" or the "rich neck aristocrats." Wealthy business executives kept their own planes at the Easton Airport and commuted to their command posts in Washington and Philadelphia. While the wealthy reflected different points of view on local politics and the direction of Talbot, they were united at least in the fact that they had fled both the city and suburbia and wanted a place where they would not be stalked by the specter of crime and their investment could appreciate in value.

The Gold Coast's most famous celebrity is novelist James Michener. A sometime resident and frequent visitor to Talbot County, Michener brought a touch of glamor to the Gold Coast when he was doing research in Talbot for his book, *Chesapeake*. Indeed, Michener's rides on oyster boats, plane flights over the Bay, and visits to the Maryland Room in the Talbot County Free Library were nearly as newsworthy as the book he was writing. Michener met the Gold Coast society through the activities of the Cheapeake Bay Maritime Museum in St. Michaels. Well-traveled, well-storied, self-deprecating, and a multimillionaire, James Michener charmed Talbot society. Everyone wanted to have a party for him; everyone wanted Michener and his wife to grace their dinner table. Talbot's squires loved *Chesapeake*. It confirmed their belief that they were living in one of the nicest and most historic areas in America.

* * *

There are three nuggets on Talbot's Gold Coast: Easton, Oxford, and St. Michaels; and the towns are as popular with county residents as they were in the colonial era. Each has withstood the stresses of time and changing economic life. And today there is a new spirit of optimism in these towns as if they have suddenly come alive after shaking a centuries-old languor.

Easton is the old colonial capital of Maryland's Eastern Shore. During the colonial period, transportation problems necessitated two capitals in the colony, Annapolis and Easton. After the Revolution this arrangement was ended, though Easton was still a major legal center and hostelry. History records that in 1809 Easton was an important medical center and headquarters for some of the most clamorous lawyers on the Eastern Shore. In that year the Maryland Assembly passed the Eastern Shore Compact which recognized the Eastern Shore as a distinct political entity. As such, the law provided that one of the two United States senators must come from the Eastern Shore. Such was the power of Talbot's gentry in Annapolis that the compact's original purpose was to prevent the Eastern Shore from having *two* senators. This compact was not repealed until 1896 despite its obvious contravention of the United States Constitution that forbade state governments from adding state qualifications for federal office holding.

Politics and law were the lifeblood of Easton; when Talbot's gentry went to Annapolis, the lawyers went with them. William Eddis, the social gadfly of colonial Annapolis, was prompted to remark of the Eastern Shore in 1770 that "a litigious spirit is very apparent in this country." As is often the case, the legal disputes were more over money than principle. The main instigator of trouble in this sense was Talbot's Matthew Tilghman. An active leader of Maryland's antiproprietary party, Tilghman strenuously objected to Lord Baltimore's personal bureaucracy of tax gatherers and fee grabbers. The Lords Baltimore got about £32,000 a year from the province, a matter that did not sit well with the gentry who would have liked to grab a few fees for themselves.

Even today Easton likes to think of itself as a colonial town. The late Eastern Shore historian, Norman Harrington, once wrote that despite the predominant Victorian architecture, "the town has a pseudo-colonial image of itself." At the moment, many of the old houses in Easton, which a few short years ago were crumbling relics from the nineteenth century, are being refurbished. Many retirees from Baltimore have come to Easton to savor either the joy or curse of having an old house to maintain. But they become members of the Historical

Society of Talbot County or Historic Easton, Inc. and historical preservation consumes their resources and monopolizes their energies.

Also, old ideas die hard in Easton. At the county court-house on Washington Street you can still see the statue that was erected in 1916 to honor the ninety-six soldiers from Talbot who served in the Confederate army. During the Civil War, the wealthy planter, Tench Tilghman II, was a rabid secessionist and tried without success to raise arms for the rebels. In June 1861, four hundred Union troops from Baltimore raided the armory at Easton and confiscated all the ammunition and muskets. More than three hundred men from the county served in the Union army during the Civil War but they have been conveniently forgotten. Many of these patriotic soldiers were blacks who later established a little village called Unionville on the Miles River.[8]

Not all of the Gold Coast's history has dealt with money. Easton was once a major center for the Quaker fellowship; and today you can still visit the Third Haven Meeting House which was built there in 1682-1683. In 1700, William Penn, the great Quaker proprietor, held a meeting under one of the massive oaks there that included Lord and Lady Baltimore. The Quaker conscience was always troubled about money and slaves in Talbot County. When Quakers spoke out against the evils of their day, they were greeted with hostility or indifference. In the colonial period the Quaker fellowship on the Eastern Shore was quite extensive, ranging from Somerset to Kent Island. Many of these Quakers had fled religious persecution on Virginia's Eastern Shore. Today only a handful of Quakers remain in Easton and Third Haven Meeting House is both a historical landmark and a house of worship.

The town of Oxford is a lazy little tidewater village whose roots stretch deep into Talbot's past. Oxford's cool summer breezes, relaxed atmosphere, and convenient harbor on the Tred Avon River for sailing vessels have made it a popular port of call since the colonial period. From a mariner's standpoint Oxford could not be more convenient. It is built on a milelong peninsula that has a deep creek behind it that in the colonial era was deep enough for oceangoing ships.

Ship captains were loading tobacco at Oxford as early as 1658, and it soon became an important customs port and trading center. Oxford was also one of the original thirty towns laid out by Lord Baltimore for his Maryland Plantation, but it was the merchants rather than the lord proprietor who turned Oxford into a prosperous seaport.

The town's fortunes in the colonial era were inextricably linked with that of Foster Cunliffe & Sons of Liverpool. This British mercantile company traded in tobacco, beaver pelts, general merchandise, and slaves, and in 1738 the firm sent young Robert Morris to be their chief factor or trader in Oxford. A man of humble birth, Morris was a shrewd trader and made a fortune for Foster Cunliffe and himself. The local inn and main street of Oxford continue to bear Morris's name.

Most of the profits were in slaves as Talbot planters eagerly bought Negroes for their tobacco farms along the Tred Avon and Miles rivers. Soon other London merchants came to Oxford and the town flowered. Planters made Oxford their social center and the streets of the town were often thronged with carriages and individuals who dressed in the latest London fashion. Access to deep water and dense oak forests made Oxford a natural as a shipbuilding center and the town soon had six boatyards.

In 1742 Robert Morris received an assistant from Foster Cunliffe in the form of Henry Callister to help him in his work. Although relations between the two factors were often cool, the men respected each other. Callister had a keen eye for social observation, and nouveau riche planters did not impress him. He kept a copious notebook of the day-to-day activities of Oxford, much to the delight of today's local historians. When a ship arrived, a small cannon was fired to alert the planters, and the people of Oxford flocked to the dock, eager to receive letters and inspect the London dry goods and general merchandise. If there were slaves on board, they were quickly auctioned off. Usually the ship captain would treat the townsmen to a keg of rum to induce spirited bidding.

In 1750 Robert Morris died as a result of a freak accident. During a naval salute a piece of cannon wadding struck him and shattered his arm above the elbow. Within a few days he was dead. His young son, Robert Morris, Jr., however, would have his father's financial talent and would ultimately go on to fame and glory in Philadelphia as the financier of the American Revolution.

By the late colonial period, however, the tobacco economy of the Eastern Shore began to decline and the fortunes of

Oxford-Bellevue Ferry. Photograph by Pat Vojtech.

Oxford suffered as a result. The only excitement to stir the town was the arrival of 208 French-speaking Acadians in 1753. These wretched refugees from the French and Indian War were not welcomed by the town, and Henry Callister had to appeal for food and shelter for them on "the principles of humanity." Anti-Catholic xenophobia was widespread in Talbot at this time and feelings against the French were high. Wrote one observer: "Even the charity they received was grudgingly bestowed." Callister had persuaded local planter Edward Lloyd to feed and clothe the Acadians but this did not last long as the Talbot aristocrat was never very receptive to the poor, especially poor outsiders. Ultimately most of the Acadians were settled in Somerset County and other Eastern Shore communities.[9]

During the French and Indian War Oxford's tobacco trade with England suffered greatly. Local soil exhaustion and the rise of the new competitive port of Baltimore sounded the death knell of this small tidewater port. What little prosperity remained was destroyed by the commercial interruptions of the American Revolution. By 1793 Oxford was in a sad state and one observer wrote:

> The once well-worn streets are now given up in grass, save a few narrow tracks made by sheep and swine, and the strands have the appearance of an uninhabited island than where human feet had ever trod . . . .[10]

After 1840, Oxford would become an important oyster and tomato processing center but it did not recapture the state of colonial grace from which it had fallen. By the early twentieth century, Oxford was a raucous watermen's town and port of call of the Chesapeake's oyster fleet. Today the ships of Foster Cunliffe that docked at the wharves of Oxford have been replaced by a sleek armada of yachts owned by millionaire industrialists. Oxford was created by wealth and now it has been reclaimed by businessmen, bankers, investors, and speculators. The watermen and ship chandlers are long gone and the boatyards repair pleasure vessels rather than build cargo ships. Oxford now has a recreational aristocracy. The wealthy began to move into Oxford in the 1970s. There were plenty of architecturally sound old homes to restore; the town had an historic ambience; and it was ideally suited for yachtsmen. Also, the town was within easy striking distance of the metropolitan centers of Baltimore and Washington. Within a decade, old genteel but slightly down-at-the-heels Oxford took on the new shiny patina of wealth, and Oxford local Hazel Newham would complain, "Hardly any of the people who we knew are still here." With the new wealth came a kind of big-city standoffishness that bewildered and annoyed the natives. The outsiders, they complained, didn't take much trouble to find out who lived next door. Property values soared; and local taverns became trendy restaurants for the yachting crowd.

It got so bad, says one Tred Avon oysterman, that "you have to go clear out of town to have a beer at a workingman's bar." The gentrification of Oxford was particularly hard on blacks who constituted an important part of the community. In the enclave of the wealthy there was no room for black cannery workers and boatyard mechanics.

Yet some of the natives made huge profits in real estate and not all of Oxford's inhabitants thought that an influx of wealthy outsiders was bad. Fletcher Hanks, for example, a former seafood packer, thought the gentrification of Oxford a good thing and saved the village from lapsing into economic and architectural decay. Nor were all of Oxford's newcomers retired millionaires and yachtsmen. Many less affluent but well-educated couples were seeking a quiet beautiful place to live and raise a family.

When Peter Dunbar grew fed up with university life in central Pennsylvania, he spread a map of the Atlantic coast on the kitchen table and began to study the possibilities of finding a new life in a tidewater community. For Dunbar and his wife, Nancy Wilson, Oxford met all their criteria. It was beautiful, safe, and serene and not too far distant from friends and relatives. "We chose location first, " said Dunbar. "The matter of earning a living was secondary. I was a skilled engineer and handy with a boat and I envisioned that if all else failed, I'd tong oysters. At the time we were romantic. We had been formed by the consciousness-raising of the 1960s, and were not interested in corporate America." Oxford was more staid than the Dunbars had anticipated, but they adapted to local conservative ways and soon joined the Oxford Civic Association.

In the 1970s there was a considerable amount of tension in the town over economic development. Many of the natives welcomed tract homes and townhouse development plans because it gave work to locals. The outsiders like Dunbar and others wanted to keep Oxford in its pristine form. Planning and zoning was the battleground. Says Peter Dunbar: "It is hard to argue with people who have been poor for generations who are now sitting on zoning boards that economic growth is a bad thing."

While zoning arguments raged in Oxford, the influx of outsiders continued and a house that once sold for $70,000 skyrocketed to $300,000. Many of the new people became active in community life and the Oxford Citizens Association gradually worked out several zoning compromises with the town government. "Now we are part of the establishment," laughs Nancy Wilson. "We hope to be able to keep Oxford quiet, secure, and safe. We'll see what happens."

Peter Dunbar became the first Ph.D. to join the Oxford Volunteer Fire Department. Within the same year the fire department accepted blacks and women as members. Only eight hundred people live there most of the year. Oxford is a small town with small resources, Dunbar reflects. "It's a little scary when you think that if a million dollar property catches fire at 3:00 A.M., the fire department consists of me, a minister, and the pregnant woman down the street."

For the moment, at least, Oxford is a serene place. In summer the town expands to about two thousand but it remains a place where you can still close up every bar in town and be in bed by midnight. The old Robert Morris Inn still commands the strand along the Tred Avon River. Travelers stop to feed the ducks before crossing the river on the Bellevue ferry and are enchanted by the town's colonial setting. The rich tobacco factors of the colonial era created Oxford; perhaps today's affluent émigrés to Oxford will keep it prosperous.

Unlike Oxford, St. Michaels is no longer a sleepy port town. It has become a tidewater tourist mecca, created in part by the nationally acclaimed Chesapeake Bay Maritime Museum. Tour buses regularly rumble through the streets and traffic in summer in St. Michaels is often bumper to bumper. Antique shops line Talbot Street with eye-catching names like Sentimental Journey and Hodgepodge Collectibles. In fact natives complain that St. Michaels should be renamed St. Teeks—"for all we have here now," complains local resident Jane Lowe,"are antiques and boutiques." Such complaints, however, do little to deter the day-tripping Washingtonian. The shops of St. Michaels are filled with the kind of instant tradition that appeals to middle-class metropolitan taste.

The town lost an important zoning battle over whether or not a new hotel could be constructed in the heart of town and the traffic for the St. Michaels Harbor Inn and Marina has added further to the congestion of the village. The fern bars have invaded St. Michaels, too, and when an old building suddenly is transformed into a "mews," you know that something strange has happened to this old watermen's town.

Despite the tourist invasion, St. Michaels is still one of the most charming villages on Maryland's Eastern Shore. Modest white frame houses on shady side streets display American flags on summer afternoons and provide a setting worthy of a Norman Rockwell painting. The town harbor and wharves are still an important entrepôt for Chesapeake watermen, and at various times during the day you can watch them unloading their catches of crabs and oysters on the town dock.

St. Michaels is the oldest town in Talbot County and it was a trading center as early as the 1630s. Many of the houses in St. Michaels date from the colonial period and a walk through the town is a walk through American history. St. Michaels was an important shipbuilding center and the town played an important role in the War of 1812. Here were equipped many of the privateers that preyed upon British oceangoing commerce. According to local history, the shipyards of St. Michaels constructed vessels that were responsible for the capture or destruction of over five hundred British merchant ships. So great a threat was St. Michaels, that the British attacked the town on August 9, 1813. The town imposed a blackout, and its shrewd citizens placed lanterns in the trees to misdirect the cannon barrage, thus fooling the British. Only one house was struck and it is known as the Cannonball House.

After the War of 1812 St. Michaels became an important seafood processing center and was the watermen's capital of Talbot. The Miles River was crowded with bugeyes, schooners, and other vessels of the oystering and coastal trade. "Every boat carried a jug of rum against the cold," remembered Frederick Douglass, the fugitive slave who lived for a time in St. Michaels, and the village was "an unsaintly as well as unsightly place." Outsiders were rare in St. Michaels and, even as late as the 1950s, the town was more important as a grain milling and hardware center for watermen and farmers than it was as a tourist attraction.

In the 1960s St. Michaels awoke from the somnolence of rural life when the Chesapeake Bay Maritime Museum was founded. The museum was dedicated to the lore and history of the Chesapeake and its attractive and tasteful exhibits made it a mecca for Bay country visitors. After a shaky start on a minuscule budget, the museum recruited Jim Holt, a wealthy corporation executive, to be its administrator. Holt and his wife owned a vacation home in Bozman and he was eager to retire from directing the Latin American operations of the Honeywell Corporation. The Holts easily fit into the circle of Gold Coast society and within a short time the struggling museum was the darling of Talbot philanthropy. Said former museum aide Sandy Buchman: "Jim Holt was well off in his own right, he was both shrewd and modest and he traveled in the right circles."

Within a decade Holt turned a small struggling museum into a premier institution on the Eastern Shore. When Holt retired, the museum had seventeen structures on eighteen acres and more buildings were being added to create a "Waterman's Village." The museum is the home of skipjacks and other sailing craft that are disappearing from the Chesapeake maritime industry; and you can see artisans and shipwrights working there. Therefore, the museum is preserving the skills of the past as well as interpreting them. Each year the museum's 100,000 ticket-buying visitors help fuel the local economy, a matter of great consequence to the revenue-conscious town.

Most Chesapeake watermen have been ambivalent about the museum since its inception. They fail to see why tourists would be so excited about the day-to-day drudgery of a Chesapeake waterman's life. Some are openly critical and blame the museum for transforming the town into a kind of Chesapeake Williamsburg where watermen are appreciated as heritage objects rather than as working men and women. "The museum," argues ex-waterman Varley Lang, "doomed St. Michaels for us. Our Boshell's Boat Yard got turned into a hotel and the museum won't let oyster trucks on its docks."

Many locals who have been distressed by the metamorphosis of St. Michaels worry that Tilghman Island will suffer a similar fate. Tilghman Island is the last major community of watermen left in the county, and it is being similarly pressured. Says veteran skipjack captain Pete Switzer: "These government civil service types can come down here and buy a $70,000 house on Tilghman for weekends and think it's a great bargain. For a waterman that is a fortune. I fear that many of us will end up living in trailers before too long."

*   *   *

Easton, St. Michaels, Oxford, and Tilghman may not yet be household words on the Atlantic seaboard. However, these communities in Talbot County and others like them in the tidewater are among the fastest growing and most affluent in the United States. While large cities like Baltimore continue to decline and the suburbs seem besieged by traffic and tract houses, small towns on the Eastern Shore are attracting people. Many Americans have never felt comfortable with cities and have found them to be, in the words of Thomas Jefferson, "a cancer on the body politick." They don't like the suburbs either because they are sterile. More and more people with college degrees are opting for what they call on the Eastern Shore "the simplicity of life and rural atmosphere." If these new migrants to Talbot County and elsewhere on the Shore have anything in common beyond their educational background, it is their self-centered individualism. They have opted for something that they call quality of life over family ties and roots in the community of their birth. They want the good life—the weekends on their sailboats, the parties on Peach Blossom Creek, the easygoing commercial life of Easton, and the freedom from the racial and social pressures of modern urban life. They could have made more money elsewhere, but they chose not to.

According to Peter Dunbar and Nancy Wilson, themselves metropolitan emigrants to Oxford, the people who come to Talbot County and the Eastern Shore dance to the beat of their own drum. "They love the region so much," says Dunbar, "that careers and income become secondary." In Oxford, St. Michaels, and Easton, you can find waitresses and bartenders with college degrees; and in Oxford you can hire a carpenter who is an expert in Shakespeare.

"Tourism has picked up the county and made it possible for young people to stay and work," adds Robin Wightman, an Easton YMCA leader. "Ten years ago there were no jobs in Talbot unless you wanted to tend bar." Now it is possible to stay and work, she says, but there is still little upward mobility.

"You'll get a job and stay in it." But there are other compensations. Talbot has become a thriving artistic community, and many of the wealthy patrons allow artists and writers to live cheaply in cottages and carriage houses on their estates.

The only question is how long will it last? Many people in Talbot worry about what will happen when the terrain cannot take more wells and septic tanks, when traffic begins to clog roads that were once pleasant country lanes. Thoughtful citizens like Jane Lowe, the widow of Thomas Hunter Lowe, former speaker of the House of Delegates, have seen the road to St. Michaels from Easton become "a race track of automobiles and fast-flying trucks." All the tourists are anxious to get to St. Michaels and on weekends that place is as congested as any city. "We locals avoid it on Saturdays," says Lowe.

For Easton businessman Jerry Hutchins, Talbot still offers a genteel way of life but he worries that the county is becoming a bedroom community. Low taxes and low education budgets will do little to redress Talbot's socioeconomic problems, he argues. Whether folks like it or not, Talbot is changing rapidly, Hutchins concludes. "It has been sitting here for too long. We are too close to metropolitan areas to remain bucolic."

With town property values escalating and rural property restricted by the County Land Use Plan to two-acre lots, many police officers, schoolteachers, clerks, and skilled workers are unable to live in the community in which they work. Also, the soaring demand for recreational property has had a disastrous impact on one group of people in Talbot, the watermen. Oxford and St. Michaels used to be quiet fishing villages. Now for many residents they are weekend retreats from life in Washington; and you will find few watermen residing in either community. They have either sold out or been pushed out by higher rents and property taxes.

Black residents of Talbot County have also felt the pressure of increased cost of living. Talbot has one of the highest percentages on the Eastern Shore of elderly black residents.[11] The black community of Oxford has been largely displaced by gentrification; and the black community of Bellevue immediately across the river and accessible by ferry is beginning to be surrounded by upscale housing development. Furthermore, blacks still feel the sting of Talbot's racism.

In 1986 Miles Gray, a black hotel executive at the Tidewater Inn in Easton thought that he had found "a piece of heaven" when he moved to Tilghman Island. He rented a secluded waterfront home on two and a half acres of land. Gray's initial enthusiasm for the place, however, waned as he and his wife and children began to get "a lot of funny glares." When Gray entered the local stores, the people would suddenly grow quiet and not resume talking until he left. In response to the cold shoulder by the community, the Gray family began to shop in St. Michaels.

Shortly thereafter in April 1986, a group of rowdies at the McDaniel Country Store halfway between St. Michaels and Tilghman planned a visit to the Gray family. In the early morning, the group erected a Ku Klux Klan cross on the front lawn of Gray's residence and set it ablaze. It was a clear message that blacks, especially middle class "blacks who wore suits," were not welcome on Tilghman Island. Although most watermen denied any knowledge of the cross-burning incident, information led the police to four whites who were subsequently fined and jailed for their heinous acts. Miles Gray's "piece of Heaven" was shattered by the incident and the black professional quit his job at the Tidewater Inn, and moved his family to a more hospitable metropolitan environment. Although the Talbot County government claimed that the cross burning was an isolated incident, the black community saw it as part of Talbot's racism.

In February 1987, the town of Easton tightly controlled a twenty-five-minute Ku Klux Klan rally that was staged to support the criminals who had participated in the cross burning. Few people attended. Several blocks away, meanwhile, a biracial crowd of over four hundred staged a counter-rally for decency and fair treatment of blacks in Talbot. According to Police Chief Edward Blessing, "The spectators at the rally were in complete disagreement with the Klan and the onlookers were more curious than anything."[12]

✳   ✳   ✳

The passions of the Gold Coast are reserved for yachting. Nearly everyone in Talbot of financial means owns a boat and participates in the local yachting culture; and county harbors and coves bob with craft whose value far outstrips the annual wage and net worth of the average citizen. At the bottom of the scale are "stinkpotters" and dilettantes—owners of powerboats and unskilled owners of sailboats who do not know the difference between a spinnaker and a boom vang. Most of these Sunday sailors are content to remain at fancy anchorages in Oxford and St. Michaels; and their boats are little more than floating cocktail lounges. As you move upward in the culture, you meet the status-conscious doctors and lawyers who are drawn to boating because it allows them to hobnob with the better sort and because sailing is a rather classy way of getting back to nature on Chesapeake Bay. At the top are the serious sailors, the men and women who live for the yachting. It is they who crew the great Chesapeake log canoes, test their skills on sleek yachts, and sometimes wager their lives against a stormy sea. The true yachtsmen of Talbot has only one yardstick of value judgment: are you good helmsman or crew? All else is secondary. These are the men and women of the regattas. They will drive hundreds of miles just to crew in a race and pay a king's ransom for a craft that will help them win a regatta. They speak the language of boats, lines, sails, and navigation; and these yachtsmen may very well be the privileged heirs of a maritime culture that has nearly vanished in the Chesapeake Bay country.[13]

In 1909 Robert Barrie and his brother, George, first drew attention to the Chesapeake Bay for America's yachting elite. These two fun-loving wealthy New Englanders were the first of the blue-chip set to cruise the Bay, and their articles, which were originally published in the British magazine, *Yachtsman*, were later issued as a book entitled *Cruises, Mainly in the Bay of the Chesapeake*. The Barrie brothers approached their adventure with the élan and panache of veteran yachtsmen. In the summer of 1908 they cast off to explore the Chesapeake from the Corinthian Yacht Club at Essington, twelve miles below Philadelphia on the Delaware River. Their boat, *Mona*, rivaled any of today's opulent craft. The cutter was forty-two feet long with an eight-foot beam, drew five feet, four inches, and had a stateroom, saloon, forecastle, galley, and toilet. To assist them, the Barries brought their cook and two sailors.

Once through the Chesapeake and Delaware Canal, they proceeded to sail down the Bay. From the Elk River, they headed for the Turkey Point light and took advantage of the spanking breeze to run across the Bay to Havre de Grace. Occasionally they anchored, swam, or rowed along the shore in their small skiff. Suppers on board were worthy of the cuisine of Delmonico's, and the Barries capped their evenings with copious tumblers of Scotch whiskey.

A westerly breeze carried them to Tolchester Beach in Kent County, and they were able to tack back across the Bay toward Annapolis before the wind died and stranded them in the Magothy River. The Barrie log continues to make a yachts-man envious: "Next morning the clanking of chain and slatting of sails awoke us about six o'clock, and as there was a fine north-north-west breeze we immediately joined the concert, and were soon slipping out with the fleet. In the Bay we found a regular fleet of schooners running wing-and-wing. Immediately after breakfast we followed suit, and were soon over the twenty miles to Bloody Point Bar, on the south side of Kent Island; here we got the wind on the beam, set balloon staystail, and had a most glorious bit of sailing across Eastern Bay . . . . "[14]

The Barries had their perilous times as well. In Annapolis a swift running tide nearly caused their boat to be smashed at a drawbridge, and fierce summer squalls tested their seaman-ship. When the Barries returned to their yacht club on the Delaware River after several days on the Bay, they were ready for a good meal and a few stiff drinks. Not a bad cruise at all, this Chesapeake, said they.

Since the publication of the Barries' adventures, there has been a proliferation of guidebooks to sailing the Chesa-peake. Many of the old Bay anchorages that the Barries used have become thriving modern "boatels" replete in some cases with showers, flush toilets, electricity, and restaurants. In Crisfield, for example, yachtsmen can tie up in a modern clean marina at Somers Cove that even has a private swimming pool for its patrons.

The Chesapeake yachting season officially begins with the blessing of the fleet at St. Michaels in May and the sailboats participating in the event are traditionally decorated with flowers, flags, and pennants. The boats then assemble near Navy Point and a memorial wreath is tossed into the water in memory of those who have lost their lives while sailing. As summer proceeds, the sailors sharpen their skills with week-end cruises up the Choptank River and daring sprints before the wind on the Miles and Eastern Bay. Such training is necessary because the August regattas are exceptionally stren-uous, dangerous, and competitive.

The jewel of the regattas, of course, is the Annapolis-Ox-ford Race, and it is one that few serious yachtsmen miss. Over a hundred yachts vie for trophies and set their spinnakers in a strong tide for Oxford. This regatta is a major tourist attraction and Oxford is abuzz with armchair mariners with binoculars. Discerning sailors will be able to see the pennants of the Annapolis Yacht Club, the Naval Academy Sailing Squadron, the Corsica River Yacht Club, the Miles River Yacht Club, and the Tred Avon Yacht Club as the boats fly before the wind. As in most regattas on the Chesapeake, the Miles River Yacht Club is represented by nearly a score of boats. Unless the skippers have to tack in light air, the race to Oxford is always a thrilling adventure. The yacht clubs have a wide popular following in Talbot County and their adventures are always breathlessly reported in the Easton *Star-Democrat.*

The late author Douglass Wallop enjoyed sailing out of his home port of Oxford and loved the races so much that he penned a delightful novel about yachting called *Regatta.* It is a comic tale of highjinks, stupidity born of inexperience, and romance during the Annapolis-Oxford Regatta and may very well be the best novel written about yachting on the Chesapeake. Wallop was best known for his book *The Year the Yankees Lost the Pennant,* which later became the Broadway hit *Damn Yankees.* The well-to-do author and dramatist regularly sailed the Tred Avon River and many of his fellow yachtsmen found their lives as sailors and partygoers chronicled in his novel *The Good Life.*

The most graceful vessels that sail on Chesapeake waters are often called "butterflies of the sea." These are the Chesapeake log canoes. Once the proud Chesapeake log sailing canoes were the mainstay of local oystering and commerce in the Chesapeake. Today there are two dozen left. Log canoes owe their origin to the Indians who dug out whole tree trunks and turned them into Bay craft. In the early 1800s Eastern Shore shipbuilders adapted the method by chopping a craft with an adz and other tools out of several whole logs attached together. Often these logs were sized, squared, and roughly cut to shape by the unaided eye, wrote nautical historian M. V. Brewington. When its lines were smoothed out, the canoe was fitted with mast and sail and became a reliable small vessel for tonging oysters on the Chesapeake. As the canoes were fairly swift on the water, it was inevitable that men would race them; and by 1840 there were log canoe races held at St. Michaels every Fourth of July. According to Brewington, the race resembled more a stampede than a regatta:

The contestants hauled the sterns of their canoes
upon the beach; sail was taken in and furled, and
the crews went ashore. On a signal, all hands rushed
for their canoes, shoved off, fixed their rudders,
made sail and set out. The wild melee made by such
a start can be readily imagined: upset canoes, tan-
gled gear, and high language.[15]

By the 1880s there were hundreds of log canoes in use
on Chesapeake Bay and it was during this decade that most
of the racing canoes still in use were constructed. The racing
canoes had, in addition to the foresail, mainsail, and jib of the
work canoes, a large balloon jib and a stay sail. Thus the log
canoe was heavy with sail and required a small crew to lean
out far on stabilizer boards to keep the craft from capsizing.

These swift flying unstable craft are a pleasure to watch
on the Miles and Choptank rivers; and in August their regattas
cause traffic jams on both rivers as yachtsmen turn out to
follow the fleet. The canoe's narrow hull and oversized sail pose
a constant threat of capsizing and one or two vessels get
knocked down in the water every season. Given the large
numbers of jellyfish in the Chesapeake in August, log canoe
captains don't like to end up in the water. Today's fleet of the
Chesapeake Bay Log Sailing Canoe Association includes boats
that were originally used for commercial fishing as well as
vessels designed especially for racing.

Judge John C. North II of St. Michaels owns three Chesapeake log canoes and is the dean of the fleet. A circumspect
former country judge, North only becomes animated when the
conversation turns to log canoe racing. Log canoes are a
passion with this fastidious barrister, and his *Jay Dee, Island
Bird*, and *Island Blossom* are maintained to a high degree of
perfection. The first was built in 1931 by the judge's great
uncle, John B. Harrison, and the latter two were built in 1882
and 1892, respectively, by North's great-grandfather, William
S. Covington. Thus, Judge North is not only a yachtsman but
a keeper of a family tradition that links the Miles River region
with a vanished era of Chesapeake maritime commerce.

The log canoes are expensive to maintain. "Today's old
Chesapeake log canoes," laughs North, "are kept together with
epoxy glue, Kevlar, and fiberglass. This allows the boat to
maintain its original strength which it would not have after a
hundred years of sailing." Log canoes are rarely sold; and

almost never sold to outsiders beyond the Eastern Shore. Yet they are highly prized craft and a vintage log canoe on today's market would easily command $12,000.

The sailors of log canoes are special people, adds North's wife Ethel. It is not the province of the nouveau riche weekend sailor. "To handle a log canoe," says Ethel North, "you have to know a lot about sailing and have a crew that is equally knowledgeable." At any moment a wrong move can capsize the boat. "It is the speed and danger of the log canoe that attracts men."

On a brilliantly clear mid-September morning, house guests sit on the veranda of Judge North's spacious summer home on the Miles River waiting for the crew and helpers to arrive. The lawn runs from a white picket fence marked with a log canoe plaque down to a small long dock and the river. Judge North scampers about in old work clothes preparing for the day—there is equipment to be gathered and a decision has to be made on the weather. It seems a perfect September Saturday. The azure sky has a few powder-puff clouds and there is a good wind. "Too good a wind," worries Judge North. "We could get easily knocked down out there on the river." When fellow members of the Miles Yacht Club arrive, North has a long discussion with them as to whether to cancel the race because there is too much wind. North chooses his words carefully as if the conversation were a legal brief that he might one day have to pick apart. After much talk, the yachtsmen decide to delay for an hour in hopes that the wind will lessen.

In the kitchen Ethel North has prepared a lunch of heaping platters of tossed salad, baked beans, potato salad, and hot dogs to fuel the men for the afternoon races. The men wolf down the food. They know they will need all their energy when the race begins. As they munch on hot dogs, North and his friends talk constantly of fetch, the distance that waves have to go before they hit land. This morning the Miles is a bit choppy and the fetch not to their liking. But by noon the wind has eased and North and his friends decide to hold the race. "That wind will blow us quick all the way down to Crab Alley Bay," laughs Ross Dabney, North's jib tender. Dabney is an English professor at Sweet Briar College and a fervent racer. On this day he has driven up from Virginia specifically to be part of North's crew. Anthony and Simon Black, two Chesapeake transplants from South Africa, round out North's crew, and they are joined by neighbors and friends to carry the long heavy ship mast down to the water and the bobbing log canoe.

The three log canoes are part of a race for the coveted "Captain Jack Higgins Trophy" named after the late boatwright and captain of the log canoe *Noddy*. This race is also for points toward the High Point Trophy which is awarded by the Log Canoe Association for the most racing points during the sailing season. Because of the varying strengths and speeds of the canoes, each boat has an "allowance" or handicap in seconds per nautical mile. Thus the *Jay Dee*, which is the fastest log canoe in the fleet, has no handicap while the *Island Bird* has a handicap of 86.40 seconds.

Once the canoes are launched, they tack up river past Perry Cabin to the Chesapeake Bay Maritime Museum harbor where the racing committee boat awaits them. The skippers review their race charts while waiting for the red warning ball to be lowered. When it falls, off they go like shimmering butterflies skipping on a shiny glass sea. The *Island Blossom* with Douglas Hanks at the helm lunges forward and cuts across the water effortlessly. A retired Oxford realtor, Hanks has been sailing on Chesapeake waters since he was a boy. He is one of the toughest skippers to beat in any race and is well nigh indefatigable in a log canoe. Judge North in the *Island Bird* is fiercely competitive as well. A gentleman of the old school, Judge North does not stint on tradition. While most skippers are dressed in shorts and polo shirts, Judge North sails in a white shirt and white trousers just as they did in the 1920s.

The boats glide swiftly past the North house and Ethel North happily waves at the sailors. Hugging the far shore, the canoes lean heavily in the wind and the crews scamper far out onto the long stabilizing planks to keep the vessels from tipping. For a moment the log canoes seem to be scudding before the wind on their port sides. In a moment they are gone downriver toward Eastern Bay. It is a brilliant fall afternoon and Doug Hanks, Judge North, and the other skippers know the happiness of swift vessels under full sail with good friends. The white sails of a dozen log canoes counterpoint the dark Miles and the azure sky; and on this day in Talbot County the log canoe race is the closest thing to bliss that a man can find on the Gold Coast of Maryland's Eastern Shore.

In 1949 Homer Bast, a Talbot historian, described the county as a community where the tenor of life, the customs, and social outlook had not varied in three hundred years. The gentry ran Talbot County in the colonial period; they run it today, he noted. His other observations may apply to contemporary Talbot as well: It's a county with "an intensely conservative citizenry, reluctant to embark on radical social or economic reforms . . . and more respectful of a good boat handler or horseman than of a scholar or artist." Facing the future, Bast predicted that "if there remain a spot in America where a man with a certain minimum of resources can live a life of independence and dignity among his neighbors, that spot would be Talbot County, Maryland."[16] Bast did not define what that "minimum of resources" was to lead the good life in the county. Suffice it to say that in Talbot especially, wealth is not without its advantages.

12

Choptankia

Man is the last wild creature.

—Wallace Stegner

No river in the Chesapeake region has done more to shape the character and society of the Eastern Shore than the Choptank. It is the noblest watercourse on the Eastern Shore. At its mouth is a superb sound several miles wide ringed with outside islands. Inland the Choptank River curves gently through a network of creeks and coves past the pleasant town of Denton. In the colonial period the Choptank nurtured Cambridge from a fledgling outpost into a thriving tobacco and grain seaport and became Dorchester County's principal highway of commerce. In the 1930s H. L. Mencken, the feisty journalist for the Baltimore *Sun*, lambasted Cambridge and Dorchester County as a bastion of racist hayseeds. In a pique, Mencken called the county "Choptankia" and the name is probably more apt than he realized.

Dorchester County is named for Sir Edward Sackville, the first Earl of Dorset in England, and was "erected" in 1669. The town selected as a county seat was named after Cambridge, England. After that, all comparison with the mother country ceased. Dorchester was a huge territory of rivers and marshland that during the colonial period encompassed much of Caroline county and modern Delaware. A brawling population of redemptioners, parvenu merchants, and penniless aristocrats carved out homesteads and fought among themselves as much as with the Indians.

In the eighteenth century Cambridge was little more than a tough frontier settlement, a center of trade that connected British commerce on the Bay with tobacco farms and the Choptank Indian trail that ran across county to New Market. Astute planters and businessmen like Henry Hooper carved out manors for themselves along the Choptank and by 1739, Hooper owned over 2,500 acres which he incorporated into Warwick Fort Manor plantation. Lord Baltimore kept over six thousand acres of Dorchester for himself but never erected anything on it. Today the town of Vienna resides on one hundred acres of Lord Baltimore's original patent. The Ennals, Gary, and Hooper families came as close to landed aristocracy in the colonial period as one could get in Dorchester County. Today you can still see the kind of landed estates that these seventeenth and eighteenth century traders and land specu- lators put together when you sail up the Choptank River and Gary Creek past Spocott plantation. Spocott was first patented to Stephen Gary in 1662 and has been home to Dorchester's rich and influential ever since. For generations it has been "the home place" of the Radcliffes, a talented family of lawyers and farmers.

The country lawyers who crowded the small courthouse in Cambridge on court days were a raucous lot given to petty litigation, horse races, and public drunkenness. Either out of conviction or boredom, the court conducted witch trials and attempted to tax bachelors into the arms of matrimony. Those who dared to slander the good court of Dorset risked the penalty of having a hole bored through their tongue!

For the land-hungry planters of colonial Dorchester the most vexatious problem was the Nanticoke Indians. This small tribe inhabited some of the best territory in the county, and Dorset's local history is a dismal chronicle of frauds and hostilities devised to dispossess the Nanticokes and their smaller affiliated tribe, the Choptanks.

The Indian presence in the Chesapeake Bay country goes back as far as 10,000 years. While little remains of paleo-In- dian culture, it is possible to find fluted projectile points in farm fields that were fashioned during this period. Our first significant glimpse of the Eastern Shore Indian comes during the Archaic period (8,000 to 1,000 B.C.). By this time Indians were living in well-defined areas in bands of twenty-five to fifty people and using stone axes for making log canoes. Because of their chopping and scraping tools of polished stone, we can surmise that they were deer hunters. Writes Indian historian Frank W. Porter: "Because they did not know how to grow their own food and did not have any domestic animals, the Archaic Indians had to travel with the change of seasons to find food." By about 900 A.D. the Indians of the Eastern Shore had learned how to plant corn and had an active commerce with tribes on the western shore. At the time of their first contact with whites in the seventeenth century, the Indians had garden plots and lived on a diet of fish, oysters, crabs, hominy, nuts, and fresh vegetables. The Indians had also developed a sophisticated technique of harvesting fish from the Bay by constructing fishing weirs. These V-shaped fences were made of sticks driven into the bottoms of streams and rivers. The center part of the weir contained a large opening which led to a woven basket where the fish were trapped.

Indians lived in large huts or wigwams that often were fourteen feet wide, ten feet high, and twenty feet long and were covered with mats of woven bark. The division of labor was strictly by sex. Men hunted, fished, and decorated their bodies with elaborate tattoos. Women farmed, made corn pone with deer fat, and stored dried beans and corn for winter. Evidence also suggests that the Indians of the Eastern Shore were well organized into tribal councils.

The religious beliefs of Eastern Shore Indians were remarkably sophisticated. They believed in the spirit-God Manito, giver of all good things, and feared Okee, the powerful evil spirit. Indians also believed that if they lived a good life they would go to a place of happiness after death. If they lived an evil life, they would suffer in the hereafter. On certain occasions, the Indians of the Eastern Shore mummified their dead. Two Indian practices especially attracted the Europeans. The Indian consumption of native tobacco, albeit for religious and ceremonial purposes, gave rise to smoking in Europe and a cash crop economy in the New World. Wampum, polished white and purple shells on leather strings, gave the colonists an understanding of the material concerns of the aborigines.[1]

By the end of the seventeenth century, the Nanticoke and Choptank Indians on the Eastern Shore of Maryland had withstood nearly seventy years of mounting pressure and conflict created by continuous contact with the white settlers.[2] The Europeans came first to trade in beaver pelts and later to build tobacco plantations out of the wilderness. In the process the Indians became acquainted with English perfidy and alcohol.

While the English Crown gave away land in the New World, it left it to the discretion of the grantees as to how to deal with Indians. In most cases Indian treaties and charters were overlooked and ignored. Although Lord Baltimore recognized the Nanticoke tribe, the proprietor was vague about assuring the Indians their territorial domains. When the Eastern Shore began to receive large numbers of English settlers in the late seventeenth century, the Nanticokes had already been weakened by years of raids by the Susquehannas from the north. Also, as nomads, it was hard for them to defend their land before the onslaught of farmers. Furthermore, many ambitious settlers, unable to get grants of land from Lord Baltimore, bought land directly from the Indians and then produced these Indian deeds as proof of their title to the land. According to Frank Porter, "The large scale encroachment of Indian land vastly exceeded the ability of the Proprietor of Maryland to control it."[3]

Between 1642 and 1698 the Nanticokes, frustrated by land-hungry settlers and unscrupulous traders, retaliated by either staging raids or threatening war to protect themselves and their lands. The English responded swiftly. On July 4, 1647, Captain John Price and a squad of forty men sailed across the Bay to show no mercy to the Indians, to destroy their corn, burn their houses or kill them, and thus make them unable to live free and to become wards of the colony.[4] The last Nanticoke wars took place in 1677-1678 and the Indians were easily suppressed. In 1698 the Maryland Assembly consolidated its Indian policy by placing the Nanticokes on three reservations in Dorchester—the Choptanks were assigned to land on the Choptank River adjacent to Secretary Creek; the Nanticokes were settled on two parcels of land, Chiconey at the confluence of the Nanticoke River and Marshyhope Creek and at Broad Creek.

Indian historian Frank Porter relates one incident that vividly portrays the conflict between Indians residing on reservations in Dorchester County and Englishmen who schemed to get their land. In 1723 Captain John Rider and Isaac Nicols attempted to steal a large parcel of Indian land. When they arrived on the reservation they found only one Indian resident there. The Indian, William Asquash, the son of the late Nanticoke emperor, was thrown off his own land and his cabin set afire. The Indians who returned in the fall of the year found that Rider had built a house on their land and they, in turn, burned it. In the legal squabble that followed, Rider argued that he was not a trespasser but legally entitled to the land as Maryland law stipulated that all land abandoned by Indians reverted to the colony. The Indians argued that they had not abandoned the land but had been following their subsistence strategy. The court decided the case against the Indians.[5]

By 1720 many Nanticokes began to leave the Eastern Shore and migrate northward to live with the Iroquois. After the rumors of an Indian insurrection in the Pocomoke swamp in 1742, persecution and harassment of the small tribe of Nanticokes increased in Dorchester. In 1759, a delegation of the remaining members of several tribes living on reservations on the Eastern Shore told the governor of Maryland that they were very small in number, suffering from a shortage in food, and being violently removed from their land. Finally, in 1767 the Choptank and Nanticoke Indians were invited by the General Assembly of Maryland to sell their lands and move to New York.[6] Practically all the Nanticokes left their homes on the Eastern Shore and migrated eventually to the Grand River Iroquois Reservation in Canada. When the Nanticokes left Dorchester they carried their sacred relics with them. During and after the Revolution, some seven thousand acres of Indian land were confiscated in much the same way that Tory lands were.[7]

By 1852 there was still a small remnant of Nanticokes living in Canada; and in that year an Indian named Billy Nanticoke petitioned the Maryland legislature for an annuity which was to be paid to them in consideration of the land they lost in Dorchester and elsewhere before and during the American Revolution. The legislature refused to grant the claim.[8]

Land grants were originally intended to secure the Indians against the encroachments of the white man. Yet their reservations on the north side of the Nanticoke River amounted to some four thousand acres, hardly a large amount of land for a seminomadic people and hardly a buffer against the spread of white English culture. The tragedy of the Nanticokes was simply that the British tried to turn them into farmers. Also, the British concept of property as an individual right rather than a tribal one, made it easy for the British to trade liquor for land rights. Rather than emigrate as the Nanticokes did, the Choptanks chose to remain and assimilate into the population. Many of the Choptanks intermarried with blacks and poor whites, and by 1840 their little tribe had disappeared.[9]

In 1608, according to Captain John Smith's estimates, there were about 3,000 Nanticoke Indians on the Eastern Shore. In 1756 there were about 140 Indians still resident on reservation lands in Dorchester. By 1907 the ethnographer James Mooney reported that there were only 100 Nanticoke and Wicomico Indians left on Delmarva and all of these were of mixed blood. The census of 1980 recorded 16 Indians living in Dorchester County of unknown tribal origin.[10]

*   *   *

During the eighteenth century, trading ships from London and Liverpool called regularly at Cambridge for lumber and tobacco and, by the eve of the American Revolution, the town boasted a High Street aristocracy living in spacious homes that rivaled in genteel comfort anything in the Chesapeake. Even today people on the Eastern Shore remember fragments from an old poem that proclaims:

> High Street, Cambridge, and there you are.
> A smiling street and an olden way,
> Where shadows go by of the dames that dwelt
> In the Dorset gardens of yesterday.

When the Revolution started, recruiters for General Washington's Army encountered serious problems in Dorchester. Thomas Sparrow, the recruiting officer for the county, reported that in attempting to recruit men for the patriot army, he was nearly murdered by Dorchester citizens who still believed in a king. Given the unpopularity of the militia on the Eastern Shore, the gentry co-opted the lower classes into supporting the Revolution by claiming that service in the militia was the one way that the poorer classes could earn some money, rise in social rank, and experience opportunities for leadership.[11]

In the nineteenth century Cambridge became an important seafood packing center and its river boats opened up the economy of what is now Caroline County. The river served as a highway for schooners laden with thousands of baskets of

Cambridge waterfront. Photograph by Pat Vojtech.

Autumn "honkers," Photograph by Pat Vojtech.

peaches and tomatoes bound for Baltimore. The Civil War disrupted county life as the community struggled with the issues of unionism and secession. Dorchester remained solidly in the Union fold during the Civil War and did not tolerate talk of secessionism. Unionism in Dorset was largely the work of Governor Thomas Holliday Hicks. A Dorchester native and former county sheriff, Hicks had climbed the ladder of local politics by adhering to the Know-Nothing Party, an anti-Catholic, anti-immigrant movement. When the Democratic legislature met in Annapolis to debate whether Maryland should join the South in secession, Hicks bowed to Unionist pressure and pulled every political wire at his disposal to keep the state in the Union. A stubborn, pragmatic man, not much given to political philosophy, Hicks refused to see Maryland sullied by disunion. Throughout 1861, Hicks played a delicate balancing act. The Governor shrewdly convened the state legislature in Frederick where lawmakers would be surrounded neither by secessionist hotheads nor Lincoln's army. While Hicks complained of Lincoln's military despotism in sending troops to occupy Baltimore and the Eastern Shore, the governor gave a cold shoulder to entreaties from Richmond to join the Confederacy. In the end Hicks bowed to the forces of old patriotism, military necessity, and geography. For Maryland Unionists, it was the truculent governor's finest hour. Thus it is more than a bit ironic that Hicks came to this position after more than a decade's agitation for the secession of the Eastern Shore from the state of Maryland![12]

With its safe harbor and strategic position on the Eastern Shore, Cambridge grew to be an important vegetable and grain port in the decades following the Civil War. The town became an important seafood packing center and one of the principal ports of Maryland's oyster fleet. The town throbbed with a lively commercial spirit and its economy benefited from a significant immigration of Germans, Irish, and blacks from other regions in the South. Both seafood and vegetable packers grew rich and powerful; and with the advent of the twentieth century, Cambridge would become the personal fiefdom of Albanus Phillips, the tomato packer and catsup king. They say in Dorchester that Albanus Phillips was one of the toughest men who ever strode the docks of Cambridge. Phillips loved to hunt and helped establish the Bishop's Head Gunning Club, one of the first game reserves in the county. He loved the marshes of the region and delighted in sailing on the Choptank, but he hated men who crossed him or defied him in business, and he reserved his special hatred for labor unions.

Born in 1871, Albanus Phillips was every inch the self-made man. He went to sea on a coasting schooner while still a boy and later made a sizable income as an oyster wholesaler. In 1899 he organized the Phillips Packing Company in Cambridge and in a few short years had the largest canning and packing operation in the town. In the 1920s Albanus Phillips marketed his canned tomatoes and sweet potatoes all over the United States, and it was commonly said that Cambridge was dominated by Phillips Packing. If Albanus Phillips didn't like you, you didn't work in his packinghouses or canneries and that was that.

During the Depression, men labored for miserable wages in Phillips canneries and the American Federation of Labor (AFL) attempted to unionize the plants. When his workers formed the AFL-backed Cambridge Workers Association in 1937, Phillips vowed to break the union and hired a special guard force to intimidate the workers. The workers went on strike and fought Phillips's goons, but the tomato packer refused to negotiate with them. The workers demanded a wage of forty cents an hour and a forty-hour week. Soon the CIO Canneries Union also came to town and Phillips clashed with them the following year. Throughout 1937 the two thousand workers at the Phillips canneries stoned policemen who came into the plants. July 1937 was especially tense. Strikers were shot at by Phillips's armed guards, and finally the National Labor Relations Board was called into Cambridge to quell labor hostilities and restore order. The Phillips Company was subsequently ordered to "cease and desist" from "unfair labor practices" by the National Labor Relations Board after charges were filed by both the AFL and the CIO. Yet the rebuked packer remained defiant. He said that his wages were the same as all of the other packers and he saw no need to change them. It was not until World War II that the Phillips canneries were unionized, but the workers never had much leverage. The farmers had to sell their snap beans and tomatoes to Phillips or else their crops would rot in the fields and they would not tolerate cannery strikes. Changes in consumer tastes rather than the unions finally undid the Phillips Packing Company. The advent of frozen foods resulted in a poor market for tinned tomatoes and vegetables. When Phillips finally ceased its operations in the 1960s, an era had passed. No more would the big canneries dominate the economic life of Maryland's Eastern Shore.[13]

*　　*　　*

At first glance Cambridge seems to be a sleepy, lazy river town. Northerners and visitors have seldom been impressed with Cambridge because the town is slow to reveal its secrets. As early as 1872 a writer for *Scribners Magazine* criticized the town. While he liked the hotels and shady streets of Cambridge and found Dorchester "a land of serenity and dignity," its confines were "too narrow for youthful enterprises; it must ever be a nook. It has no imperial possibilities."[14]

What writers and news reporters often miss is the simple fact that Cambridge and the men of Dorset are part of a wild environment. Civilization has yet to tame Dorchester County completely. It was the wildness that attracted Annie Oakley in 1912 when she and her husband came to Cambridge. Annie first saw the great marshes and the Choptank River when she toured in the town with a Wild West Show. Later when rodeo shows became passe and her career was starting on the skids, she packed her guns and settled briefly with her husband in a modest house on Hambrooks Bay. Occasionally the locals were startled by rifle fire when Annie Oakley chose to knock walnuts out of the trees with bullets for recreation.[15]

What Annie Oakley sensed in 1912 applies today. "There's something about them boys up in Dorchester," says a Somerset watermen. "A lot of 'em are wild and don't care about things too much." In Dorchester boats and guns are as common as pickup trucks and lawnmowers; and heaven help the local businessman who won't let his men take off for the first days of dove season! Shooting dove sharpens the eye and is good practice for hunting the elusive diving sea duck. Dorset is also a land where men like to prog the marsh for turtles and talk of the big drum fish that they pull out of Chesapeake Bay. In essence Dorchester County is where the wild things are; it is a land where hunters in the old days used swivel cannon to slaughter thousands of canvasback ducks at night from low-slung "coffin boats" on the marsh. It is a land where people still become hypnotized by the painted sky of a Chesapeake sunset and dream of floating far away down the Bay in the evening mists.

Dorchester's legislative affairs are looked after by a shrewd, highly opinionated, marsh progger named Fred Malkus. The dean of Maryland politicians, Malkus has been in the Maryland state legislature for over forty years and is unbeatable on his native ground. Malkus likes politics and trapping muskrat on the marsh in equal amounts and is the spokesman for Dorchester's defiant individualism. Folks in Dorchester want to be left alone to do pretty much as they please, and Malkus looks after their interests. Some say Fred Malkus is the last of the old-time politicians, a breed of hard-drinking, plain-talking country lawyers and farmers who lived and practiced the political conservatism they preached. In Annapolis some legislators treat Malkus as a curious anachronism, but most take him seriously when it comes to matters affecting the farmers and watermen on the Eastern Shore. Malkus came to Dorchester from Baltimore at the age of three and never left. Local politicians concede that it is tough to beat a man like Malkus who knows practically everyone in Dorchester County by his first name. When he won his eleventh term in the Maryland Senate, folks in Cambridge bought his legislator's chair and gave it to him as a gift. Even though he is in his seventies, you will find Fred Malkus hip-booted and out on the marsh during muskrat season.

Perhaps the most interesting of Dorchester's characters is its droll and complex novelist, John Barth. A prolific writer and proud native son of Cambridge, Barth is not exactly a sociable man outside of a tight circle of friends and relatives. A man with large plastic glasses and bald head, Barth looks more like an Eastern Shore bank clerk than a world-class novelist. Barth came of age in Cambridge, and his view of life was shaped by the racism of the South and the fierce individualism of the Eastern Shore. His parents operated a candy store in a working class section of Cambridge, and Barth came up during a time when Cambridge was still the feudal barony of Albanus Phillips. Yet Barth was a thoughtful boy given to long dreamy moments watching millions of geese take flight for a distant home from the marshes of Dorchester. A scholarship to Johns Hopkins rescued him from a dead end in Cambridge and allowed him to pursue a career in writing. But spiritually John Barth has never left the Eastern Shore. In his mind he is out on the Blackwater Marsh watching a monochromatic sunset.

While Barth blazed to fame with his picaresque novel of Eastern Shore colonial life, *The Sot-Weed Factor*, it is his first book, *The Floating Opera*, that is most revealing about life on the Eastern Shore. Cambridge in the 1930s and 1940s is the setting for this humorous existential novel, and the themes developed in this work serve as counterpoints for Barth's later works.

Taking his cue from the James Adams Floating Theater, a showboat that plied the rivers of the Chesapeake in the period after World War I, Barth constructs his own opera around a fictional theater boat. Todd Andrews, a fifty-year-old small-town bachelor lawyer, relives the day ten years before when he decided to commit suicide by blowing up the show-boat—cast, crew, and audience. He had changed his mind (in true existentialist tradition) only because suicide, like every other action in his life, would have been without meaning. Throughout the story, Barth sketches an intriguing portrait of society and manners in Dorset. We meet cannery house barons and drunken corporate chieftains with their big houses on the Choptank. The old destroyed Cambridge Hotel comes to life with its irascible tidewater denizens.

In using the Eastern Shore as a philosophical stage, Barth's Todd Andrews comes to terms with life by discovering in time that it is better to choose among relative values than to reject all values by way of suicide. Thus, like most of Barth's novels, *The Floating Opera* centers on the absurdity inherent in all human beliefs. What remains is the will to prevail and an acceptance of the almost comic nature of all existence. Barth's novels, for the most part, are life's spiritual odysseys set on the Eastern Shore. For Barth the Eastern Shore is a kind of metaphor for the borders of human experience just as the marsh is the border between land and water, a zone of life and decay where the primal functions of birth and death are going on.

*   *   *

These days the new religion of Dorchester County is economic development; and the town fathers of Cambridge are more than anxious to put the past behind them. Cambridge still continues to get an unfair press on race, complains business executive, Edward Evans. "Everytime the metropolitan newspapers write a story about our town the lead is 'racially troubled Cambridge.' Yet we are talking about events that happened over twenty years ago. Although we have come a long way, we're still referred to as 'racially troubled Cambridge' and it hurts us economically."

Today in Cambridge the city has blended the love of waterfowling with economic development to produce the Grand National Waterfowl Hunt, an event that combines "good shooting with refined company." Nicknamed the "Celebrity Hunt," the Grand National annually hosts a spirited three-day adventure in waterfowl shooting. The invitation-only event draws the big name sportsmen—men and women who follow all the great community-sponsored hunts of America. They shoot in the National Quail Hunt in Oklahoma, the One Box Pheasant Hunt in Nebraska, and the One Shot Antelope Hunt in Wyoming. After these hunts, they stalk big game in Africa or fly to Australia to fish for giant marlin on the Great Barrier Reef.

The Grand National began in 1983 as the brainchild of Jim Bugg. A Dorchester resident and entrepreneur who founded Century 21 Real Estate, Bugg was interested in organizing a sport activity that would uphold the local gunning tradition as well as foster much needed economic development in the community. "We wanted people to learn that in addition to having great waterfowl, Dorchester is a good place to work and to live," says Bugg.

The club's approach to economic development is strictly soft sell. No one who comes to the hunt as a "new shooter" pays a penny, says club official Jim Benjamin. Financial support for the event comes from a large patrons organization, membership dues in the club, and local donations. Each year the club culls a list of two hundred prominent people from the world of entertainment, public affairs, and industry. The governor of Maryland is the honorary chairman of the event and invitations to the hunt go out with his signature on them. According to Benjamin, the club usually gets around twenty new hunters each year. Members of previous hunts, the "old shooters," are always welcome, but they must pay their own way. As Hunt Club officials like John Tieder are quick to point out, there is a substantial informal communications network of monied and powerful people in this country. And Jim Benjamin adds that "the Grand National Waterfowl Hunt is one way of putting the word about Dorchester out on that network."

During its short tenure, the hunt has already reaped some economic dividends. Ed Evans, president of the Cambridge Wire Cloth Company, notes that industries like the diesel engine firm of Johnson and Towers, Inc. and Western Publishing have expanded their operations in Cambridge because their executives joined the hunt. "When executives come to the Hunt," says Ed Evans, "they also have a very good chance to size up our county. We have a lot to offer in terms of our wage base and community support."

It is a wet December Sunday afternoon and the Econo Lodge in Cambridge is jammed with hunters, club members, and media reporters. The invitations have resulted in an intriguing mix of sportsmen that includes an Oklahoma oil wildcatter, several investment counselors, a textile millionaire, professional baseball players, country and western stars, and a former astronaut. While most of the "new shooters" gravitate toward the table displaying exquisitely tooled Baretta shotguns that will be awarded to the top marksmen of the hunt, the media focuses its attention on the famous country singer Lynn Anderson, baseball pitcher Mike LaCoss of the San Francisco Giants, and space aviation pioneer Wally Shirra. Hank Thompson and his wife Anne round out the country touch to the hunt. Known as the "King of Country Swing Music," Thompson has promised to play for the club one night during the hunt. The hunt also attracts outstanding women marksmen like April Jones and Oksana Sparks from Wyoming and Texas.

The hunting and entertainment schedule of the Grand National is a strenuous one that combines early morning waterfowling with benefactors' parties that go on into the night. Most of the hunters, though, are unfazed by the attention they receive. They tease one another about how many points they will score in the waterfowl shooting.

Before dawn on Monday morning, the hunters are ferried by car to selected Dorchester host farms and preserves for a morning of goose shooting. The overcast weather brings the geese into the fields and the hunters have a glorious time, ultimately bagging over a hundred geese.

That night the hunters board a bus and head for the Cambridge American Legion. The second night of the hunt is stag night, an event that no self-respecting hunter in Dorchester County misses. Presiding over the stag night are the

Turlocks, a hardy band of coonskin- and leather-wearing joke-
sters who are a unique tribe on the Eastern Shore. They call
themselves Turlocks after the characters in James Michener's
Chesapeake. A Turlock, says Tom Flowers of his fellow tribes-
men, is "a muskrat reborn as a Dorchester waterfowler."

To the delight and roar of the crowd at the Legion hall,
Chief Turlock Russell Smith ascends the stage. Wearing a
shoulder-length coonskin hat, Smith peppers the audience
with buckshots of jokes and bawdy social commentary. "Now
all you tightwads get up here," bellows Smith, "and place your
bets on the duck. See if you can win a couple hundred bucks."

Hunters purchase numbered chips that correspond to
numbers on a board in the bottom of a duck cage. "When the
duck is placed in that cage, he's going to get excited and take
a squat," yells Russell Smith. "If he squats on your number,
you win!" In less than a minute the duck makes up his mind
and fills the wallet of a happy Eastern Shoreman. While a
twangy country band plays loud music, the celebrity hunters
and guests attack tables piled high with soft-crab sandwiches,
crab cakes, oysters, and fresh roast goose.

In the Tuesday morning darkness a bus deposits the
hunters at the tiny village of Fishing Creek off the Honga
River. Two large charter fishing boats wait at the dock to
carry the hunters down the river and out into Chesapeake
Bay for a morning of sea duck hunting. The hunters grab an
impromptu box breakfast of ham and egg sandwiches and
stow their guns and gear. In a short while the boats pass
Hooper Island and roll gently in the Bay as the hunters await
their contacts. Within minutes John Tieder roars out of the fog
in his large powerboat. Heavily dressed in foul-weather gear,
Tieder coordinates the distribution of the hunters from the
"mother boats" to small craft that bob in the waves with decoys
to await the sea ducks. "There are three thousand sea ducks
out here, I estimate," says Tieder. "Let's see who the good
shooters are."

Shooting sea ducks is a high art. Those who have done it
say it is the most exciting sport on Chesapeake Bay. The
prolific sea duck is the artful dodger of the Chesapeake. Sea
ducks fly in rapid jerky movements and are capable of plung-
ing and diving erratically. According to seasoned hunters,
shooting sea ducks is kind of like shooting doves while bounc-
ing on a trampoline.

Communication between boats is difficult and one hears only muffled shots on the water. As visibility improves, April Jones suddenly stands up in her boat, takes quick aim, and bangs down a sea duck. Her husband, Tom, bags one also. Meanwhile John Tieder keeps a nervous eye on the weather; and as it worsens, he revs up his boat. "I'm going to gather them up," shouts Tieder. "It's getting bad out here and they've probably had enough."

Twenty minutes later a band of thoroughly chilled hunters scramble on board, including the shivering but enthusiastic April Jones. "I thought I was in a shooting gallery. They were devils to hit," she laughs. "There is definitely nothing like this back home in Wyoming." Hunt officials check the final—a dozen sea ducks and an equal number of boxes of expended shells.

Back at the dock at Fishing Creek, the hunters wait for the bus in the cold drizzle. Only John Tieder's retriever, Will E. Hunt, seems to have any energy and the dog happily gobbles the remains of the ham and egg sandwiches. Some, like Allen "Slim" Flinchum, are tired but happy hunters. Impervious to the elements, the wealthy construction executive sips a cold beer. "The shooting was good today, real good," he reflects.

After a hot lunch and several whiskeys at a Hooper Island restaurant, the hunters reboard their bus. As they cross the great marshes of Dorchester, they see fields black with geese that have flown in through the fog to feed on harvest corn. In December, when the sky on the Eastern Shore turns gray and the mists seep up from the salt marshes of Dorchester onto the farmlands, you can hear the piercing noise of thousands of honking geese. It is that wild call of migrating birds that stirs a man's blood and sense of wonder and makes life in the Choptank River country an adventure. Man and nature come together in Dorchester County and it is still the place where the wild things are.[16]

13

Arcadia

*It has always been easy come, easy go on the Shore, with
all that connotes both good and bad.*
—Hulbert Footner, *Rivers of the Eastern Shore*

W hen Giovanni da Verrazano sailed into Chincoteague
Bay in 1524 and beheld a magnificently forested coast,
he called it Arcadia, a simple innocent, virgin land. In the
service of King Francis I of France, Verrazano sailed to the New
World aboard the *Dauphine* with a crew of fifty men in search
of a water route to China. Sailing up Chincoteague Bay, he
spent three days exploring the land that is now Worcester
County, Maryland. [Not all scholars agree that Verrazano
explored the coast of Worcester. Samuel Eliot Morison, a
prominent historian of New World exploration argues in his
work, *The European Discovery of America*, that Verrazano
actually landed at Kitty Hawk, North Carolina.] Verrazano
came across a naked Indian brave of remarkable beauty who
was very much frightened at the sight of white men. Like most
people who have since come to the beaches of Worcester, the
Italian took a souvenir back to the King, in this case the terrified
Indian he had kidnapped. The Indian reaction to this incident is
unrecorded, though it probably contributed to the distaste the
Indians had for English colonists stranded on their shores.

Henry Norwood sailed to Fenwick Island from Jamestown
in 1647 on the ship *Virginia Merchant* and visited the Assateague barrier island at length. He spent some time with the
Indians, though he was not well received. Norwood and his

company nearly perished for lack of food and water, even though both were in abundance in nearby forests. The Englishmen were reduced to eating rats. When one English woman in the company died, wrote Norwood, "It was my advice to the survivors, who were following her apace, to endeavor their own preservation by converting her dead carcass into food, as they did to good effect." Thus did Arcadia have a less than auspicious beginning.[1]

In the colonial period Englishmen took their cue from the Indians and established salt works on the coast. "Making salt from the sun" was an important economic activity and there were salt works in both Worcester and the Eastern Shore of Virginia during the period from 1630 to 1852. The most important salt works was that established at Sinepuxent Inlet during the American Revolution operated by the Baltimore Salt Company. As patriot salt needs increased during the war, the Maryland government used Hessian prisoners of war to man the salt works.

The men who lived on the Worcester Coast often profited from tragedy as wrecks were common in winter storms. In 1750 a Spanish ship, *The Grayhound*, was beached on Assateague during a storm. News of the disaster quickly spread to the coastal communities. The coast men, however, treated the disaster as a windfall. They cut up the decks of *The Grayhound* for lumber and carried off everything they could lay their hands on. One enterprising coastman arrived with several oxcarts and transported the ship's cargo of mahogany planks to Snow Hill where he sold it to a local merchant.[2] While Marylanders occasionally plundered wrecked vessels, the Virginians had an even worse reputation. Accomack County, Virginia, was popularly known in the eighteenth century as a land of plundering pirates. Vessels that were wrecked in Accomack waters were fair game for the thieves.

The nefarious business of looting wrecked ships on the shoals of Assateague Island reached such a point that the Maryland Assembly finally appointed a state wreck-master in Worcester County in 1790. The wreck-master was authorized to send armed deputies to the scene of a wreck to keep the vessel from being looted. The Maryland Assembly further enacted a provision in law that stipulated that looters of distressed vessels on the Worcester Coast would be executed without benefit of clergy. Few wrecks were plundered after that time.[3]

Most of the early settlers in Worcester County took lands along the Pocomoke River or came inland from the sea and acquired land patents to the area around which the town of Berlin is located. As an organized county Worcester is a latecomer, having been chartered in 1742 out of lands mostly from Somerset County. Worcester bears the name of the Earl of Worcester who, in the seventeenth century, was one of Lord Baltimore's staunchest English Catholic allies.

While Worcester was primarily a naval stores economy, providing masts and lumber for ship construction, it did have a significant seafaring population. As anyone from the town of Berlin will tell you, this land is the birthplace of the famous naval hero of the War of 1812, Stephen Decatur.

Born near Berlin in 1779, Stephen Decatur was the offspring of a revolutionary war naval officer. Decatur followed in his father's wake, and in 1804 the young naval officer distinguished himself in dashing hand-to-hand combat with the Tripolitan pirates in the Mediterranean. At that time American commerce was being preyed upon by Moslem princes along the coast of what is now Libya and Tunisia, and Decatur's fleet restored law and order for American shipping with grapeshot and cutlass. During the War of 1812 Decatur battled the British fleet on the high seas of the Atlantic and though he was ultimately outnumbered and defeated, he became America's foremost naval hero of that era. In addition to his swashbuckling naval exploits, Steven Decatur was also author of the morally dubious postwar maxim that at one time graced the lips of every school child in America: "Our country! In her intercourse with foreign nations may she always be in the right; but our country right or wrong!" Stephen Decatur did not live long enough to test his maxim. He was shot and killed in a duel on March 22, 1820, on the western shore.

Slavery and the tobacco culture took hold in Worcester as it did elsewhere on the Eastern Shore, but it never amounted to much. Much of Worcester was swampy, and the dense forests of cypress trees that continue to fascinate visitors were a much easier source of income. Cypress was highly valued for shipbuilding because it was extremely sturdy and did not rot. Therefore, during the colonial period, one found a society of woodsmen and rivermen who were as adept in the swamps of the great Pocomoke forest as the original Indian inhabitants. The chief activity of these woodsmen was in making cypress

246

shingles which they hacked by hand, using heavy iron blades called frows. The shingles were used throughout the Eastern Shore both for roofs and siding. By 1860, however, most of the great stands of cypress in the Pocomoke forest had been cut; and what you see today along the Pocomoke River are cypress trees of relatively recent growth. The forests of the Pocomoke River bred a fierce sense of independence in its inhabitants. Blacks and poor whites were well tolerated if they proved that they could cut a living from either the soil or the forests. The career of Jacob Armstrong is a case in point.

Jacob Armstrong was born a slave in Worcester County sometime before the American Revolution. Little is known of Armstrong's early life save that in 1783 his master, a white planter named Charles Bishop, manumitted him and his wife, Comfort, and two of his four children. The other two children had been sold to planters who did not share Charles Bishop's convictions. This manumission occurred in the democratic afterglow of the American Revolution and was no doubt prompted by religious sentiment as well.

What unfolds is the story in the county land records of a man working at a seemingly exhausting rate as a farmer and forest worker. Armstrong was bound to rescue his two slave children and to acquire enough wealth so that the fortunes of his family would be secure. Armstrong spent his first five years as a free man working for others. In spite of low wages and discrimination against free blacks, he and his wife accumulated enough money to buy a fifty-acre farm called Acquango Savannah. The farm was located near the Pocomoke forest, a short distance from Snow Hill. As the land was exceedingly swampy, Armstrong had to cut drainage ditches to make it productive. Each year he bought more undeveloped forest and swamp land and turned it into productive fields. By 1822 Jacob Armstrong owned over six hundred acres and was the owner of one of the largest farms in the county. Were he not black, he would have been welcomed into the local gentry as few of that class had as much land as Armstrong. With the profits from his farms, Armstrong purchased the freedom of his two children and also engaged in moneylending and land speculation. Armstrong's willingness to extend credit to other poorer free black farmers was of extreme importance to the development of Worcester's free black community, writes historian Tom Davidson, because at this time whites were usually unwilling to extend credit to blacks under any terms. Individuals like Jacob Armstrong helped break the cycle of dependency that kept emancipated blacks tied to their former masters. When he died in 1825, Jacob Armstrong had demonstrated in his life and work that even oppressed blacks could, through hard work, carve out their own personal Arcadia in the forests of the Pocomoke.[4]

The swamps and forests of the Pocomoke River also were the home of one of the most interesting industries to emerge on the Eastern Shore in the early nineteenth century, Worcester's great iron furnace. Fortunately, the Nassawango Iron Furnace, as it is properly called, has been rescued from the ravages of vandals and the encroachments of the Pocomoke swamp. Today it is a museum and popular landmark on Maryland's Eastern Shore.

There was interest in iron manufacture in Maryland as early as 1719 when the Maryland legislature offered one hundred acres of free land to anyone who would set up furnaces and forges in the colony. While the pig iron industry grew slowly in Maryland, its manufacture did not meet much royal resistance from British iron manufacturers because they profited from its resale in the mother country.

The Pocomoke swamp was rich in bog iron, a low grade but easily smelted ore, and Eastern Shoremen dug ore out of the swamp as early as 1788. While other entrepreneurs had attempted to operate an iron furnace and produce pig iron, it was not until 1832 that the operation became profitable. In that year Thomas A. Spence, a Worcester County judge, formed the Nassawango Iron Furnace Company and purchased over five thousand acres of land adjacent to the furnace.

During the 1830s there was great national demand for pig iron and the Nassawango Iron Furnace Company profited immensely. Iron Furnace grew to be a company town of over a hundred homes and it contained a general store, a blacksmith shop, a grist mill, a saw mill, a school, and a church. The town even boasted a hotel for visitors. As late as 1838, Furnace Hill, as the town was called, had a population of four hundred.

In the midst of the forest primeval several hundred workers carved out an industrial economy. Gangs of laborers went into the swamp, dug up the ore and hauled it by boat up Nassawango Creek, and thence by a man-made canal to the furnace. Other groups of lumberjacks cut down trees and created large charcoal ricks to provide fuel for the furnace. Then the large brick furnace was carefully packed with bog iron and oyster shells and fired up. A huge bellows, propelled by a waterwheel turning in the sluice of the canal, fanned the charcoal fire and heated the iron to molten capacity. When the furnace was ready, the workers tapped it and the molten iron poured on the casting floor into moulds that resembled a sow and her little piglets, hence the name pig iron. When cooled, the iron bars were carried by boat down the Nassawango Creek to the Pocomoke River for shipment to Baltimore and beyond.

For an iron smelting operation located deep in the heart of a swamp, the Nassawango Iron Furnace Company was an exceptionally efficient operation. Sadly, its demise was due to events totally beyond its control. By 1848 the great Mesabi iron range of Minnesota began to produce iron ore of exceptionally high quality and the demand for crude low-grade pig iron collapsed in America. With it collapsed the dreams of Judge Spence and the Nassawango Iron Furnace Company. Spence attempted to keep the furnace operating and bankrupted himself. By 1854 the iron furnace was a ghost town; and before long the swamp began to reach out to reclaim it.[5]

In the twilight of a summer afternoon there is an eeriness to the old iron furnace. The imposing high brick furnace stands in the midst of a small clearing surrounded by dense forest. Locals say that ghosts haunt the grounds, and that if you listen carefully, you can hear their moaning sounds as the evening winds blow through the Pocomoke Swamp. The dreams of an industrial community in the forest are now history and only the Pocomoke River and its great swamp endures.

The Indians called the river Pocomoke or dark water. The Pocomoke is a mysterious river colored by swamp tannin and other chemicals of forest runoff. It begins as marshland in Delaware and trickles southward as a primeval stream through the Pocomoke swamp and dense stands of cypress trees. Canoeists often launch their craft from Whiton Crossing, a few miles south of Powellville off Route 354, and paddle through the swamp eleven miles to Snow Hill. For those who have canoed the swamp, there is nothing like it for mystery and natural splendor in Maryland. The swamp is full of deer. It is also a bird-watcher's paradise, being home to scarlet tanagers, the rare ruby-throated hummingbird, fourteen kinds of warbler, blue herons, and egrets. Up until the Civil War, the Pocomoke Swamp was the haunt of brown bear, and bear trapping in the swamp was a popular sport with woodsmen in Worcester.

Often the Pocomoke is no more than twenty feet wide; and on occasion you have to use a bow saw to trim away tree limbs that block the stream. There is a cathedral-like silence in the swamp and little from the outside world penetrates the swamp's junglelike foliage. In 1971 the Pocomoke River was the first river in Maryland to receive protection as a "Wild and Scenic" watercourse; and as you paddle across the duckweed floats in the swamp and listen for the occasional screech of an owl, you will understand the river's wild beauty.

In the seventeenth century the Indians used the Pocomoke Swamp as their final redoubt when the English settlers took their land. Few colonists cared to penetrate its ghostly vastness and from its woods came the few desperate Indian raids in defense of Nanticoke and Assateague tribal homelands that are recorded in seventeenth century local history. Runaway slaves also found refuge in the swamp, and on its periphery were Worcester's first settlements of free Negroes.

Five miles downstream from Whiton Crossing at Porter's Crossing, the Pocomoke widens considerably, and, if you are quiet and observant, you can spot ospreys at roost in a tall cypress tree. Approaching Snow Hill takes a bit of caution; for by this time the river is wide enough to admit motorboats and the Pocomoke has more than its share of dipsomanic mariners.

The Pocomoke River is an environmentalist's dream, a unique body of water flowing through the pristine swamp and forest. The protectors of this woodland arcadia are a diverse group ranging from devout bass fishermen concerned about chemical runoffs in the river to people like the late Salisbury businessman Stanton Adkins. A wealthy lumber merchant and builder, Adkins donated a large tract of the Pocomoke swamp on the Nassawango Creek to the Nature Conservancy, largely because he wanted to keep the place as it is. Adkins reasoned that there had to be some place for wildness left on the Eastern Shore and the swamp was it. A brass plaque attached to a tree deep in the forest memoralizes his donation. The swamp also has its activists; and none are more vocal defenders of the river and the swamp than Joe and Ilia Fehrer.

Transplanted Baltimoreans and inveterate canoeists, the Fehrers have lived in Snow Hill for over twenty years. Joe Fehrer came to the Eastern Shore in 1971 to manage land acquisitions for the newly created Assateague National Seashore. Ilia Fehrer plunged into volunteer activities, and with the wit, determination, and organizational abilities of a former schoolteacher, she began speaking out for environmental sanity and conservation on the Eastern Shore.

Since their retirement the Fehrers have been a batallion of two in defense of Worcester's marshes, forests, and wetlands. Ilia Fehrer serves as chairman of the Worcester Environmental Trust, a position that often brings her into disputes with her less-environmentally-sensitive neighbors. The Fehrers also speak out in the press and their opinions often fill the letters to the editors sections of local papers like the *Salisbury Daily Times*. The Fehrers have often waged uphill battles with local farmers over fertilizer runoff in the Pocomoke. In the beginning the farmers scoffed at them, but now they take them seriously. In the end the Fehrers and their conservation allies succeeded in developing a plan with the state Department of Natural Resources to begin to control the pollution of Pocomoke waters. While "non-point pollution" (fertilizer and chemical runoff), has not ceased, efforts have now begun to keep the river a safe haven for man and nature. Local citizens have the Fehrers and the Nature Conservancy to thank for that. Says Ilia Fehrer: "There are always environmental problems cropping up. But basically, the river's in good shape."

After Snow Hill the river courses lazily to the Chesapeake and meets the salt waters of Pocomoke Sound south of Shelltown. Pocomoke City is the river's dowdy queen. Today there is not much here to interest tourists, and perhaps that is how the locals prefer it. The market ambiance of this small river town is low key, and the churches are filled on Sundays. Before 1878 Pocomoke City was called Newtown and was an important ferry point on the north–south highway on the Eastern Shore and an inland port for ships coming up from the Chesapeake Bay. Pocomoke was also an important shipbuilding center, dating from the seventeenth century. The deep waters of the Pocomoke River made Pocomoke easily accessible to large Bay vessels and the wharves of the town were often crowded with large schooners filled with fertilizer and lumber. In the 1820s and 1830s Pocomoke City was a riotous riverfront town, known for its gambling, cockfights, drinking, and swearing. Many parsons on the Eastern Shore worried that Pocomoke City was the citadel of the ungodly, as it was well known that black conjurers and root doctors practiced their craft in the town to a large black and white clientele. Even today in the Pocomoke area one has little difficulty finding spiritual readers, psalmists, and assorted healers with contacts in the beyond.[6]

The steamboats began to visit Pocomoke regularly in 1868 and the trip from Pocomoke City to Baltimore that took several days by coasting schooner could be made in a day on steamboats like the *Helen, Maggie,* or *Sue.* With the steamboats came the drummers, country salesmen vending a whole variety of finished goods from dresses to shoes to eyeglasses to a curious farm population anxious to have anything that was "up-to-date." The drummers stayed in boardinghouses or at the local hotel, drank heartily, played cards until the wee hours, and gave as much business as they took. Some astute drummers speculated in hides purchased in one of Worcester's five local tanneries for sale later in the garment center of Baltimore.

On Saturdays the farmers came to Pocomoke in their horse-drawn wagons and peddled their goods for sale just like the drummers. Every wagon had, in season, large amounts of fresh fruit, potatoes, turnips, cucumbers, several squawking chickens, and flour. Farmers would come in from as far away as thirty miles and would often spend the night sleeping in the homes of relatives or at one of the Methodist churches if there was no room for them elsewhere. That way of life, however, has vanished. The automobile and new highway construction on Route 13 took the traffic and the commerce from Pocomoke City, and the steamboats and schooners that once came upriver disappeared after World War II.

In the modern era, Worcester is in fact two counties. Most of Worcester remains agricultural with small crossroads hamlets like Girdletree and Stockton. In fact, to travel Route 12 in Worcester is to travel through countryside and communities that have changed little since the 1930s. The general stores and country post offices conduct business on a first-name basis and visitors from distant parts are met with a friendly curiosity. The other part of Worcester County, which inhabits an almost totally different social universe, is Ocean City, the beach resort whose taxes support most of the county. In the words of one Girdletree local, "Ocean City is the tail that wags the dog in Worcester public life." Worcester County currently has the lowest state income tax rate in Maryland and local taxpayers are thankful for that. Yet in the country byways of Worcester, people worry that Ocean City is bringing too many unwelcome changes to county life. They watch the hordes of beach-bound automobiles on Route 50 in summer, shake their heads, and wonder.

*   *   *

For thousands of city dwellers in Baltimore and the Washington suburbs, Ocean City is the only reason to visit the Eastern Shore. Generations of Marylanders have vacationed in Ocean City since the turn of the century. Each summer an endless stream of traffic pours along Route 50 bound for Ocean City, the beaches, and fun. Ocean City can be as wild and fast as a roller coaster on a hot July night. It can also be as sedate as an autumn breeze on a September afternoon. After Labor Day, retirees and middle-aged vacationers recapture the town and the resort becomes more tranquil.

Everyone has an opinion about Ocean City. The conservationists see it as a development nightmare. High school youths and college kids march like lemmings to the sea to savor the social life, the booze, and occasionally illicit drugs. The high school youths are especially troublesome. The security forces in the hotels and motels call them "June Bugs" because every June when school lets out, the kids scamper to Ocean City to frolic and get drunk. As one local observer put it, "The frequent buzz from the police sirens is an indication that some of the June Bugs need pest control."

Ocean City has many images. It's a family place, a raunchy place, a romantic strand of the Atlantic all rolled into one. It is also a very open gossipy place where everyone seems to know one another and many of the hotels and restaurants are still managed by third and fourth generations of the same families. There is a pulse to Ocean City that throbs with vast transfusions of money, a resort where men and women gamble on boardwalk businesses that will net them more money in three months than they could earn in a year. Ocean City is also a racket, a speculator's bubble in real estate, a place where people hustle the outsiders and each other.

In the wild summer carnival of Ocean City you will see everything from tattooed female motorcyclists to lobster-red bathers to skin-head punks with pierced noses to strolling mothers with children and doting grandparents. Today's Ocean City is a neon giant that dominates the sleepy economy of Worcester County. City authorities count the vacationers by the number of toilets flushed and water consumed on any given day, a most interesting form of demographics. In summer over 200,000 tourists jam the resort and the boardwalk becomes a bedlam of humanity punctuated with body sweat and the smell of popcorn. People who normally would not give fast food a second look join long lines and pay exorbitant sums for a cardboard container of french fries laced with salt and vinegar.

The dreams that people have of Ocean City are of the town that once was. In their mind's eye on a gloomy winter evening in Glen Burnie, Towson, and Baltimore, people see an Ocean City that stretched from the Sinepuxent Inlet to 15th Street, the traditional boundary of the town. Everyone was friendly and the pace of life was relaxed. The only local scandal concerned Bobby Baker, the snappy-suited Washington wheeler-dealer and owner of the Carousel Motel who fell from grace in the Lyndon Johnson administration. Charter fishing boats were cheap; the beach was free; and the surf was clear, cool, and invigorating. North of 15th Street was empty dune land. You could picnic there and skinny-dip in the waves. The town was as corny as a kewpie doll and as sweet as saltwater taffy.

Vacationers come even though the Ocean City of their youth is no more. That town vanished in the 1970s when a building boom led by the construction of high-rise condominium complexes altered the landscape of this barrier island and made it a northern variant of Miami. Today's Ocean City throbs to the sound of disco music. Its trendy bars and restaurants cater to a fast urban affluent set that is looking, always looking to meet someone.

*   *   *

Ocean City traces its history as a resort to the 1870s when it served as a primitive boardinghouse and cottage community for fishermen and urban sufferers of hay fever. Worcester County natives like Jenkins Henry, Lemuel Showell, and others sensed the commercial potential of the barrier island as a summer holiday site and worked with New York promoter Stephen Taber to establish a town. They called their new creation "The Ladies' Resort to the Ocean." Once the promoters got assurances of a railway connection to their fledgling resort, they were able to get investors to support the construction of the Atlantic Hotel. Using Stephen Taber's fifty acres as a site, the promoters laid out their town into 205 building lots. Thus did Ocean City begin as a real estate promoter's dream and thus has it been ever since.[7]

Trains crossed the Sinepuxent Bay in 1878 and the Baltimore, Chesapeake, and Atlantic Railroad ran its Ocean City Flyer from the ferry wharf at Claiborne in Talbot County to the depot on Philadelphia Avenue in Ocean City. By the 1880s three hotels were providing almost round-the-clock service to tourists who came not to bathe in the ocean but mainly to watch it. It was not until the turn of the century that large numbers of visitors actually began to swim in the Ocean City surf. In the early days of Ocean City, rates at the best hotels ranged from $12 to $15 a week. Yet, the resort was more known for its local Catholic monastery than its hostelries.

Ocean City until the Great Depression was primarily a town of fishing camps and seafood houses. Out beyond the surf, pound fishermen erected stationary nets on the sandy ocean floor and hauled in major catches. In 1916, for example, Ocean City seafood processors shipped on one day a catch of 1,787 barrels of fish that required a train of twenty express cars bound for New York and the Northeast.[8]

By the 1930s Ocean City boasted twenty hotels, and guests to the resort were met at the train depot and their luggage taken by oxcart to their hotel. Guests took all their meals in the hotel dining room and counted on their host to provide them with an entertaining stay.

The automobile transformed Ocean City. After the opening of the Chesapeake Bay Bridge in 1952, Ocean City was an easily accessible half-day ride, and a flood of vacationers poured across the Eastern Shore in their new cars. In the postwar prosperity of the Eisenhower era, money was easy and Marylanders wanted fun, relaxation, and an ocean breeze. By 1960, Ocean City, during the high vacation days of July and August, boasted over 100,000 vacationers. By the tourist season of 1975 that number had swollen to 250,000. The town grew so fast that in the two-year period from 1971 to 1973 over

Ocean City on the boardwalk. Photograph by Pat Vojtech.

Pocomoke City bridge. Photograph by Pat Vojtech.

6,000 condominium permits were granted to builders by the city. This expansion was accompanied by considerable dredging and filling of marshes on the bay side of the island. Oceanfront lots that once sold in the 1920s for a hundred dollars, now commanded fortunes. In Ocean City self-promotion is the coin of the realm, and Ocean City is a veritable publishing house for tourist and real estate literature. If your mailbox is lonely, just write to the Ocean City Chamber of Commerce and you will receive more fan mail than a rock group. The town boosts its 145 streets, its beaches, its amusements, its real estate investment possibilities, and its condominiums to the point of evangelical frenzy. What it does not stress is the congested lone coastal highway (Route 528) that runs the length of the resort and is one of the most hazardous roads in Maryland. Locals refer to it grimly as "Six Lanes of Death" and pedestrians cross it at their peril. But undeterred, Ocean City is widening the highway.

On the weekend, in summer, everyone seems to arrive in Ocean City at once. Traffic backups can make tempers hot, especially after a long drive on Route 50. Small wonder, then, that after checking into the motels, vacationers throng the thirty-odd saloons and bars, the five county-run liquor stores, the fifteen wine shops, and numerous six-pack vending 7-Eleven stores.

The next day Maryland's obsession with the beach begins and in the mid-day heat hundreds of thousands of bodies bake on the sand. Old men play cards beneath the shadow of beach umbrellas, kids build sand castles, married women gaze curiously at the well-endowed lifeguards, and young men stroll the beach in search of "a perfect 10." As the water until late August is cold, few stay in the ocean for very long.

Presiding over the teeming mass of resort life is Ocean City Mayor Roland "Fish" Powell. In summer the mayor can more often be found on the boardwalk glad-handing tourists than in his office. Powell is a native of Ocean City and has watched it grow. When he was a boy his mother ran a twelve-bedroom boardinghouse on Dorchester Street, and Fish Powell has worked the tourist trade ever since. The mayor doesn't remember how he got the nickname "Fish," but he remembers carrying the appellation to grade school. When Powell was growing up Ocean City was a small fishing town with dirt streets paved with oyster shells and lined with whitewashed telephone poles. Yet Powell hasn't found the growth of Ocean City to be all that bad. Without the resort's economic growth, Powell notes, it would have been impossible for many residents to live and work here.

Fish Powell knows, however, that not all growth in Ocean City has been good. Drugs have become a big business in Ocean City. Local law enforcement agencies find the problem overwhelming as they are seriously undermanned. In 1987 Worcester County had only one full-time narcotics officer, and the influx of cocaine has kept pace with the growth of the resort. Says Worcester County Sheriff Dan McAllister: "The enforcement problem is greatly increased with four major highways . . . providing a drug delivery corridor from Florida north through Virginia to Pocomoke, south from New York, and east from the Baltimore-Washington D.C. area."

Drugs enter Ocean City by plane and mail as well. Once police intercepted a mail delivery of hashish from Amsterdam. "All we can do now," complains Sheriff McAllister, "is scratch the surface." Local authorities worry that most crimes in Ocean City such as robberies, burglaries, and thefts seem to have a drug connection. According to a recent study of Worcester County, the crime rate jumped 14 percent in 1986 in Worcester County with 500 more crimes reported than in the previous year. "The drugs triple in the summer and it's an increase we can expect every year," concludes McAllister. Thus the resort's fast lane is a street of snow that until recently was not on the social map of Ocean City.[9]

It was inevitable that a resort that grew as fast as Ocean City would have its development blues. The influx of tourists from Baltimore and Washington has been both its greatest strength and its greatest weakness. Over the past two decades, to accommodate the mass of urban vacationers, developers have poured concrete and asphalt over every open spot of this fragile five-mile-square island. At the height of the summer season, this former health refuge for sufferers of hay fever resembles more a drag strip; and the garish strip development of stores, shoppers' marts, motels, beer joints, and condominiums only gets worse. Realizing that in the future congestion and overdevelopment may make the resort less attractive to vacationers, the city has drafted a twenty-year plan that seeks to increase tourism while restraining metropolitan sprawl and development. Planners for Ocean City also worry that Ocean

City's land shortage will place intense pressure on farm and recreational land west of the resort, thus intensifying metropolitan blight rather than curing it. At the moment, however, there is one bright spot on Ocean City's troubled metropolitan horizon. Automobile gridlock is getting so bad in the resort that ultimately traffic congestion may limit Ocean City's complete development. In the past the automobile made Ocean City into a megaresort; in the future the automobile may force the city to restructure itself in new ways.

*   *   *

No doubt Nature will also cast its die on the fate of Ocean City as well. Ocean City sits squarely in the Atlantic Ocean storm surge and hurricane zone. Storm surges are great walls of water that come sweeping along the coastline near the area where an ocean storm makes its landfall. Giant waves hammer at everything in their path and tear away buildings, wharves, piers, and boardwalks. Three fierce storms have hit Ocean City since it became a resort: 1916, 1933, and 1962. On August 23, 1933, a severe northeast storm crashed upon Ocean City and slashed an inlet across the island that separated Ocean City from Assateague Island. The inlet was so deeply cut by the storm that it was almost completely navigable. The storm swept away the fishing camps, damaged the hotels, and destroyed the railroad bridge across Sinepuxent Bay. For Ocean City residents, however, the storm of 1962 will always be "The Big One." On March 6, 1962, a storm struck Ocean City with such intensity that many beachfront properties were uprooted. High waters flooded downtown Ocean City and rescue workers had to evacuate town residents by boat. The storm caused $20 million in damage and the town averted mass drownings and havoc only because the resort was luckily empty of tourists at the time. In some places on the island the water covered the strand five to eight feet deep. These storms hit the Delmarva coast with ferocious intensity and with little advance warning.

Federal authorities at the National Oceanic and Atmospheric Administration in Washington have long been warning people who choose to live in Atlantic coast communities like Ocean City of the risks associated with hurricanes and storm surges. Barrier islands, like the one on which Ocean City is located, are the most unstable coastal lands currently used by people. They continually move and shift in response to natural forces. They are geologically young, these barrier islands, and have been ever changing over the milennia. Barrier islands like these rise and submerge along the Atlantic coast. When left alone these islands shift and adjust, destroying old beaches and creating new ones in the process. Towns try to halt this process with engineering works, dikes, and bulkheads but they can do little to stem the coastal retreat process. Ocean City and the state of Maryland are spending millions to pump sand back up onto the receding beach. The late mayor, Harry Kelley, played the role of King Canute in Ocean City and ordered a fleet of bulldozers into the waves to push sand up onto the beach. Winter storms ultimately frustrated the bulldozers and one hurricane may cause the beach replenishment program to come to naught. Yet like Harry Kelley and King Canute, Ocean City believes that it can hold back the waves with seawalls, groins, and jetties. The resort may be courting disaster.

Gilbert White, an environmental geographer at the University of Colorado, has noted that "the most rapidly growing site for catastrophic events in the United States is the Gulf of Mexico and the Atlantic coast of the country."[10] Using statistics drawn from studies of storms and wave conditions, scientists have concluded that a twenty-five-foot deepwater wave offshore is capable of flooding Ocean City. A storm that produces such waves is expected to occur at least once every twenty-five to thirty years. Significantly the scientists point out that the high-rise condominiums of Ocean City were built in the 1970s when the hurricane cycle was in an unusual lull. The condominiums have yet to be tested by a storm as fierce as that of 1933 or 1962.

In September 1985, hurricane Gloria struck Ocean City, tearing up the boardwalk and depositing sand and rubble on the city's streets. Ocean City fared well, however, and Mayor Fish Powell proclaimed: "We came out of it smelling like roses." Scientists fear that the resort's future may not be as flowery, however. Behind their scientific calculations is the knowledge of the infamous hurricane, Camille, that deluged Pass Christian, Mississippi, with a twenty-five-foot storm surge in 1969. Also, sometimes fiction has more truth than reality. No one can read John D. MacDonald's thrilling suspense novel, *Condominium*, without shuddering at the thought of high-rise apartment buildings snapping like matchsticks in a hurricane.

*   *   *

Assateague Island is an alternative to the boardwalk Babylon of Ocean City. A thirty-seven-mile-long island, Assateague is part of the National Seashore Park system. Maryland owns most of it and today it remains a largely unspoiled state park. The state also maintains a well-run guarded beach and campground. The campground is often crowded and vacationers bring the blight of urban civilization with them. Nature pays them retribution by visiting them with swarms of pesky salt-marsh mosquitoes and fierce biting greenhead flies. Those who wish to explore the beach in solitude can hike south and enjoy the wildness of this barrier island. Here you will find beaches that have changed but little since French and Spanish explorers first spotted them in the sixteenth century.

Assateague is also the home of wild ponies, and vacationers are advised not to be too friendly with them—they kick and bite. They are also as skillful as a boardwalk moocher and will try to con you out of sweets and vegetables. No one is exactly sure about the origin of these little ponies. They are shrouded in the romance of the novel *Misty Of Chincoteague*; and folklore has it that they were descended from the horses that swam away from shipwrecked Spanish galleons. Others cite pirate legends and tales of wrecked English ships where large numbers of escaping horses and cattle swam to the island. What is certain, however, is that as early as 1671 large numbers of ponies were running wild on Assateague Island and on the Eastern Shore, and both the Maryland and Virginia colonists found them a nuisance because they ate crops and destroyed fields. In short, on the Delmarva coast the ponies were more troublesome than Blackbeard the pirate.

As courts in Maryland in the seventeenth century ruled that all unrestrained livestock could be captured, the first of what came to be the famous pony pennings probably occurred at that time. Certainly by the nineteenth century the capture and sale of Assateague ponies had become an important local industry. The pony men of Assateague were a distinct class, wrote a journalist for *Scribner's Monthly* in 1877. They were tough bulbous fellows "with a sponge-like capacity for absorbing liquor . . . ." Once or twice a year these men corraled the ponies of the island and sold the foals. The fractious ponies often proved more than a match for the pony men and vacationing excursionists from the mainland were often delighted by the spectacle of cursing pony men lassoing and haltering a herd of kicking, biting, squealing, horses.[11]

The ponymen and their way of life have long vanished from Assateague but the marshes and swamps that sustained their way of life are still there. From the old ferry landing on the west side of the upper island you can follow a marked canoe trail that will take you south on Chincoteague Bay. The shallow waters of the Bay shimmer in the sunlight and occasionally you will want to get out of your canoe and search for crabs and clams. There are several canoe basins along the way where you can camp. In late afternoon westerly breezes keep the mosquitoes away, but while the land breeze prevails on the island, man is prey to the insects.

Little remains of the lifesaving stations that once dotted Assateague and the Delmarva Coast. In Ocean City at the inlet, one of the stations has been turned into a museum to allow visitors a glimpse of what was once an important service. From the colonial period up through the modern era, ships have foundered in the waters off Assateague. In 1873 the United States Congress authorized the establishment of lifesaving stations to rescue victims of shipwrecks along the Atlantic coast. And by 1874 there were eight such stations established between Cape Henlopen in Delaware and Cape Charles in Virginia. The men who manned these isolated beach stations were often quite busy. Between 1874 and 1915, notes local historian William H. Wroten, Jr., the Assateague Lifesaving Station was called into action 174 times. These men often fired Coston rockets to warn ships that they were getting close to the island's shoals. At times they plunged into the surf in their sturdy rowing rescue boats and ran hawsers out to stranded vessels to rescue cargoes and crew. The stations were usually not manned during the summer months when the Atlantic was placid. But during the other nine months the stations maintained a keeper and crew of six to eight men on duty twenty-four hours a day. The men patrolled the beach on foot and on horseback. When they spotted a vessel in distress, they launched their boat through the often chilling breakers. When they attempted to reach a beached vessel in the surf, they fired a line by cannon out to the boat. Once the line was secure, they attached a metal bulletlike rescue car to the line and hauled the crew to safety on the shore. William H. Wroten summed up their lives:

The surfmen, as they were called, lived a lonely, hard, and busy life—one of constant danger in the daily battle with the sea and the weather—all for a month's pay of about $20.00 plus room and board . . . . About the only other contact they had with people came from the rescued crews of disabled vessels, which were given food, shelter, and clothing until taken to the mainland.[12]

The Life-Saving Service was discontinued in 1915 and its duties were taken over by the United States Coast Guard. Also, with the decline of the coastal trade of sailing vessels, there were fewer wrecked and disabled vessels along the Delmarva coast. The waters off Assateague continue in winter to be dangerous, however. In December 1959, the cargo ship *African Queen* struck a shoal off Assateague and broke in two. Fortunately the Coast Guard arrived promptly on the scene and rescued the captain and crew of forty-five.

As with so much of the Eastern Shore, Worcester's society is rapidly changing and its heritage risks being plowed under by real estate developments like Ocean City. How long, people ask, will it remain Arcadia? Towns like Berlin, which once boasted inns and hotels, are little more than bedroom communities for people who work and do most of their shopping in Salisbury or Ocean City. Recently a group of investors transformed the Atlantic Hotel into a Victorian-era showpiece, and Berlin's antique shops cater to the tourist trade. The town, however, no longer serves as much of a commercial center. West of Ocean City along the Sinepuxent Bay, trailer courts and subdivisions spring up like toadstools after a spring rain. The developments have fancy names like Mystic Harbor, as if a prefab home or box trailer could have anything mystical about it. The homes seem as transitory as their restless occupants. When Hollywood filmed *Violets Are Blue* in Ocean City, the moviemakers constructed an artificial neighborhood in West Ocean City to portray an idyllic resort setting. It was a clean, wholesome, long-established neighborhood and at night you could look out across the water to Ocean City and see the giant Ferris wheel near the boardwalk sparkling in the night. When the movie was finished, stagecrews tore down the set and took it all away. Thus it is still easy come, easy go in Maryland's Arcadia with all that connotes—both good and bad.

Part Four

Explaining the Region

14

Two Faces of the Eastern Shore

*If you have not had the luck to be born on the Eastern Shore
you cannot know its people.*

—Sophie Kerr

*The real Eastern Shoreman's an oyster
Cuz he just stays put where he's at!*

—John Creighton

When you cross the Chesapeake Bay Bridge you are on
the Eastern Shore. After that opinions differ about the
nature of the region and what attractions it holds for the visitor
and native. In many respects the Eastern Shore is a creature
of tourism, a "proud traditional community of upright and
industrious farmers and watermen." It is of such images that
National Geographic television specials are made. It is to the
interest of every one in the tourist trade to keep the Eastern
Shore as old-fashioned as possible. Even when developers
build new condominium tracts, they give them names that will
evoke the heritage of the Eastern Shore. Add the word "Chesapeake" to the word "estates" and you have a realty winner every
time. Tourists expect to see watermen in workboats; and
indeed they would be delighted if Eastern Shoremen still used
horses or mules to pull their plows. For the tourist the scent
that blows across the land must be a mixture of honeysuckle,
salt water, and Old Bay Seasoning.

The land on the Eastern Shore used to be owned by
farmers, small-town families, and timber companies. Now land

is increasingly owned by corporations, real estate syndicates, foreign investors, urbanites, and retirees. The greatest change on the Eastern Shore in the twentieth century involves the sale of farmland. In Kent County, for example, more than 10 percent of the tillable land has been sold in recent years to Dutch, German, and South American investors at prices up to $4,000 an acre. According to the *Kent County News*, a short while back foreigners quietly bought fifty-one farms for a total price of $28 million. A lot of land along the Route 50 corridor is being held idle because ownership has passed into the hands of nonfarming speculators or developers. Even cropland along the corridor suffers from the "impermanence syndrome" as farmers are unwilling to make permanent improvement to the land or in structures and machinery because they know that the land will be developed or urbanized. Also urban buyers of rural land rarely have much idea of how much land they really want or how much they really need.

Besides, real estate investors and tourists want an idealized version of the agrarian world. They want carefully manicured fields; they don't want noisy farm tractors or combines or the odor of chicken manure or the penetrating stench of hog lagoons. As a result, some of the most fertile farmland in Wicomico and Queen Anne's counties is now paved over with subdivisions and convenience stores.

The result of this development is that the public image of the Eastern Shore of Maryland and its private reality seem to be rapidly diverging. Everyone wants to keep the Eastern Shore as it is. The realtors are usually the loudest spokesmen for "tradition."

The Eastern Shore is full of places that offer instant tradition these days. Shantytown in Ocean City affects the tone of an old watermen's village; St. Michaels with its antique stores sells duck decoys and pie safes manufactured in New England for tourists hungry for a bit of Eastern Shore heritage. Weekend mariners can take a cruise on a Chesapeake skipjack or ride on a replica of a Chesapeake steamboat, *The Maryland Lady*, on the Wicomico River; and hardware stores do a thriving business selling clam rakes and wire crab pots to people who haven't the slightest interest in using them more than once.

Each year Route 50 adds more billboards and businesses and soon the highway will be a Chesapeake version of a

Turkish bazaar. Maryland's "reach the beach" traffic programs do little more than encourage urban motorists to clog the highways on summer weekends. And the land becomes alive not with the sound of music but with the agony of late Sunday traffic jams and the sound of crying, exhausted, and sun-burned children.

Every native Eastern Shoreman wants his region to re-main the way it was when he was growing up. But these days it's hard to stand in the path of progress. Last stands are far from popular, and most Eastern Shoremen know what hap-pened to General Custer. Ironically, outside people come to the Eastern Shore simply because they want to get back to the land and sea and live a "last stand" kind of life. Much to their surprise, however, they find that the natives are selling them out to the modern world of motels, shopping centers, and fast-food restaurants. Whatever is good and true about the Eastern Shore will at some future date, no doubt, end up as a heritage piece at the Chesapeake Bay Maritime Museum at St. Michaels.

It is a sad irony that the way of life and beauty of the Eastern Shore should show its worth now that it is nearly gone. For centuries the people have lived a provincial life here and they have been resourceful in wresting a livelihood from soil and sea. Eastern Shoremen had a commonality of interest and they were willing to work until they died or took to their beds. Of course, life on the Eastern Shore was at times drab and uninteresting—such is the way of rural society in the tidewater. But progress has its price and perceptive natives wonder whether the price is worth paying.

Once at the county courthouse squares on the Eastern Shore, men in overalls and high-topped shoes played checkers, smoked hand-rolled cigarettes, and talked mostly of mules. A man with a good strong mule was an important asset in the community; he could make a crop. Mules could stand the Eastern Shore summer heat better than horses and they lived longer. Mules were swapped and bought; and it took a smart man to understand how to get his best work out of what some people mistakenly called a dumb beast. Mules, though, went out with the Depression of the 1930s on the Eastern Shore. Much like oxen teams, which were used to drag timber out of the forest, mules exist now only for private recreation. Some-times in the cool of a late summer day, you will see an old black

Skipjacks on the Choptank River; City of Crisfield *in the foreground.*
Photograph by Pat Vojtech.

man in bib overalls behind a mule and a single blade furrow plow. An unused rototiller sits in the garage. The machine is easier and cheaper to maintain, but the man just can't seem to get back into nature's cycle without the mule.

Yet the man and his mule are an anomaly. Today farmers disk the land using tractors with insulated air-conditioned cabs. They cannot hear the joyful cry of egrets that plunge out of the sky to snatch insects out of the freshly turned earth.

While the Eastern Shore of Maryland is no longer a remote region, there is still much remaining that is distinctive. Statistics from the Maryland Department of Agriculture reveal that although half of the farms in Maryland that were operating in 1950 have now disappeared, there is still plenty of farmland on the Eastern Shore. Some land lost to commercial development has been replaced by land gained from cleared forest and local farm experts state that there is probably as much land on the Eastern Shore today under cultivation as there was before the Civil War. There have been casualties, of course. Since 1978 Wicomico County, according to the Maryland Census of Agriculture, has lost nearly a hundred farms and is well on its way to becoming a metropolitan county with a small part-time agricultural component.

Elsewhere on the Eastern Shore the outlook for the agrarian life is much more encouraging. Today's Eastern Shore farm is a small-scale operation and farmers have to be exceedingly resourceful in order to survive. Farmers usually supplement their cropland income with money gained from poultry houses and part-time jobs. Truck farming is beginning to return to the Eastern Shore as the numerous roadside stands and "pick your own" operations attest. Also, farmers are beginning to experiment with aquaculture and there are already flourishing operations in "Louisiana" crawfish in Worcester County. Farmers are developing the technology for catfish and stripped bass production. Bruce Nichols of Worcester County, for example, has invested in crawfish aquaculture and produces about 20,000 pounds of crawfish a year on about 20 acres of ponds. He sends the crawfish to Baltimore and gets $2.10 a pound. "Crawfish," says Nichols, "will eat anything, crop residue, table scraps, grass clippings, dead chickens, almost anything organic." Crawfish production can complement poultry and grain production and currently there are twelve growers on the Eastern Shore.

Over the past thirty years, total Maryland farmland has diminished by some two million acres while the population of the state has increased by that amount. Statisticians extrapolating on this trend argue that all the farmland in the state will be lost in sixty years. Thus, when viewed in this context, the continued vitality of agriculture on Maryland's Eastern Shore is indeed surprising. "Eastern Shore farmers still have a variety of options," says Maryland Extension Agent Joe Trumbauer. "They can grow truck crops for the nearby cities or raise grain for the local chicken industry. As long as the metropolitan market for poultry remains strong, Eastern Shore farmers will be all right." Trumbauer also notes frankly that "we are just at the point where non-farm income is beginning to exceed farm income in agricultural households."[1]

It has often been suggested that the loss of family farms witnessed in the past several years in America will culminate in a system devoid of them around the year 2000. In the future experts predict that there will be about fifty thousand agri-mega units in the country. If this happens, the price of food will soar. At this writing Americans spend about 12 percent of their disposable income for food. Because of the family farmer there are still hundreds of commercial banks in existence. Farmers are the key element in community life in non-metropolitan America. Certainly on the Eastern Shore the farmer has been the keystone of the region's commercial prosperity. In 1986 Wicomico Agricultural Extension Agent Brad Hilty reported that a typical Eastern Shore farmer with three hundred acres of corn, two hundred acres of soybeans, and one hundred acres of wheat would have produced an income of $65,800.

In the future, population growth will largely determine agriculture's fate in the region. Presently agriculture has been able to flourish in the context of very small population growth. Even Wicomico County, which has perhaps one of the fastest growth rates on the Eastern Shore, is growing at the very modest rate of 1.2 percent a year. And, at a time when the Maryland state population averages about 442 persons per square mile, the Eastern Shore is relatively empty. Big population counties on the Shore like Wicomico and Cecil have 174 and 182 persons per square mile respectively; and remote Dorchester has a population of but 50 persons per square mile.[2] How long this vast green space on Maryland's Atlantic and Chesapeake shore will remain is anyone's guess. Each year one sees more and more long-distance commuters taking up residence in Queen Anne's and Talbot counties. Some even commute to jobs in Washington and Baltimore from Cambridge! Currently the commuter traffic gridlock in Anne Arundel County precludes massive settlement of long-distance commuters on Maryland's Eastern Shore. That process awaits the development of high-speed monorail trains across the Bay with direct service to Washington.

Meanwhile, the land abides. "There is much confusion between land and country," Aldo Leopold, the famous naturalist, once wrote. "Land is the place where corn, gullies, and mortgages grow. Country is the personality of the land, the collective harmony of its soil, life, and weather."[3] Conservation practices are much more in vogue now in the region and the forests are well maintained and scientifically harvested. Often the riches of the countryside are intangible; the beauty of a twelve-point stag in a Worcester County meadow, a cornfield full of wild geese on a cold winter morning, or a waterman tonging oysters on the Miles River. And the beauty of the landscape is being rediscovered by native and tourist alike. Everyone hopes, perhaps nervously, that the land will be there for the next generation.

*   *   *

From a political standpoint the Eastern Shore has seen its power decline over the years. Since the new Constitution of 1967 reapportioned the state legislature, tidewater counties have been reduced to playing a grumbling second fiddle in the house of delegates and senate. Before 1967 rural politicians ran Maryland, and theirs was a power out of all proportion to the number of citizens on the Eastern Shore and in western Maryland. As historian George Callcott has noted, in the years 1776 to 1920 the Eastern Shore produced 65 percent of the state's governors; members of the region's banking, business, legal, and farming communities ranked among the state's political elite.[4] While political life is still lively on the Eastern Shore, its leaders have been eclipsed in state power politics by a new and somewhat brash political elite from Baltimore and the suburbs of Washington, D.C. There is little room in Annapolis for the haughty patrician style of Eastern Shore politics today; and those who have not changed with the times have become political caricatures rather than political leaders. Quips one seasoned pol in Annapolis: "You can always tell the Eastern Shore crowd. They're the anti-boys. They're against everything from mass transit to environmental protection to welfare to gun control, to tax reform, racial integration, and planning and zoning." Such an observation may be harsh, but it does have the ring of truth to it.

Over the centuries Eastern Shoremen have embraced tradition more often than they have clamored for change. And who is to say that they have been completely wrong? Community life on the Eastern Shore is dominated by local elites who care about their towns and villages. Though crime and divorce rates are climbing, they are still low by national standards; and people still walk at night without fear of the shadows. The cycle of the agricultural seasons gives a certain regularity and uniformity to Eastern Shore life; and the past offers continuity and stability in the face of often unwelcome changes.

The novelist Sophie Kerr once wrote that unless you are born on the Eastern Shore you cannot know its people. They are an amazing and baffling people. On the surface they seem agreeable, pliable, acquiescent, and gentle, she noted, but actually "they are strong and rigid, set in a pattern of extreme individualism, passionate and willful when roused, unforgiving and unforgetting of any transgression against their mores."[5]

Eastern Shoremen are too independent and too set in their ways to be swayed too much by outsiders. Their raw-boned individualism is their history. Since the colonial period these people have had to battle the tides, the weather, and a grasping gentry in order to live in peace. They have democratized a society that until the Civil War at least was little more than feudal. Church and home were the primary navigation points of everyday life.

Despite its lack of wealth and its racial problems, the Eastern Shore has always been recognized as a land of pleasant living. Oysters, fish, terrapin, and crabs are native to its waters and very few men in the Chesapeake have known hunger. Colonists in the colonial period often complained that times were hard and they were "reduced to eating oysters." Slaves often balked at being fed terrapin. Both foods are now luxuries in most parts of the country. Here they are local staples. The region is rich in wild ducks and geese, and a man with a fishing rod, a gun, and a few acres can indeed live quite well.

The Eastern Shore is also the land of the Chesapeake beaten biscuit, that strange concoction of flour, water, lard and baking soda. Whacked into a tough dough with the flat side of an ax handle and baked hard, a beaten biscuit does not have a shelf life—it has a half life. In times past it has been the constant friend of the Eastern Shoreman. Fill your pockets up with beaten biscuits and they will sustain you through a day's hard work. You can use the leftover crumbs for bait; whatever biscuits are left can be eaten tomorrow or even the following week. At Wye Mills, a short distance from the famous Wye Oak, stands Orrell's Bakery, the only commercial establishment in the region devoted to making Chesapeake beaten biscuits. This staple has been around since the seventeenth century and novelist John Barth has written of them better than any man in the region in his novel *The Floating Opera:* "I recommend three Maryland beaten biscuits for breakfast. They are as hard as a haul seiner's conscience and dry as a dredger's tongue and they sit for hours in your morning stomach like ballast on a tender ship's keel. They cost little, are easily and crumblessly carried in your pocket and if forgotten and gone stale are neither harder nor less palatable than when fresh." And like the Chesapeake beaten biscuit, the Eastern Shoreman is tough on the outside, and stable and enduring on the inside.

Thus there are two faces to this intriguing abundant land. One looks to a past that enmeshes the people in a web of tradition, community life, provincialism, and absurd prejudices. The other looks to the future and welcomes change with a rough unfettered individualism. And like most people, Eastern Shoremen set little store by consistency.

Ancient, serene, and beautiful is the Eastern Shore. Its heritage of three centuries is its greatest strength and it is a unique blend of soil, soul, and sea. The vision of America that Maryland's Eastern Shore has to offer is one that has largely disappeared in modern times of sprawling metropolitan national growth. It is a vision of settled communities, of families black and white involved in the seasonal processes of agriculture, seafaring, and church life. It is a vision of strong kinship bonds and shared experiences. On the Eastern Shore the past continues to anchor the present and offers stability in contemporary life. All of us, to survive in the turbulent present, need to define a way of life for ourselves and our families; and in discovering the Eastern Shore we learn something about the gentle cycle of the passing of days and the meaning of human relationships. For in discovering the Eastern Shore we may be able to find something within ourselves that we had long thought was irrevocably lost.

"There is a history in all men's lives, figuring the nature of times deceased," Shakespeare wrote, and the Eastern Shore abounds in stories of courage, creative energy, and resourcefulness. It is of such things that noble visions and great lives are made that resist the erosion of time and circumstance.

Notes

1. On the Eastern Shore

1. Dickson J. Preston, *Talbot County: A History* (Centreville: Tidewater Publishers, 1983), 316-317.

2. Gilbert Sandler, "Few Remember Life Before the Bridge," *Maryland Magazine*, Summer 1983, 2-9.

3. Quoted in Michael Foss, *Undreamed Shores: England's Wasted Empire in America* (New York: Scribner's, 1974), 155.

4. Hammil Thomas Kenny, *The Placenames of Maryland, Their Origin and Meaning* (Baltimore: Maryland Historical Society, 1984); Stanley Pargelis, "An Account of the Indians of Virginia," *William and Mary Quarterly* 16 (April 1959): 228-243.

5. Robert L. Swain, Jr., "The Chesapeake Bay—Origin of the Name and the First Explorers," in Charles Branch Clark, *History of the Eastern Shore of Maryland and Virginia* (New York: Lewis Historical Publishing Co., 1950), 3 vols., 1:1-14; Edward A. Arber ed., *Travels and Works of Captain John Smith, Part II* (New York: Burt Franklin, 1910), 412-433.

6. James C. Mullikin. "The Separatist Movement and Related Problems,1776-1851," in Clark, *Eastern Shore of Maryland and Virginia* 1:464.

7. W. Halstean, *The Eastern Shore of Maryland, Soil and Climate Unsurpassed* (Easton: Privately printed, June 1879).

8. Newton Dennison Mereness, *Maryland as a Proprietary Province* (New York: Macmillan Co., 1901); Raphael Semmes, *Captains and Mariners of Early Maryland* (Baltimore: Johns Hopkins University Press,1937); John Herbert Claiborne, *William Claiborne of Virginia* (New York: G.P. Putnam's Sons, 1917); Paul Wilstach, *Tidewater Maryland* (Cambridge, Md.: Tidewater Publishers, 1969), 40-42.

9. George Alsop, *Character of the Province of Maryland* (1666; reprint, Baltimore: Johns Hopkins University Press, 1880), 36.

10. Arthur Pierce Middleton, *Tobacco Coast: A Maritime History of Chesapeake Bay in the Colonial Era* (Newport News, Va.: Mariner's Museum, 1953); Paul G. Clemens, *The Atlantic Economy and Colonial Maryland's Eastern Shore: From Tobacco to Grain* (Ithaca: Cornell University Press, 1980); Aubrey C. Land, *Colonial Maryland, a History* (Millwood, New York: KTO Press, 1981).

11. Alsop, *Character of the Province of Maryland*, 68-69.

12. Joseph A. Leo Lemay, *Men of Letters in Colonial Maryland* (Knoxville: University of Tennessee Press, 1972), 77-110.

13. Ebenezer Cooke, "The Sot-weed Factor or a Voyage to Maryland, 1708," reprinted in John D. Shea, *Shea's Early Southern Tracts* (Baltimore: Privately printed, 1865); *see also* Edward H. Cohen, *Ebenezer Cooke: The Sot-weed Canon* (Athens: University of Georgia Press, 1975), 6-27, 60-70.

14. John Thomas Scharf, *History of Maryland from the Earliest Times to the Present Day*, 3 vols., (reprint Hatboro, Pa.: Tradition Press, 1967), 2:13; Gloria L. Main, *Tobacco Colony: Life in Early Maryland, 1650-1720* (Princeton: Princeton University Press, 1982), 110.

15. Quoted in Eugene Irving McCormac, *White Servitude in Maryland, 1634-1820* (Baltimore: Johns Hopkins University Press, 1904), 64.

16. Quoted in Scharf, *History of Maryland* 2:17.

17. Abbot Emerson Smith, *Colonists in Bondage: White Servitude and Convict Labor in Maryland, 1607-1776* (Chapel Hill: University of North Carolina Press, 1947), 130-133, 278-306.

18. Ibid., 260. Indentured servants in Barbados staged a bloody rebellion in 1649 against their inhumane treatment.

19. Russell R. Menard, "Immigrants and Their Increase: The Process of Population Growth in Early Colonial Maryland," in Aubrey C. Land et al., *Law, Society and Politics in Early Maryland* (Baltimore: Johns Hopkins University Press, 1974), 88-105; Arthur E. Karinen, "Maryland Population, 1631-1730," *Maryland Historical Magazine* 54 (December 1959): 365-407.

20. *Archives of Maryland* (Proceedings of the County Courts, 1648-1688), Series 7 (Baltimore: Maryland Historical Society, 1937), 54:519.

21. *Archives of Maryland* 54:671.

22. *Archives of Maryland* 54:78, 121.

23. *Archives of Maryland* 54:xvii-xviii.

24. *Archives of Maryland* 54:116.

25. *Archives of Maryland* 54:121; the Bradnox career is detailed in pp. 116-122, 130-133, 138-142, 167-171, 173-180, 217-220, 224-229.

26. *Archives of Maryland* 54:9.

27. *Memoirs of the Bordleys*, p. 46 as quoted in Scharf, *History of Maryland* 2:8; Main, *Tobacco Colony*, 224.

28. Lorena S. Walsh, "Urban Amenities and Rural Self-Sufficiency: Living Standards and Consumer Behavior in the Colonial Chesapeake, 1643-1777," *Journal of Economic History* 43 (March 1983), 109-117.

2. The Wye Country

1. Gregory A. Stiverson, *Poverty in a Land of Plenty: Tenancy in Eighteenth Century Maryland* (Baltimore: Johns Hopkins University Press, 1977).

2. James Martin Wright, *The Free Negro in Maryland, 1634-1860* (New York: Columbia University Press, 1921). As early as 1664 the Maryland Assembly had passed laws forbidding sexual intercourse and marriage between whites and blacks in the colony.

3. Paul Wilstach, *Tidewater Maryland* (1931; reprint, Cambridge, Md.: Tidewater Publishers, 1969), 123-124.

4. A full account of the early Bennett and Lloyd families is contained in Dickson J. Preston, *Wye Oak, the History of a Great Tree* (Cambridge, Md.: Tidewater Publishers, 1972).

5. John Beale Bordley, *Essays and Notes on Husbandry and Rural Affairs* (Philadelphia: Budd and Bartram, 1801); Hulbert Footner, *Rivers of the Eastern Shore: Seventeen Maryland Rivers* (New York: Farrar and Rine-

hart, 1944), 299; *Dictionary of American Biography* 2:460-461; Frederick G. Emory, *Queen Anne's County* (Baltimore: Maryland Historical Society, 1950), 271; Scharf, *History of Maryland* 2:49; Stiverson, *Poverty in a Land of Plenty*, 84.

6. Gregory A. Stiverson and Phebe R. Jacobsen, *William Paca: A Biography* (Baltimore: Maryland Historical Society, 1976); an account of the subsequent fate of the Paca family is contained in Preston's *Wye Oak.*

7. An excellent example of the pioneering work of the Wye Institute on Maryland's Eastern Shore is *A Profile Study of the Eastern Shore* (Centreville, Md.: Wye Institute, 1964). It was the first major study by a foundation of the socioeconomic problems of the region.

8. Boyd Gibbons, *Wye Island, the True Story of an American Community's Struggle to Preserve Its Way of Life* (Baltimore: Johns Hopkins University Press, 1977).

3. From the Sassafras to the Susquehanna

1. Scharf, *History of Maryland* 2:2-8.

2. Bayard Taylor, "Down On The Eastern Shore," *Harper's New Monthly Magazine* 43 (September 1871).

3. Paul Wilstach, *Tidewater Maryland*, 181-183.

4. The best available work on Augustine Herrman is Earl L. W. Heck, *Augustine Herrman* (Richmond: William Byrd Press, 1941).

5. Louis Dow Scisco, "Notes on August Herrman's Map," *Maryland Historical Magazine* 33 (December 1938), 343.

6. George Johnston, *History of Cecil County, Maryland and the Early Settlements Around the Head of Chesapeake Bay and on the Delaware River* (1881; reprint, Elkton, Md.: Regional Publishing Co., 1967), 37-99.

7. Johnston, *History of Cecil County*, 252.

8. The Cecil County Bicentennial Committee, *Cecil County in the Revolutionary War* (Elkton, Md.: Cecil County Public Library, 1976).

9. Angus Davis, "The Town That Lumber Built," *Maryland Magazine*, Summer 1976.

10. *Cecil Whig*, September 2, 1843 (Reprinted in the *Cecil Whig*, April 9, 1986.)

11. Ralph D. Gray, *The National Waterway: A History of the Chesapeake and Delaware Canal, 1769-1965* (Urbana: University of Illinois Press, 1967), 67, 70, 75; Edward Noble Vallandigham, *Delaware and the Eastern Shore* (Philadelphia: J.B. Lippincott, 1922), 41-55.

12. *Pride and Progress, Annual Report on Cecil County*, (Elkton, Md., March 1986).

4. From Kent to Caroline

1. Robert L. Swain, "Chestertown as a Port before the Revolution," in Clark, *The Eastern Shore of Maryland and Virginia* 1:331-341.

2. Footner, *Rivers of the Eastern Shore*, 310-312.

3. J. Hall Pleasants, ed., "Letters of Molly and Hetty Tilghman, Eighteenth Century Gossip of Two Maryland Girls," *Maryland Historical Magazine* 21 (March and June 1926), 20-39, 123-149.

4. Ibid.

5. Clark, *The Eastern Shore of Maryland and Virginia* 1:448-451.

6. Fred W. Dumschott, *Washington College* (Chestertown, Md.: Washington College, 1980).

7. David C. Holly, *Steamboat on the Chesapeake: Emma Giles and the Tolchester Line* (Centreville, Md.: Tidewater Publishers, 1987), 100-101.

8. Kenneth L. Carroll, "Nicholites and Slavery in Eighteenth Century Maryland," *Maryland Historical Magazine* 79 (Summer 1984), 128.

9. Edward M. Noble, *History of Caroline County* (Federalsburg, Md.: J.W. Stowell Co., 1920); additional information on Caroline County is available in Mary Anne Fleetwood, ed., *Voices from the Land: A Caroline County Memoir* (Queenstown, Md.: Queen Anne Press, 1983).

5. Main Street Methodists

1. William Henry Williams, *The Garden of American Methodism: The Delmarva Peninsula, 1769-1820* (Wilmington, Del.: Scholarly Resources Press, 1984), 44-58.

2. George H. Corddry, *Wicomico County History* (Salisbury, Md.: Peninsula Press, 1981), 115-116.

3. Charles Jones Truitt, *Historic Salisbury, Maryland* (New York: Country Life Press, 1931), 81-101.

4. Richard W. Cooper, *Profile of a Colonial Community: Salisbury Towne and Wicomico County on Maryland's Eastern Shore* (Baltimore: Gateway Press, 1986), 198-215, 221-224.

5. Richard W. Cooper, "Wicomico Has Historic Courthouse," *Salisbury Daily Times*, February 28, 1986; Barbara Audet, "The Great Salisbury Fire of 1886," *Salisbury Daily Times*, October 16, 1986.

6. John C. Hayman, *Rails Along the Chesapeake, a History of Railroading on the Delmarva Peninsula, 1827-1978* (Salisbury, Md.: Marvadel Publishers, 1979), 65-94.

7. Haynes Johnson, "The Mob and the Profit Motive," *Washington Post*, March 12, 1986.

8. Phil Patton, "Fowl Play: The Great Chicken War," *New York Magazine*, November 19, 1979.

9. Don Singleton, "Chicken on Sunday, Monday, Tuesday, etc." *New York Daily News*, February 3, 1980.

6. Semper Eadem

1. Walter C. James, "What the Tangier Sound Means to Me," *Marylander and Herald*, September 2, 1976.

2. Somerset County Folklore File, Maryland Room, Enoch Pratt Library, Baltimore.

3. "The Happy Days of Millard Tawes," *Baltimore Sun Magazine*, October 8, 1967.

4. Clayton Torrence, *Old Somerset on the Eastern Shore of Maryland* (Baltimore: Regional Publishing Co., 1973), 23-55; Boyd S. Schlenther, ed.,

The Life and Writings of Francis Makemie (Philadelphia: Presbyterian Historical Society,1971), 13-28.

5. John R. Wennersten, "The Travail of a Tory Parson: Reverend Philip Hughes and Maryland Colonial Politics, 1767-1777," *Historical Magazine of the Protestant Episcopal Church* 44 (December 1975).

6. Adam Wallace, *Parson of the Islands, A Biography of Joshua Thomas*, (Philadelphia: Methodist Home Journal, 1870).

7. "The War News," *Baltimore Sun*, September 17, 1861; Clark, *Eastern Shore of Maryland and Virginia* 1:544.

8. Jack Wennersten, "Renegades and Raiders of the Chesapeake," *Chesapeake Bay Magazine*, October 1983; *see also* "Operations on the Potomac and Rappahannock Rivers, January 5 to December 7, 1861," *Official Records of the Union and Confederate Navies in the War of the Rebellion, IV & V* (Washington, 1896).

9. Ibid. *See also* William J. Kelley, "Baltimore Steamboats in the Civil War," *Maryland Historical Magazine* 37 (Summer 1942), 42-52.

10. L. Allison Wilmer, et al., *History and Roster of Maryland Volunteers, War of 1861-1865*, 3 vols. (Baltimore: Guggenheim Weil and Company, 1898), 1:626-627; *see also Records of the War of the Rebellion*, Series III, 1:933-34, 606; Harold Bell Hancock, *Delaware during the Civil War* (Wilmington: Historical Society of Delaware,1961), 126.

11. Charles Lewis Wagandt, *Mighty Revolution, Negro Emancipation in Maryland* (Baltimore: Johns Hopkins University Press, 1964), 159, 164-184; "Proceedings of the Committee on Elections," Maryland House of Delegates, *Journal*, February 10, 1864, Appendix 9-13; *see also* Maryland House and Senate Documents, January Session, 1864, *Report of the Committee on Elections on Contested Elections in Somerset County* (Annapolis, 1864).

12. John T. Handy, *Rehobeth Presbyterian Church* (Philadelphia: Kennett News and Advertiser Press,1956), 19.

13. C. Z. Keller, "Agriculture in Somerset County," *Marylander and Herald*, May 8, 1953; Frank H. Ruth, "Strawberries," *Little Journeys through the Eastern Shore* (Salisbury, Md. Privately printed, 1927).

14. *38th Annual Report of the Commissioner of Labor and Statistics in Maryland, 1929* (Baltimore, 1930), 26-39.

15. Jack Wennersten, "Behind the Wire: When the Afrika Korps Came to Somerset County," *Maryland Magazine*, Autumn 1982.

7. Slavery

1. Roger Ekirch, "Exiles in the Promised Land," *Maryland Historical Magazine* 82 (Summer 1987), 95-122.

2. Land Records, Somerset County Court House, Princess Anne, Maryland; Torrence, *Old Somerset*, 306-310.

3. Jeffrey Richardson Brackett, *The Negro in Maryland: A Study of the Institution of Slavery* (reprint, New York: Negro Universities Press, 1969), 33.

4. Allan Kulikoff, *Tobacco and Slaves: The Development of Southern Cultures in the Chesapeake, 1680-1800* (Chapel Hill: University of North Carolina Press, 1986), 37.

5. A good account of the slave trade in the eighteenth century is contained in Jay Coughtry, *The Notorious Triangle, Rhode Island and the African Slave Trade* (Philadelphia: Temple University Press, 1981)

6. Philip D. Curtin, *The Atlantic Slave Trade, a Census* (Madison: University of Wisconsin Press, 1969).

7. Kulikoff, *Tobacco and Slaves*, 66.

8. Thomas E. Davidson, "Free Blacks in Old Somerset County, 1744-1755," *Maryland Historical Magazine* 80 (Summer 1985), 151-156.

9. Brackett, *Negro in Maryland*, 52-53.

10. Kenneth L. Carroll, "An Eighteenth Century Episcopalian Attack on Quaker and Methodist Manumission of Slaves," *Maryland Historical Magazine* 80 (Summer 1985), 139-150.

11. Brackett, *Negro in Maryland*, 80-81.

12. Roger Bruns and William Fraley, "Old Gunny: Abolitionist in a Slave City," *Maryland Historical Magazine* 68 (Winter 1973), 369-382.

13. Brackett, *Negro in Maryland*, 81.

14. Sarah Bradford, *Scenes from the Life of Harriet Tubman* (reprint, New Jersey: Citadel Press, 1961).

15. Brackett, *Negro in Maryland*, 91.

16. Frederick A. Douglass, *My Bondage and My Freedom* (reprint, New York: Arno Press, 1968), 171-172; Dickson J. Preston, *Young Frederick Douglass: The Maryland Years* (Baltimore: Johns Hopkins University Press, 1980), 1-156.

17. Ted Giles, *Patty Cannon, Woman of Mystery* (Easton, Md.: Easton Publishing Company, 1965); M. Sammy Miller, "Patty Cannon: Murderer and Kidnapper of Free Blacks, A Review of the Evidence," *Maryland Historical Magazine* 72 (Fall 1977), 422. Miller asserts that "it was Patty's murder of whites that eventually led to her capture." Local historian Jerry Shields asserts that Patty Cannon may have died a natural death. "Nothing in official records indicates that she took poison or otherwise committed suicide." Jerry Shields, *The Infamous Patty Cannon in History and Legend* (Dover, Del.: Biblioteca Literaria Press, 1990), 13.

18. General Advertisement for September 6, 1853, Thomas Sudler Mss, Maryland Historical Society, Administrative Accounts, Somerset Records, 1853.

19. Ibid.

20. Frederick Bancroft, *Slave Trading in the Old South* (Baltimore: J.H. Furst Co., 1931), 39-41, 120-121. Abolitionists regarded Austin and Richard Woolfolk and their six-member family as the most infamous slave traders in the South.

21. Ibid., 28-37, 39-44, 118.

22. Ibid., 651; William Calderhead, "The Role of the Professional Slave Trader in a Slave Economy: Austin Woolfolk, "A Case Study," *Civil War History* 23 (1977), 195-211.

23. Robert W. Todd, *Methodism of the Peninsula* (Philadelphia: Methodist Episcopal Book Rooms, 1886), 173.

24. Bancroft, *Slave Trading*, 120-121; Clark, ed., *The Eastern Shore of Maryland and Virginia*, 1:520. While slavery remained more economically viable in western shore Maryland counties like Charles and Prince George's the institution left a profound imprint on the popular consciousness of the Eastern Shore. As late as 1860 virtually one out of every three slaveholders in Maryland was an Eastern Shoreman. And as historian Charles Clark has noted, free negroes were "treated in the main like slaves." Thus on the Eastern

Shore slavery remained a standard of value and prosperity until the Civil War. See Clark, *The Eastern Shore of Maryland and Virginia;* 1:512.

25. Douglass, *My Bondage and My Freedom,* 52.; Newbell Niles Pickett, *Folk Beliefs of the Southern Negro* (reprint, Montclair, New Jersey: Citadel Press, 1968), 5.

26. Brackett, *Negro in Maryland,* 106; *Somerset County Union,* September 1, 1855.

27. Brackett, *Negro in Maryland,* 213.

28. *Somerset County Union,* November 4, 1859.

29. Brackett, *Negro in Maryland,* 87-91.; *see also* James Martin Wright, *The Free Negro in Maryland 1634-1860* (New York: Columbia University Press, 1921), 306-317.

30. Ira Berlin, *Slaves Without Masters: The Free Negro in the Antebellum South* (New York: Pantheon Books,1974), 183.

31. Property Schedules, Somerset County, Maryland, *United States Census of 1860;* Circuit Court of Somerset County, *Lankford* v. *Duffy,* May 29, 1860, Thomas Sudler MSS, Maryland Historical Society; *Baltimore Sun,* January 20, 1860; *see also* Wright, *The Free Negro in Maryland,* 259-262. Delegate Curtis W. Jacobs of Worcester County submitted a bill in 1860 legalizing the reenslavement of free blacks. While the bill passed the state assembly as a referendum to be decided in southern Maryland and the Eastern Shore, the voters turned it down.

8. Freedom's Ferment

1. Charles Branch Clark, *Politics in Maryland during the Civil War* (Chestertown: n.d.), 163.

2. Quoted in Charles Lewis Wagandt, *Mighty Revolution: Negro Emancipation in Maryland* (Baltimore: Johns Hopkins University Press, 1964), 190.

3. Remarks of John W. Crisfield, *Congressional Globe,* 37th Congress, 3rd session, vol. 33. part 1, 147-151.

4. *Baltimore Sun,* November 11, 1863; *Baltimore Sun,* October 30, 1863.

5. Freedmen's Bureau Book Number 3, Maryland and Delaware, Record Group 105, 1866, National Archives; on May 19, 1868, the Somerset County Board of Commissioners paid bounties to blacks who had served in Company H of the 19th Maryland Colored Regiment. *See Proceedings of the Somerset County Commissioners,* May 19, 1868, Maryland Hall of Records.

6. *Public Local Laws of Maryland,* Article 20, 1-28, *Annotated Code of Maryland* (Annapolis, 1888).

7. *Debates of the Constitutional Convention of 1864,* III (Annapolis, 1865), 1601.

8. Barbara Jeanne Fields, "The Maryland Way from Slavery to Freedom," Ph.D. diss., Yale, 1978, 148.

9. W. A. Lowe, "The Freedmen's Bureau and Civil Rights," *Journal of Negro History* 37 (July 1952), 236-237.

10. Fields, "Slavery To Freedom," 154-157.

11. Jeffrey Richardson Brackett, *The Negro in Maryland,* 232.

12. Ruth Ellen and John R. Wennersten, "Separate and Unequal: The Evolution of a Black Land Grant College in Maryland," *Maryland Historical Magazine* 72 (Spring 1977), 110-117.

13. *Maryland Farmer*, May 1868.
14. Quoted in Fields, "Slavery to Freedom," 174.
15. Ibid., 175.
16. *Salisbury Advertiser*, April 12, 1873.
17. *United States Census of 1880*, Maryland.
18. Fields, "Slavery To Freedom," 182.
19. Interview with Mrs. Esther Johnson Henry, Upper Fairmount, Maryland, July 1977. Mrs. Henry's father was an active leader of the black Republican organization in the 1880s and 1890s.
20. *Salisbury Advertiser*, June 9, 1894.
21. "52-Year Lynching Record Ranks Maryland 27th with 30 of 4,361 Crimes," *Baltimore Afro-american*, February 23, 1935.
22. Rose Bradley, "Back of the Maryland Lynching," *The Nation* 137 (December 13, 1933), 672-673.
23. John R. Wennersten, "The Black School Teacher in Maryland, 1930s," *Negro History Bulletin*, April-May 1975.
24. "The Maryland Lynching," *The New Republic* 76 (November 8, 1933); "Maryland's Eastern Shore," *Nation* 137 (December 20, 1933); "Maryland Storm Warning," *New Republic* 77 (December 20, 1933).
25. Arthur Franklin Raper, *The Tragedy of Lynching* (Montclair, New Jersey: Patterson Smith, 1969), 48.
26. *Worcester County Democrat*, December 12, 1931; *Salisbury Times*, December 5, 8, 15, 1931. In a recent study Charles W. Smith notes that the mob that killed Williams numbered close to 2,000. *See* Charles W. Smith, "Lynching: White Man's Justice/Negro Nemesis: An Analysis of Causation, Condonement and Resistance to Negro Lynching in the Southern and Middle Atlantic United States," Unpublished Essay, University of Maryland, Eastern Shore, December 17, 1990. It has subsequently been asserted that Elliott was killed by his mentally unstable son and not by Williams. *See* Smith, "Lynching", 23.
27. H. L. Mencken, "The Eastern Shore Kultur," *Baltimore Sun*, December 12, 1931.
28. *New York Times*, January 24, 1932.
29. *Marylander and Herald*, October 16, 1933; *Salisbury Daily Times*, October 19-20, 1933.
30. *Nation*, December 13, 1933; *Marylander and Herald*, October 20, 1933; Armwood was captured near Red Hill, Virginia, approximately three miles south of the Maryland State line, a short distance from Pocomoke City, Md. *See Salisbury Daily Times*, October 17, 1933.
31. *Baltimore Sun*, October 17, 1933.
32. *Baltimore Sun*, October 17, 1933; *Salisbury Daily Times*, October 18, 1933.
33. *Baltimore Sun*, October 19, 1933.
34. *Baltimore Sun*, October 20, 1933.
35. *Baltimore Sun*, October 19 & 20, 1933.
36. *Baltimore Sun*, October 21, 1933.
37. Ibid.
38. *New York Times*, October 19, 1933.
39. H. L. Mencken, "Plans to Put Down Lynching," *Baltimore Sun*, October 20, 1933.
40. *Marylander and Herald*, October 20, 1933.

41. *New York Times*, November 29, 1933; *New Republic*, December 20, 1933; *see also* Affidavits and Testimony of Attorney General William Preston Lane in *Punishment for the Crime of Lynching, Hearings Before a Subcommittee of the Judiciary, 73rd Congress*, January 20-21, 1934 (Washington, 1934), 115-118.

42. *Marylander and Herald*, December 1, 1933; *New York Times*, November 30, 1933.

9. The Struggle for Equality

1. *New York Times*, August 28, 1960.
2. Sterling Seagrave, "She's a St. Clair in a St. Joan Role," *Washington Post*, June 21, 1963.
3. "Cambridge, Maryland Stumbles into Racial War." *Life Magazine* 55 July 26, 1963, 18-23.
4. Robert A. Liston, "Who Can We Surrender To?" *Saturday Evening Post* 236 (October 5, 1963), 78-80.
5. *Cambridge Daily Banner*, May 26,1964; May 28,1964; February 29, 1964; December 23,1964.
6. *Cambridge Daily Banner*, May 26, 1964.
7. *Cambridge Daily Banner*, May 28, 1964.
8. *Cambridge Daily Banner*, May 26, 1964.
9. *Salisbury Daily Times*, October 23, 1964.
10. Clayborne Carson, *In Struggle: SNCC and the Black Awakening in the 1960s* (Cambridge: Harvard University Press, 1981), 255.
11. Ibid.
12. *Cambridge Daily Banner*, July 25, 1967; *Dorchester News*, July 26, 1967; *Salisbury Daily Times*, July 25, 1967; *Cambridge Daily Banner*, July 28, 1967.
13. *Salisbury Daily Times*, November 7, 1973.
14. *Cambridge Daily Banner*, November 28, 1973.
15. *Cambridge Daily Banner*, May 12, 1961.
16. Wennersten, "Separate and Unequal."
17. George H. Corddry, *Wicomico County History, 64-66*; Wennersten, "Separate and Unequal."
18. *Life Magazine* 55 (July 26, 1963), 18-23.

10. Waterland

1. Wilstach, *Tidewater Maryland*, 17.
2. United States Department of the Interior, Fish and Wildlife Service, *National Estuary Study*, vol. 3 (Washington, 1970), 78.
3. *See* Gilbert Byron, *The Lord's Oysters* (Baltimore: Johns Hopkins University Press, 1977).
4. Holly, *Steamboat on the Chesapeake*, 113-144.
5. Robert H. Burgess, ed., *Coasting Captain, The Journals of Captain Leonard S. Tawes Relating to His Career in Atlantic Sailing Craft from 1868 to 1920* (Newport News: Mariner's Museum, 1967).
6. Gilbert Byron, "These Chesapeake Men," in Harold D. Jopp, ed., *Shoremen: An Anthology of Eastern Shore Prose and Verse* (Cambridge, Md.: Tidewater Publishers, 1974), 279.

7. *Maryland Shellfish Commission Report, 1914-1915* (Annapolis, 1916), 7.

8. Ruby Covington, "Oystering in the 1890s," *Baltimore Sun*, March 7, 1971.

9. Interviews with Alex Kellam, March-April, 1980.

10. Varley Howe Lang, *Follow the Water* (Winston-Salem: John F. Blair, 1961), 29.

11. Interview with Varley Lang, July 1987.

12. Lang, *Follow The Water*, 213.

13. *Baltimore Sun*, March 11, 1979.

14. Lewis Regenstein, *America the Poisoned* (Washington: Acropolis Books, 1982), 147.

15. "Spread of a Deadly Chemical—And the Ever-Widening Impact," *U. S. News and World Report*, September 6, 1976.

16. *Baltimore Sun*, August 29, 1976.

17. *Baltimore Sun*, July 4, 1982.

18. Marianne Kyriakos and Karen Porcelli, "Holding Time at Bay," *Washington Post*, May 20, 1988.

11. Gold Coast

1. Robert L. Swain, Jr. "Origin of County Names," in Clark, *History of the Eastern Shore of Maryland and Virginia*, 2:910-911.

2. Homer Bast, "Talbot County, Maryland, A History," in Clark, *Eastern Shore*, 2:949.

3. David Curtis Skaggs, *Roots of Maryland Democracy, 1753-1776* (Westport, Ct.: Greenwood Press, 1973), 42-43.

4. Clemens, *The Atlantic Economy and Maryland's Eastern Shore*, 149, 120-167.

5. Preston, *Young Frederick Douglass*, 41-52.

6. Halstean, *The Eastern Shore of Maryland*, 1-7.

7. Norman Harrington, "The Eastern Shore's Well-Heeled Immigrants," Easton *Star-Democrat*, October 29, 1972.

8. Preston, *Talbot County*, 247.

9. Gregory A. Wood, *The French Presence in Maryland, 1524-1800* (Baltimore: Gateway Press, 1978), 68-71. Clark, *Eastern Shore*, 2:946.

10. Bast, "Talbot County," 951.

11. *The Health of Maryland* (Baltimore: Maryland Center for Health Statistics, 1985).

12. *Washington Post*, April 14, 1986.

13. *Maryland Coast Dispatch*, February 6, 1987.

14. Robert Barrie and George Barrie, *Cruises Mainly on the Bay of the Chesapeake* (Philadelphia: Franklin Press, 1909), 49.

15. M. V. Brewington, *Chesapeake Bay Log Canoes and Bugeyes* (Cambridge: Cornell Maritime Press, 1963), 27.

16. Homer Bast, "Talbot County," 982.

12. Choptankia

1. Frank W. Porter, III, *Maryland Indians: Yesterday and Today* (Baltimore: Maryland Historical Society, 1983); Jay F. Custer ed., *Late Woodland*

Cultures of the Mid-Atlantic Region (Newark, Del.: University of Delaware Press, 1986)

2. Frank W. Porter, III, "A Century of Accommodation: The Nanticoke Indians In Colonial Maryland," *Maryland Historical Magazine* 74 (June 1979), 175.

3. *Ibid.*, 177.

4. *Ibid.*, 180.

5. *Ibid.*, 184.

6. John Thomas Scharf, *History of Maryland* 1:428.

7. Philip A. Crowl, *Maryland during and after the Revolution* (Baltimore, 1943).

8. Scharf, *History of Maryland* 1:84-144; Porter, "A Century of Accomodation," 186. *Report of the Select Committee on the Claims of the Nanticoke Indians Made to the House of Delegates* (Annapolis, 1853).

9. Elias Jones, *New Revised History of Dorchester County* (Cambridge, Md.: Tidewater Publishers, 1966), 181-188.

10. Porter, "Century of Accommodation," 188.

11. Skaggs, *Roots of Maryland Democracy,* 171.

12. *Dictionary of American Biography* 7: 166; Jones, *History of Dorchester,* 135; George L. Radcliffe, *Governor Thomas H. Hicks of Maryland and the Civil War* (Baltimore: Johns Hopkins University Press,1901), 12-13.

13. *Baltimore Sun,* June 24, 1937; June 21, 1937; June 28, 1937; July 2, 1937; July 3, 1937; July 9, 1937; July 24, 1937; November 13, 1937.

14. *Scribner's Monthly,* March 1872.

15. Walter Harper, "Annie Oakley, She Packed Her Gun and Moved to Cambridge," *Shorewoman,* Summer-Fall 1980.

16. Interview with Edward Evans, December, 1986; John R. Wennersten, "Dorchester County's Celebrity Hunt," *Maryland Magazine,* Autumn 1987.

13. Arcadia

1. Quoted in Reginald V. Truitt and Millard LesCallette, *Worcester County, Maryland's Arcadia* (Snow Hill, Md.: Worcester County Historical Society, 1977), 11-12.

2. *Archives of Maryland* 28: 493-494.

3. William B. Marye, "The Sea Coast of Maryland," *Maryland Historical Magazine* 40 (June 1945).

4. Thomas E. Davidson, "Jacob Armstrong: Pioneer Black Capitalist on Maryland's Eastern Shore," *The Maryland Pendulum* (Maryland Commission On Afro-American History and Culture), vol. 4 No. 6., 1986.

5. Informational materials, Furnace Town Museum; Joseph T. Singewald, *The Iron Ores of Maryland* (Baltimore: Johns Hopkins University Press, 1911); Louis J. Kuethe, "A List of Maryland Mills, Taverns, Forges, and Furnaces of 1794," *Maryland Historical Magazine 31 (June 1936),* 155-169.

6. Hulbert Footner, *Rivers of the Eastern Shore,* 68-85; for social life in old Pocomoke, *see* James Murray, *History of Pocomoke City, Formerly New Town, from its Origin to the Present Time* (Baltimore: Curry, Clay and Company, 1883).

7. Truitt and LesCallette, *Worcester County,* 108-109; Marye, "Sea Coast of Maryland."

8. Truitt and LesCallette, *Worcester County*, 77.

9. Michael Naidus, "Cocaine Law Enforcement Finds Catching Up Hard to Do," *Maryland Coast Press*, May 1, 1987.

10. Gilbert F. White, *Natural Hazards* (Cambridge, Mass.: MIT Press, 1975), 57; James E. DiLisio, *Maryland, A Geography* (Boulder, Colorado: Westview Press, 1983), 53.

11. *Scribner's Monthly*, April 1877.

12. William H. Wroten, Jr., *Assateague* (Cambridge, Md.: Tidewater Publishers, 1972), 44.

14. Two Faces of the Eastern Shore

1. *1982 Census of Agriculture, Maryland State and County Data*, Part 20, U.S. Department of the Census, 1984; *Salisbury Daily Times*, March 23, 1987; Interview with Joe Trumbauer, July 3, 1988.

2. *Maryland Statistical Abstract, 1986-1987* (Annapolis: Maryland Department of Economic and Community Development); *Salisbury Advertiser*, December 24, 1986.

3. Aldo Leopold, *A Sand County Almanac* (New York: Oxford University Press, 1966), 165.

4. George H. Callcott, *Maryland and America, 1940 to 1980* (Baltimore: Johns Hopkins University Press, 1985), 10-16.

5. Sophie Kerr, "Maryland's Eastern Shore," in *Sound of Petticoats and Other Stories of the Eastern Shore* (New York: Rinehart and Company, 1948), 318.

Index

(Page numbers for photographs are in italics.)

289